SEEING RED

Hollywood's Pixeled Skins

AMERICAN INDIAN STUDIES SERIES

Gordon Henry, *Series Editor*

- *Shedding Skins: Four Sioux Poets*
  Edited by Adrian C. Louis | 978-0-87013-823-2
- *Writing Home: Indigenous Narratives of Resistance*
  Michael D. Wilson | 978-0-87013-818-8
- *National Monuments*
  Heid E. Erdrich | 978-0-87013-848-5
- *The Indian Who Bombed Berlin and Other Stories*
  Ralph Salisbury | 978-0-87013-847-8
- *Facing the Future: The Indian Child Welfare Act at 30*
  Edited by Matthew L. M. Fletcher, Wenona T. Singel, and Kathryn E. Fort | 978-0-87013-860-7
- *Dragonfly Dance*
  Denise K. Lajimodiere | 978-0-87013-982-6
- *Ogimawkwe Mitigwaki (Queen of the Woods)*
  Simon Pokagon | 978-0-87013-987-1
- *Plain of Jars and Other Stories*
  Geary Hobson | 978-0-87013-998-7
- *Document of Expectations*
  Devon Abbott Mihesuah | 978-1-61186-011-5
- *Centering Anishinaabeg Studies: Understanding the World through Stories*
  Edited by Jill Doerfler, Niigaanwewidam James Sinclair, and Heidi Kiiwetinepinesiik Stark | 978-1-61186-067-2
- *Seeing Red—Hollywood's Pixeled Skins: American Indians and Film*
  Edited by LeAnne Howe, Harvey Markowitz, and Denise K. Cummings | 978-1-61186-081-8

SEEING RED

Hollywood's Pixeled Skins

Edited by · LeAnne Howe · Harvey Markowitz · Denise K. Cummings

American Indians and Film

Michigan State University Press · East Lansing

♾ The paper used in this publication meets the minimum requirements of ANSI/NISO Z39.48-1992 (R 1997) (Permanence of Paper).

Michigan State University Press
East Lansing, Michigan 48823-5245

Printed and bound in the United States of America.

19 18 17 16 15 14 13   1 2 3 4 5 6 7 8 9 10

LIBRARY OF CONGRESS CATALOGING-IN-PUBLICATION DATA
Seeing red : Hollywood's pixeled skins : American Indians and film / edited by LeAnne Howe, Harvey Markowitz, and Denise K. Cummings.
p. cm. — (American Indian studies series)
Includes bibliographical references.
ISBN 978-1-60917-368-5 (ebook) — ISBN 978-1-61186-081-8 (pbk. : alk. paper) 1. Indians in motion pictures. 2. Western films—United States—History and criticism. I. Howe, LeAnne. II. Markowitz, Harvey. III. Cummings, Denise K.
PN1995.9.148S44 2012
791.43'6552—dc23
2012028494

Book design by Charlie Sharp, Sharp Des!gns, Lansing, MI
Cover design by David Drummond, Salamander Design, www.salamanderhill.com
Cover artwork is *Edward Curtis, Paparazzi* ©2006 Jim Denomie
and is used courtesy of the artist. All rights reserved.

Michigan State University Press is a member of the Green Press Initiative and is committed to developing and encouraging ecologically responsible publishing practices. For more information about the Green Press Initiative and the use of recycled paper in book publishing, please visit *www.greenpressinitiative.org*.

Visit Michigan State University Press at *www.msupress.org*

Contents

Introduction

Establishing Shot

The first appearance of the movie review, or at least its direct ancestor, followed quickly on the heels of the 1896 unveiling of "Edison's greatest marvel," the Vitascope: a "curious object" that was capable of projecting moving life-size, color images on a white backdrop.[1] While the *New York Times* reporter who covered this highly publicized premiere had more to say about the "marvel" itself than the content and artistic quality of the several featurettes it projected (many of them, admittedly, plotless), he did pronounce the films "all wonderfully real and singularly exhilarating"[2] (Ebert translation: "Two Thumbs Up"[3]).

As the century turned, and movies became increasingly sophisticated in their cinematography and narratives and gradually morphed from single to multi-reels, the contents of the articles reporting on film and the film industry correspondingly evolved. By the end of the first decade of the twentieth century, the staffs of several trade papers, most notably *Moving Picture World* and *Moving Picture News*,[4] included film critics who provided their exhibitor-subscribers with opinion pieces on the state of the motion-picture business, as well as plot summaries and critical evaluations of forthcoming and newly released moving pictures.

Given the concomitant rise in U.S. nationalism and world influence beginning in the early twentieth century, it should come as no surprise that some of these features focused on the challenges of creating movies that both reflected and promoted American identity and exceptionalism. Consider the editorial "What Is an American Subject?," which appeared in the January 22, 1910, edition of *Moving Picture World*. The inspiration for this piece emerged from its author's discovery of two growing sentiments among U.S. motion-picture exhibitors, both in keeping with the nationalistic temper of the times: first, "the desirability of providing American film subjects for American motion picture audiences . . . [as] against the imported film that . . . usually has the drawback of not dealing with a subject suitable for an American audience," and second, the "urgent necessity of American subjects made by American labor." The editorial went on to report that in actual fact, "Out of the forty films commented upon in the last number of *Moving Picture World*, exactly one-half are foreign subjects and were made abroad. Of those that were made in this country . . . not more than ten are of American themes . . . distinctly American in characterization, scenery, and surroundings." Turning once again to feedback from exhibitors, the author observed:

> There seems to be amongst exhibitors, among whom we have made the inquiry, a strong and increasing demand for Indian and Western subjects, and here probably we get the most satisfactory answer to our own question. Indian and Western subjects may fairly be considered American, because they deal with the aboriginal or original life of the pioneers of the country.[5]

As if to appease these exhibitors' appetite for "Indian and Western subjects," D. W. Griffith's *Ramona*, a seventeen-minute dramatization of Helen Hunt Jackson's social reform cum romance novel, opened a short five months after the publication of the *World*'s editorial.[6] Recognizing the importance of this premiere, the *World* prepared a "special release" featuring the film with contributing editor Louis Reeves Harrison[7] awarded the plum of covering the event. Being both a news feature and a review, Harrison's article provided readers with some interesting tidbits on the premiere itself, including a demographic analysis of the packed house (mostly male, and "rather above than below the average in quality") and the shortcomings of a "mediocre" vaudeville act that preceded the moving picture. Finally arriving at his assessment of *Ramona*, Harrison's prose suddenly mutated from prosaic to hyperbolic. "*Ramona*, as played," he proclaimed, "is a powerful drama of natural love." Continuing his praise, he stated:

> It is set amid scenes of surpassing beauty, so sympathetically chosen as to lend the whole play a pure spirit of poesy; scene and dramatic art are so harmoniously blended that the picture play is a veritable poem. The producers have advanced a step in the evolution of a new art and blazed the way for additional, greater achievement.[8]

The advancement in film art was evidently not the only kind of "evolution" Harrison had in mind. In his description of the audience's response to *Ramona*, he reported:

> The idea of the white man's injustice to the Indian did not reach out into the sympathies of the audience at all, but it seemed as though the playwright or director, or possibly both, had consciously or unconsciously emphasized a bigger, broader, and finer theme, the great force responsible for our origin, the one which has inspired poets of all ages, but recently discovered by scientists as the most effective cause in the evolution of man. Natural Selection![9]

Although Harrison used the term "natural selection," emphasizing its importance with both caps and an exclamation point, he considered this "great force" to be at work within and among human societies as well as in the natural realm We are thus on solid ground identifying him as a social Darwinist. Unfortunately, having speculated on the evolutionary agenda of *Ramona*'s creators, he dropped the subject and turned to the task of summarizing the movie. This is a pity, since we are left to speculate as to how Harrison arrived at his interpretation. The widespread use of "social Darwinism" in the late nineteenth and early twentieth centuries to rationalize "Manifest Destiny" and the nation's continuing appropriation of Native lands may well have contributed to his identification of "social selection" as the film's "bigger, broader, and finer theme." This reading is especially compelling when one recalls that Harrison's review appeared only two years after the first Wanamaker Expedition (1908), which sought to memorialize America's "Vanishing Race" through a series of photogravure prints by Joseph K. Dixon that recreated the nobility of traditional Indian life, but ended with apocalyptic images entitled "The Sunset of a Dying Race" and "The Empty Saddle."[10]

And here we arrive at the intriguing question of where Hollywood's past and present movie makers and critics, such as Harrison, have acquired their beliefs about American Indian and indigenous peoples and cultures. While we must assume that the individuals in these two professions derived their ideas from a variety of sources, it also stands to reason that few, if any, did so through socialization (i.e., by growing up American Indian) or in-depth research. Rather, as is common with most non-Natives, filmmakers and critics alike have come by much of what they presume to know about indigenous peoples from the rich cultural assemblage of uncritical assumptions and stereotypes provided by the various popular media. It is important to note that the elements comprising this stockpile have always been sufficiently abundant and variegated to allow for the coexistence of radically divergent ideas about what type of beings Indians are and what they ought to become. How else can one explain the presence of both bloodthirsty and noble savages in films of the same era let alone in the same movie? What is essential to recall is that most such depictions are manifestations of what Robert Berkhoffer has called "the white man's Indian" and are based on representations that, in some cases, are as old as the Columbian encounter.[11]

We'll have more to say concerning the representation and reception of the Hollywood Indian after the following story about the origins of the present anthology.

[Dissolve.]

Flashback: An Account Based on True Events

Given 20/20 hindsight, it now seems inevitable that a conversation the editors of this book shared in 2003 about American Indians in movies would lead us to collaborate on *Seeing Red—Hollywood's Pixeled Skins.* The book's actual moment of conception occurred when one of us uttered that immortal Hollywood cliché "Hey kids, let's put on a show."[12] Uh, that is, "Hey kids, let's edit an anthology on Indians in Hollywood films." For a brief moment, we imagined ourselves as a threesome, one Mickey Rooney and two Judy Garlands: fresh-faced, earnest high school types cast in *Babes in Arms* (1939). While it was Rooney who delivered this line in at least three films, he and Garland together valiantly faced crisis after crisis with a song-and-dance routine until the musical's happy finale. So okay, we're not fresh-faced, nor can we sing or dance, but one of us may have actually said, "Hey kids, let's edit an anthology." And just like Garland and Rooney, we've faced some challenges in production.

Our first challenge was to determine what kind of collection we wanted to create. Because of our long-term interest in the subject of "The Hollywooden Indian" (a phrase Stanley Vestal coined for the title of his excellent 1936 article),[13] we knew from the start that we were entering a field where many had gone before. With this in mind, we decided that our first task should be to construct a typology that set forth the various kinds of resources that contained information on American Indians in film. We identified the four following types:

1. *Reference works, book-length monographs, articles, and audio and video treatments of representations of U.S. minorities, including American Indians, in a variety of media.* Recent examples of multi-minority/multimedia resources include Stephanie Greco Larsen's *Media and Minorities: The Politics of Race in News and Entertainment* (2005); *Media and Ethnic*

Minorities, by Valerie Alia and Simone Bull (2006); and Carlos Cortes's *The Children Are Watching: How the Media Teach about Diversity* (2000).

2. *Works in which film representations of American Indians are discussed as part of a more general consideration of film depictions of minorities (racial, ethnic, religious, gender, etc.).* Notable examples include Lester Friedman's *Unspeakable Images: Ethnicity and the American Cinema* (1991); *Projecting Ethnicity and Race: An Annotated Bibliography of Studies on Imagery and American Film*, by Marsha J. Hamilton and Eleanor S. Block; Lane Hirabyashi and Jun Xing's *Reversing the Lens: Ethnicity, Race, Gender, and Sexuality through Film*; Robert Toplin's *Hollywood as Mirror: Changing Views of "Outsider" and "Enemies" in American Movies* (1993); and Allen Woll's *Ethnic and Racial Images in American Film and Television: Historical Essays and Bibliography* (1987).
3. *Studies that treat film images of American Indians as part of the wider and deeper history of Indian-white relations.* Outstanding representatives of this category include Robert F. Berkhofer Jr.'s *The White Man's Indian* (1978); Ward Churchill's *Fantasies of the Master Race: Literature, Cinema, and the Colonization of American Indians*; Philip Deloria's *Playing Indian* (1999) and *Indians in Unexpected Places* (2004); and Shari M. Huhndorf's *Going Native: Indians in the American Cultural Imagination* (2001).
4. *Resources exclusively concerned with Indians as represented by the U.S. film industry.* Noteworthy examples of this category are Gretchen Bataille and Charles Silet's (eds.) *The Pretend Indians: Images of Native Americans in the Movies* (1980) and *Images of American Indians on Film: An Annotated Bibliography* (1985); *The Only Good Indian: The Hollywood Gospel*, by Ralph and Natasha Friar (1972); Michael Hilger's *The American Indian in Film* (1986) and *From Savage to Nobleman: Images of Native Americans in Film* (1995); *Celluloid Indians: Native Americans and Film*, by Jacquelyn Kilpatrick (1999); Peter C. Rollins and John E. O'Connor's *Hollywood's Indian: The Portrayal of the Native American in Film* (1998); Raymond William Steadman's *Shadows of the Indian: Stereotypes in American Culture* (1982); Elizabeth Weatherford and Emilia Seubert's *Native Americans on Film and Video* (1981); Terry Wilson's "Celluloid Sovereignty: Hollywood's 'History' of Native Americans" (1996), Neil Diamond's *Reel Injun* (2009); and *Visualities: Perspectives on Contemporary American Indian Film and Art*, edited by Denise K. Cummings.

After we had completed our typology, we considered our qualifications to address each of the categories. Since we all are specialists in one or another subfield of American Indian Studies, we quickly agreed to focus our efforts on category four: Indian representations in films.

Good enough. But as we considered the many excellent works already published on this theme we encountered another challenge: the anthology must make an original and useful contribution to our chosen subject. We asked ourselves if we could formulate a novel approach to examining filmdom's Indians that would advance this area of study. Rummaging through our mental bibliographies, we each smacked into a number of dead ends before one of us meekly proposed, "Has anyone ever analyzed Indian representations through movie reviews?" This kind of approach, it was suggested, might uncover some interesting assumptions about Indians held by persons who are not only knowledgeable about movies but who also, by and large, intend their work to be read and understood by general audiences.

We spun this idea around like a greased up lazy Susan. To our knowledge, no one had published such a book. Wonderful! But almost immediately our third challenge appeared in the guise of the following question: "What critics should we choose to be part of our anthology and why them?" In trading ideas back and forth, we soon discovered that none of us was particularly keen on including movie reviews by professional critics, so we decided to solicit reviews from colleagues. We then compiled a list of scholars from history, literature, American Studies, American Indian Studies, Indigenous Studies, cultural studies, religion, philosophy, filmmaking, and poetry whom we had reason to suspect would be interested in serving as our critics.

Jump Cut

We're happy to report that almost all those we contacted enthusiastically embraced the opportunity to moonlight as movie critics. As we did not want to smother their creativity regarding how they should go about fulfilling their new jobs, we kept our editorial directives to a minimum, and you'll encounter a great deal of stylistic variation among the reviews. For example, four of the reviews are by American Studies specialists and may include some historical commentary as well as interpretations of literary and critical theory. Fifteen reviews are by literature professors—look for references to great books and double entendres, as English professors are clever writers. Five historians wrote reviews—lots of historical context in their chapters. Three cultural anthropologists question social relations and the definition of human life in their reviews. One reviewer is a philosopher by training, while another is a poet. Still another reviewer is a professor of religion. Also included are reviews by a Native filmmaker, a cultural studies professor, and a president of a college in Nebraska. The anthology contains thirty-six reviews in all, written by reviewers with a wide range of academic backgrounds.

We did, however, pass along a few nonbinding suggestions to our newly hatched critics. We asked them to, whenever possible, base their reviews on personal experience. Make them accessible to a nonacademic audience without sacrificing intellectual content. If appropriate, be funny (well, humorous, witty, ironic, satirical and, you know, a pleasure to read).

All of the contributors took our suggestions to heart—if not in totality, at least in part. Quite a few of the authors honored our request for "experientially based" reviews by embedding their critical voice in autobiographical accounts of how they responded as children, teens, or adults to the representations of Indians in their films. All of the reviews in the anthology have been written for a general audience. And a good number of them are funny.

Having roped in our movie critics, we thought it might be fun to also give students and readers using this anthology the opportunity to play critic. After all, part of the enjoyment of reviewing movies has always been to discuss your own take on a film with your friends. Our rating system is composed of two of the most stereotyped of Indian symbols: the tomahawk and the feather. (See page 237.)

Continuous Action

Many readers may ask what method we used to select the thirty-six movies reviewed in *Seeing Red—Hollywood's Pixeled Skins*. Here we have to admit that the process was anything but scientific. There were certain films that the three of us agreed were so important in the history of the Hollywooden Indian that they had to be included. This is why the book includes four films directed by John Ford: *Drums along the Mohawk*, *She Wore a Yellow Ribbon*, *Fort Apache*, and *The Searchers*—all but the first starring one of Ford's favorite actors, John "The Duke" Wayne. A number of other movies also made our first cut, including Delmar Davies's *Broken Arrow*, Elliot Silverstein's *A Man Called Horse*, Arthur Penn's *Little Big Man*, Kevin Costner's *Dances with Wolves*, Disney's *Pocahontas*, the interactive game of *Indian in the Cupboard*, and the Native written, produced, and directed *Smoke Signals*. We thought it appropriate to include at least one film concerning Native Hawaiians, though the subject deserves a volume all its own. The movie we selected is the Bing Crosby musical *Waikiki Wedding*. We also added a film about Indians and Arabs, *Hidalgo*, a gesture to transnationalists everywhere.

After deciding on our "essentials," we began to employ other criteria to add to our list of films. The most important of these additional principles was "chronological distribution," making certain that each decade, from the 1920s into the twenty-first century was represented by at least one film. As you will note, the distribution turned out to be far from uniform; *Wolfen* is the only film included in the 1980s category. Given the fact that chronology had played such an important role in our selection of movies, we were initially inclined to list the reviews in order of their films' respective release dates. After much deliberation we didn't arrange them temporally, reasoning that our book was not being written to make a historical argument, specifically, that cinematic Indians had changed over time in such and such ways. Rather we agreed to organize them thematically based on what our critics had to say about their movies.

Close Up

Humor plays an important place in this anthology. Let's begin with the collection's title. Over the years there have been scores of books published with the title *Seeing Red*, dealing with such wide-ranging topics as anger management, the federal surveillance of suspected communists and, our own favorite, "the rapture of redheads." However, none of these works, in our opinion, boasts a subtitle quite as alluring as ours. To give credit where it is due, the use of the phrase "Hollywood's Pixeled Skins" was generously granted to us by Ojibwe author Gordon Henry, who adapted it from one of the lines in his poem "Liquored Up."

Prefacing each review is a diary entry by "Hollywood," personified as an arrogant, cantankerous, and pseudo-omniscient industry mogul. Once again we are beholden to another—this time, one of our contributors, Dean Rader—for allowing to us to capitalize on his idea. From his point of view (and our POV on steroids), Hollywood up close is part *Wizard of Oz* (the giant, floating head before Toto outs him), part pre-converted Gordon Gekko ("Greed is Good"), and finally part Louis B. Mayer ("Don't make these pictures any better. Just keep them the way they are"). Many of you can probably think of other parts, but these were the ones that came to our minds.

Freeze Frame

While there might be some readers who consider our decision to make humor an important feature of *Seeing Red* as disrespectful and/or academically suspect, we would remind them of the important role that humor has traditionally played in American Indian societies. One of Hollywood's favorite Indian "types" may have been a stoic and grim-faced creature, frozen in both emotion and time, but as Vine Deloria's incisive (and very funny) chapter "Indian Humor" in *Custer Died for Your Sins* has demonstrated, America's Native peoples might not have survived without heavy doses of joking and teasing that served to soften the blows dealt them throughout the history of Indian-white relations. "Indians have found," Deloria stated, "a humorous side of nearly every problem and the experiences of life have generally been so well defined through jokes and stories that they have become a thing in themselves."[14] He concluded that "When a people can laugh at themselves and laugh at others and hold all aspects of life together without letting anybody drive them to extremes, then it seems to me that the people can survive."[15]

Among the oldest and most beloved vehicles of Indian humor are trickster narratives. The actions of these tales' prankish characters range from the clownish, to the ironic, to the grotesquely funny, as they go about their business wreaking havoc that, while directed toward others deserving or undeserving of such abuse, often backfires. Because of the moral ambiguity of tricksters, they resist easy categorization as either heroes or antiheroes, often occupying both of these statuses at the same time. They may thus be the creators of a community's accepted norms, but just as easily defy these same norms with reckless abandon. It is with the combination of these aspects that tricksters are often found to be a source of satire, calling on communities to rectify their hypocrisies, or making life miserable for oppressors whose inhumanity makes them deserving of retribution.

We would like to believe that the present volume carries on the tradition of the American Indian trickster. In it, Hollywood's traditional dominance in creating or reproducing inherited Indian stereotypes is challenged and lampooned. And in so doing, we laugh and hopefully feel better.

Backstory

Some readers may be lost until they learn about the backstory, or at least some of the history of American Indians in film. It's been over one hundred years since early directors, producers, and actors began making films about wild Indians, wild warrior chiefs (who just wanted to kill white settlers), and wild Indian princesses (who just wanted to love white male settlers). Occasionally a departure in plot would come along. Take, for instance, the first silent picture about American baseball in 1909. This fourteen-minute drama produced by Carl Laemmle and International

Moving Pictures (IMP), titled *His Last Game*, is the first film about American baseball, and it pits the famous Choctaw ball team against the rabble-rousing Jimtown Bar team. *His Last Game* was supposedly set in "Indian Territory," with a Choctaw "Noble Savage" dressed in braids and buckskins.[16] Soon after *His Last Game* hit the nickelodeons, other producers and directors would begin making films about American Indians.

In addition to *Ramona*, pioneering film director D. W. Griffith came out with *Indian Runner's Romance* (Biograph, 1909), a Western melodrama starring Mary Pickford and James Kirkwood as the Indians. This one-reeler tells the story of an Indian brave (Kirkwood) who discovers a gold mine. A gang of bad guys tortures Mrs. Indian Brave (Pickford), expecting her to tell them where the gold is, so they can take it. Ah, but she's a Noble Savage and won't tell. The film's two technical advisers, James Youngdeer and his wife, Lillian St. Cyr, were both enrolled members of the Nebraska Ho-Chunk Tribe. Griffith followed up *Indian Runner's Romance* by directing *The Song of the Wildwood Flute* (Biograph, 1910), starring Mary Pickford as an Indian maiden. The story involves two braves fighting over one maiden. Of course there's a bloody duel to the death. The technical advisor for this drama was American Indian actor Elijah Tahamont, stage name Dark Cloud. Tahamont was also a one-time chief of the Abenaki Tribe.

Next comes *Iola's Promise* (Biograph, 1912), which also features Mary Pickford as an Indian maiden. This time the plot has Mary being captured by cruel Indians. Her rescuer is a good white man, played by actor Alfred Paget. (Note: It costs him his own sweetie.) Three years later, in 1915, Mary Pickford stars in *Little Pal*. This time the story is set in Alaska, and Ms. Pickford plays a half-breed Eskimo girl.

During Mary Pickford's long career, she played every kind of ethnic character from the queen of Herzegovina, to a Japanese maid, to an Alaska Native maiden. She also worked with real American Indians, such as Tahamont, Youngdeer, and St. Cyr. Yet it is Pickford's meeting in 1929 with nineteen-year-old Mary Cornelius Hartshorne, a Choctaw college student at Tulsa University in Oklahoma, that adds a fascinating wrinkle to the story of Hollywood's mythmaking about American Indians.[17]

In 1929, Mary Hartshorne won the *Tulsa Tribune*'s essay contest on "Talkie Movies." Her essay was chosen over three hundred entries, and in it she discusses the necessity of achieving a good education, the value of sound recordings in such areas as speaking a second language, and social justice—three core values of Choctaw people. She was related to two prominent families in the Choctaw Nation: the McCurtains and Fulsoms. Her great-grandfather was Cornelius McCurtain, and her grandfather was Chief Green McCurtain (1902–1910). She graduated from Tulsa Central High School in 1926. She began her undergraduate studies at the University of Oklahoma, later switching to Tulsa University. An excerpt from Hartshorne's essay published in the *American Indian*, February 1929, shows how convinced she is that the talkies will be used for educating students at universities and colleges:

> Not only in a general way, however, can the talkies be of value; they can be used to great advantage in our educational institutions, as in many cases the movies have been. Students of the future will be able to spend certain hours each week learning theory, on other days they will go into the "laboratory" where they can see and hear theory put into practice. Professors whose native idiom it is cannot always be obtained to teach a foreign language, a fact which accounts for the faulty pronunciation of many who have studied a language for years. This difficulty will be overcome

> when the talkies are introduced into schools. Students of drama and public speaking may listen to famous exponents of these arts and note the harmony between voice, gesture and facial expression. Classes in science may attend lectures by the Einsteins and Edisons of their day.
>
> It may be easily seen that the cultural value of the talking screen is incomputable. But along other lines, also, will it prove itself meritable. It can, for instance, become quite indispensable to our courts of justice. Instead of sending the written record of a trial to the appellate court when a case is appealed, will it not be much more satisfactory to send a sound-film of the whole procedure, allowing the judge to hear the original case and perceive the demeanor of the witnesses?[18]

What we also found ironic about the Hartshorne essay is that it was written about the same time that Paramount Pictures was releasing *Redskin* (1929), starring Richard Dix as the Navajo Wing Foot or Yat-tay, and Gladys Belmont as Corn Blossom (see Cristina Stanciu's review of *Redskin* in chapter 1). Hollywood is making pictures about pidgin-speaking Indians at the same time a Choctaw college student wins an essay contest for elegant writing! Though naive, Ms. Hartshorne's essay is forward-looking, articulating a potential for social justice for all (something akin to equality, a core belief of Choctaws and other American Indians). Hollywood studios, on the other hand, will continue to make films that portrayed American Indians as primitive savages on the verge of extinction throughout the twentieth century. Put another way, what's up with Hollywood producers and directors? Perhaps they are still answering the 1910 question from *Moving Picture World*, "What Is an American Subject?" If it is American, it must contain representations of Indians. Even the 2011 release of comedy/drama *The Dilemma*, set in Chicago, ends with images of the Sauk war chief Blackhawk (the Chicago Blackhawks mascot) on the T-shirts that Vince Vaughn and Kevin James wear. Yeah, go team. Whatever.

One final comment. After meeting Mary Hartshorne in 1929, Mary Pickford doesn't portray another American Indian character on-screen. Of course, by that point she was reaching the end of her career. She retired from acting in films in 1933. But one wonders if the meeting had any influence on the films Pickford would choose to produce?

Montage

One spring night on Turner Classic Movies (TCM), in preparation for writing the introduction we watched Fred MacMurray and Claudette Colbert in *The Egg and I* (1947), Universal's well-wrought comedy/romance about a city couple seeking the American Dream by buying and attempting to run a chicken farm. The farm offers its own challenges, particularly to Colbert's Betty MacDonald, who was surprised by her new husband's (MacMurray's) purchase of the once-abandoned farm as a wedding gift to her. Contemporary audiences favorably received the film, which was based on real-life writer Betty MacDonald's best-selling 1945 novel of the same title. The novel, however, which has never been out of print, has been widely panned over the years for its racist descriptions of Northwest Coast Native Americans.

Okay. So, this film title may not register for many of us today as a "classic" on all counts, but it's certainly from the classical Hollywood period, and it's an entertaining film. But what does this movie have to do with American Indians in film? Well, there was one small, seemingly insignificant scene and character rendering that goes a long way towards illustrating the pervasive and monolithic image classical Hollywood perpetuated about Native peoples.

Consider this scene: Early in the film, Betty is inside the couple's farmhouse attempting to make it a "home." As she busily performs her wifely domestic duties, she is startled to see two dark-skinned figures framed in a window, silently staring at her. Anyone remember the classic extreme close-up in Ford's *The Searchers* (see the review in chapter 2) when John Wayne's niece, Debbie, first encounters a "Comanche"? The scene in *The Egg and I* is similar. A terrified Betty (the camera swiftly tracking her) frantically flees the farmhouse and runs out to find her husband, Bob, who calmly explains to her, "Oh, that's just Geoduck and his brother Crowbar, two harmless Injuns." The camera cuts back to a shot of Betty, her face indicating relief.

Denise K. Cummings recalls: As a first-time viewer of this film, I became reactionary. What's this seemingly gratuitous and racist incident doing in this film anyway? Of course, I can answer my own question. And, with a little bit of research, I learned how the film's deployment of the two minor characters actually subtends an ongoing exploitation in other period films, a detail from film history that further underscores mainstream cinema's ubiquitous misrepresentation of American Indians.

The Egg and I also features Ma and Pa Kettle (played by Marjorie Main and Percy Kilbride), who in the late 1940s and throughout the 1950s headlined their own films, beginning with *Ma and Pa Kettle* (1949) and followed by numerous sequels bearing such titles as *Ma and Pa Kettle on Vacation* (1953) and *Ma and Pa Kettle at Waikiki* (1955). In the 1949 debut title film, which stemmed from their success with *The Egg and I* audiences, Ma and Pa Kettle are rustic folk with fifteen kids who stumble upon good fortune when Pa Kettle wins a modern dream home in a contest. The characters, based on author Betty MacDonald's real-life farming neighbors in upstate Washington, are intended as comic relief, and Universal had a good run with them. The final Ma and Pa Kettle film was released in 1957 with the resonant title *The Kettles on Old MacDonald's Farm.*

Also making their filmic debut in *The Egg and I* are Geoduck and Crowbar. Geoduck is the name given to one of the generic Native characters in both *The Egg and I* and the Ma and Pa Kettle films. A geoduck is a large saltwater clam harvested in Washington State, and author Betty MacDonald further describes these mollusks in her novel *Onions in the Stew* (1955), about her life on Vashon Island. Over the years, Geoduck was played by several actors: John Berkes in *The Egg and I,* Lester Allen in the first two Ma and Pa Kettle films, and Oliver Blake in the others. Crowbar, the name attributed to the other generic "Indian" character, was played by various actors as well: Victor Patel, Chief Yowlachie, Teddy Hart, Zachary Charles, and Stan Ross. In the films, the characters are often silent, and though they sometimes provide comic relief for their white, onscreen counterparts, mostly they're treated as props.

The interchangeability of actors in their respective roles says something about Hollywood's indiscretion. In a pattern that continued to play out in many of the films reviewed in this book, classical Hollywood didn't care who played the roles (e.g., non-Natives or Natives, or non-Indians in Indian roles) so long as audiences accepted the characters as American Indians. And that's why the scene in *The Egg and I* is so maddening. The other reason is because of the scene's ideology: its message is "fear the other." This ideology was pervasive in classical Hollywood filmmaking, perpetuated over and over in hundreds of movies made before, throughout, and following the classical Hollywood period.

In *The Invention of the Western Film: A Cultural History of the Genre's First Half Century* (2003), author Scott Simmon examines the American Indian's rise in film during the silent era. Specifically, Simmon makes a compelling argument about the commercial origins and rationale for casting and (mis)representing Native Americans in films from that period. In the early 1900s, when art, technology, and the business of filmmaking were rapidly evolving in the United States, a French filmmaking company, Pathé Frères, was capturing a huge share of the international market by exporting silent films to the rest of the world. Simmon argues that one way for the United States to compete with other production companies such as Pathé was to deliver to audiences unique fare: America had the distinctive American West landscapes and the people who inhabited them, Native Americans. Thus, due to its ontological nature, its chronological positioning, and/or its capitalist impulse, early U.S. cinema advanced representations of Native Americans, most often as "the vanishing American."

The formula worked, as the well-known ascendency of the Western film genre corroborates. By the early 1930s vertical integration of the industry, and throughout the classical period in the United States, stereotypical Native Americans were shown not just in Westerns, but in the full range of film genres—from animated shorts to romance-comedies like *The Egg and I.*

Which brings us back to Turner Classic Movies (TCM). The network recently aired its thirty-film series "Race in Hollywood: Native American Images on Film" (2010), which attempts to look at the treatment of Native Americans in the movies. To TCM's credit, host Robert Osborne invited Hanay Geiogamah, director of the American Indian Studies Center at UCLA, into the studio to discuss the problems associated with cinematic representation of Native peoples, and to critique particular films screened as part of the series. Such an effort by the cable movie channel is laudable.

Many of the series' films are those reviewed in *Seeing Red*—the big-named and well-recognized star vehicles like *The Searchers*, *Dances with Wolves*, and *Thunderheart*, to name a few. As editors of *Seeing Red*, we recognize the importance of offering critical commentary about these influential films, but we also believe that films that are not so well known to all viewers are equally important. What about all *The Egg and I*'s of classical Hollywood, all those films not on TCM's list of thirty? What we mean is that millions of Americans, and movie viewers around the world, have seen, and continue to see films about American Indians that perpetuate stereotypes and convey racism. These are the films that we must talk about, consider, discuss.

Voice-Over: End Credits

Seeing Red—Hollywood's Pixeled Skins has an agenda. We hope to show why and how the images of American Indians are the mascots for American film. These essays, frequently infused with a dash (or more) of humor, emerge also to challenge the dominant ideologies concerning race that have been dished up by mainstream cinema for over a century. They are an approach for taking on the naturalization of such images; they are a model for teaching viewers to recognize both good filmmaking and the problem of misrepresentation of Native peoples. They are a method of historicizing and contextualizing cinematic representation that runs the gamut from the outright racist, to the well-intentioned, to the more recent independent productions that put forth dynamic, developed characters who reflect real-life American Indians and indigenous characters with whom young people can identify. *Seeing Red* is about social justice, a collaboration of scholars in many disciplines. The reviews show us the stereotypical representations of the past, and suggest ways we can see American Indians and indigenous peoples more clearly in the twenty-first century. From our POV, this is the message we're sending.

NOTES

1. *New York Herald*, 24 April 1896. The story of how the Vitascope became "Edison's Greatest Marvel" has more to do with entrepreneurship than invention. The creative agent in this story was actually Francis Jenkins, who introduced a projector he named the Phantoscope in Richmond, Indiana, in 1884. With the help of his new partner, Thomas Armat, Jenkins improved his invention, which they unveiled in 1895 at the Cotton States Exposition. Here it caught the attention of Frank Harrison, an employee of Norman Raff and Frank Gammon's Kinetoscope Company, which held exclusive distribution rights for Edison's Kinetoscope. Raff and Gammon were able to buy the rights to the machine from Armat (exclusive of Jenkins) and then convince Edison to claim it as his own.
2. "Edison's Vitascope Cheered," *New York Times*, 24 April, 1896 . While obviously impressed by the Vitascope's powers, the unnamed reporter nevertheless refers to the projector as "The ingenious inventor's latest toy."
3. An allusion to film critic Roger Ebert's imperious rating. Ebert has been reviewing movies for the *Chicago Sun Times* since 1967. Eight years after his start, he and the late Gene Siskel inaugurated the weekly television show *Sneak Previews*.
4. In 1931, *Moving Picture World* bought out *Moving Picture News*.
5. *Moving Picture World*, 22 January 1910.
6. Griffith's version starred a yet relatively unknown Mary Pickford who had been acting in his movies for less than a year before she was given the part. Three significantly longer Hollywood remakes were to follow Griffith's original version, appearing in 1916, 1928, and 1936. Jackson's novel also served as the basis of a popular Mexican television series of the same name. Lucy Orozco and Humberto Robles co-wrote the teleplay for this adaption, which aired on Televista in 2000.
7. In addition to his work at the *Moving Picture World*, Harrison also served as the assistant director for the film *The Price He Paid* and authored at least seven screenplays.
8. *Moving Picture World*, 4 June 1910.
9. Ibid.
10. Financed by Philadelphia department-store entrepreneur Lewis Rodman Wanamaker, each of the three expeditions had a specific goal. On the first expedition, organized in 1907, famed photographer Joseph K. Dixon captured stills of (reputedly) rapidly vanishing tribal customs. Those participating in the expedition of 1909 filmed a reenactment of the Battle of the Little Bighorn. The third and final expedition of 1913 was held in conjunction with the planned but never erected National Memorial to Native Americans on Staten Island . To demonstrate the patriotism of American Indians, expedition delegates presented leaders of selective tribes with American flags; they, in turn, signed their names under the text of the Pledge of Allegiance to the United States.

11. Robert F. Berkhofer Jr., *The White Man's Indian* (New York: Vintage Books, 1979).
12. There is a category of musicals that are now often referred to as the "Hey kids, let's put on a show" musicals. These include *Strike Up the Band* (1940), *Babes on Broadway* (1941), and *Girl Crazy* (1943).
13. Stanley Vestal, "The Hollywooden Indian," *Southwest Review* 21 (July 1936): 418–23.
14. Vine Deloria Jr., *Custer Died for Your Sins* (New York: Avon Books, 1972).
15. Ibid., 168.
16. LeAnne Howe used this film as a backdrop in her fictional novel *Miko Kings: An Indian Baseball Story* (LeAnne Howe, *Miko Kings: An Indian Baseball Story* [San Francisco: Aunt Lute 2007]).
17. LeAnne Howe is indebted to Robert Dale Parker for introducing her to the story of Mary Cornelius Hartshorne. Professor Parker uncovered her story while researching materials for his book *Changing Is Not Vanishing: A Collection of Early American Indian Poetry to 1930* (Philadelphia: University of Pennsylvania Press, 2011).
18. *The American Indian*, February 1929, p. 3.

CHAPTER 1

The Silent Red Man

Dear Diary:

By the time I get through with Richard Dix, every woman in America will wish she were sharing her tipi with this hot-blooded Redman. Can anyone spell fetishized? But dear me, his next role as a redskin is going to cost us plenty of wampum. Must kissy-kissy with the bankers. After all, the show must go on.

Love ya, Dix,

Hollywood

The Vanishing American

Jill Doerfler

So, what can you expect from *The Vanishing American*? Well, it was originally a silent film made in 1925, and as you might guess by the title, it's based on Zane Grey's popular novel of the same name. The film has been described as an "epic scale historic melodrama." Of course, "epic scale" had quite a different meaning in 1925 than it does today, so don't expect the visual impact of films like *300*—although the historical accuracy might be about the same. However, some of the scenes were filmed in Monument Valley and are quite beautiful.

The film was originally considered "sympathetic" in its portrayal of American Indians, but offers only fleeting moments of positive portrayals of American Indians. It reflects early twentieth-century anthropological views of race and human development. While physical anthropology was challenged early on by several anthropologists, including Franz Boas, it fully emerged as a field in the United States during the 1920s. Biological determinism is a major underlying theme reflected throughout the film. The characters fulfill their predetermined destinies based on their race. As you might guess, the American Indians will be doing the "vanishing" and the European Americans will be assuming control of our lands.

It becomes clear right away that there is an obsession with "race" in this film. *Vanishing* begins with a lengthy prologue that ambitiously covers thousands of years of history, where we learn about the natural rise and fall of a variety of "races." First we are introduced to the race of "basket weavers." A man comes over a rocky hillside followed by a woman carrying a baby. They walk off, and soon another "race" emerges: these are the "slab-house people," who are "more strongly developed." They don't really have to tell you this since it is clearly evident by their ability to stand completely upright and their more fashionable clothing choices. However, they, too, simply fade away, and then come the "cliff dwellers," who happen to be the first "race" that there is "definite knowledge of." These are "indolent, harmless people" who are also lazy and not very devout in their religion (this mistake will come back to haunt them).

The life of the "cliff dwellers" seems to be going along just fine; the children happily bathe in mud, and adults spend their time napping. Suddenly a priest criticizes the lazy behavior of a man, and his mother—one of only two women who are allowed to "speak" in the film—comes to his defense by calling out, "Blame not my son! Blame those idle hussies, yonder!" It would seem that women are the ones who have caused the problems for this "race." Yet, another cause is soon revealed to the audience in the intertitles. Sadly, "long years of peace had dulled the religious sense of the people." Clearly, if the men had not been so distracted by "idle hussies" they could have been busy killing each other—after all, there's nothing like a good war to rally a people back to religion!

Anyway, as you might guess, a stronger "race"—who happen to be the first of the "race" known as Indians—came in and destroyed the "cliff dwellers," but not before a priest was able to prognosticate the future: "May Paya the Father drive you into darkness as you have driven us! May he send a stronger race to grind you in the dust and scatter you through the Four Worlds of Lamentation!"

Yikes, you can guess what happens later . . . but meanwhile the Indians prevail: "And so the conquerors dwelt for ages in the land. They raided far and wide. Their numbers grew. They believed no race could be their equal." Those Indians sure *were* a confident bunch, but don't worry, it won't be long before they will be driven into the darkness by a stronger race.

Lo and behold! The Spanish arrive on their "fire-breathing monsters" (aka horses), and it only takes about two minutes for the Indians to realize that the Spanish are really "gods," and surrender. There is no real conflict, because the hierarchy of the "races" prevails naturally. God's will is done. *Thankfully*, the Spanish and other Europeans are just the most recent in a long line of colonizers, so no need for all you Catholics to feel guilty.

Just when you think the story is basically over—I mean they have covered several centuries of history in a matter of minutes, not to mention the development of several races, the film jumps to the then-present day of World War I. Richard Dix plays Nophaie, the *noble* tribal leader. Dix was born Ernest Carlton Brimmer in St. Paul, Minnesota, and became an actor after dropping out of the University of Minnesota. He went on to act in many films, both silent and early talkies. Nophaie was not his only Indian role—he also played Wing Foot in *Redskin* (1929). Perhaps they were unable to find any real Indian actors to play Nophaie; this is understandable when one considers that so many Natives had already *vanished* by the 1920s. Lois Wilson is the young, pretty, and white schoolteacher, Marian Warner.

The film continues when Kit Carson is forced to attack the Indians because they're not smart enough to surrender. If only they had realized the Americans were gods like the Spanish this could have all been avoided. Carson laments, "I'm afraid there is no other way—these Indians are my friends . . . but I must send them to their death." It is always heartbreaking when someone is forced to kill their friends, but what was he supposed to do? Allow them to go back to their conquering ways? Leave them alone to live on the lands they had reserved in treaties with the U.S. government?

Apparently, Carson was not able to send all of them to their death, because by the early twentieth century the Indians are living on a barren reservation where children tend the flocks of sheep and goats. The Indian agent, Amos Halliday, is focused on filing paperwork (boy, those whites sure do love paper), and his corrupt assistant, Henry Brooker, is really in charge. Brooker is the primary villain in the film and is involved in a horse-stealing scheme. His men even steal a horse from an Indian child. The negative portrayal of Brooker as a European American is surprising, but fits with a kind of sophisticated image.

Soon "the Indian Love Moon cast its spell over the hearts of the primitive desert children." Nophaie visits Marian, who he calls "White Desert Rose," and inquires about the Bible. (And I bet you thought the romance would never begin.) Marian is enthusiastic about sharing the "word of God" with Nophaie. However, to Nophaie's disappointment, Brooker interrupts under the pretense of school business, and he must leave. Brooker clearly wants to date Marian, but she shows no interest in him.

The next day, Brooker enters the school after the children have left and embraces Marian despite her resistance. Even though she is European, Marian is still a woman and, therefore, unable to defend herself or express her own opinions and desires. Luckily, Nophaie sees what is happening through a window and comes to her rescue. Nophaie is cast as the hero here, upsetting the natural order of the races. At this point, several other white men come in and attack Nophaie (an attempt to bring back the "natural" order), but ironically, he is able to escape on a horse.

Marian runs to Halliday, but Brooker claims that he found Marian and Nophaie together and that it was Nophaie who attacked him. Halliday instructs Brooker and his men to "bring in" Nophaie. Meanwhile, Nophaie has made it to the Valley of Marching Rocks, where Brooker and his men will never find him. Days pass and Nophaie remains safely hidden.

Unexpectedly, an army general comes to the reservation to get horses for World War I. When it becomes known that the Indians will not bring in their horses because of Brooker's previous actions, Marian suggests that if Nophaie instructs the Indians to bring in their horses, they will. With the help of a young child, Marian goes to talk with Nophaie. She explains that the government needs the horses for war: "Oh, I know—you have been unjustly treated. But Brooker and his men did that—not the Government. This is still your country. You are an American as much as any of us." Nophaie (and anyone watching the film) is quite surprised by Marian's suggestion that he is an American. Marian continues: "Yes, Nophaie! And this is a war for freedom, for the right. For oppressed people everywhere. Out of it will grow a new order . . . a new justice." Just when you thought you knew where the film was going, there is an acknowledgment that the Indians have been oppressed; the only catch is that it is not the government that has oppressed Indians, it has been "white men." I bet you thought that white men were in charge of the U.S. government; nope, two totally different groups of people. They should teach this stuff in school.

Not surprisingly the Indians do indeed bring in their horses, and many, including Nophaie, decide to enlist, with the hope that the United States will treat them with respect. Nophaie goes to say goodbye to Marian, but sees her with the general and decides not to approach her.

A few minutes later Marian sees that Nophaie is about to leave, so she brings him a copy of the New Testament. As the Indians ride off, the general comments: "Pitiful—and tremendous! Riding away to fight for the whiteman!" Oh wait, maybe the "whiteman" does have some kind of correlation with the U.S. government after all. Hmm.

Even though they're constructed as "primitive," in the film the Indians are good soldiers. Nophaie even becomes a sergeant. For added drama, these scenes have a red tint. The war ends, and Nophaie and the other Indians return home. To everyone's shock and surprise they find Brooker in charge, and he tells Nophaie that Marian and the general are married. Distraught, Nophaie goes out to the countryside and begins to pray to his God, but then realizes that he should pray to the Christian God. See, war does bring people back to religion.

Meanwhile, the other Indians are very angry because Brooker has taken much of their land and turned it into an experimental farm for the government. The Indians devise a plan to kill Brooker and burn out the other white men. Could this be the new order and justice Marian was talking about? Nope. Nophaie heads out to warn the whites.

In the meantime Marian has returned and tells Nophaie that she's not married. At this point, I was starting to think maybe Nophaie and Marian would actually end up together. But, alas, it was not to be. Nophaie is accidently shot by another Indian while trying to stop a fight. So, the "good" Indian actually isn't killed by a member of the "superior" race, but by his own kind. This, of course, serves to absolve whites and the U.S. government from any responsibility, while reinforcing the idea that the "superior" race will naturally prevail. Everyone stops fighting and gathers around Nophaie after they realize he's been shot.

Clearly clinging to a last few minutes of life, Nophaie asks Marian to read to him from the New Testament. She does, and his last words are, "I think... think... I understand." Here we're treated to a surprising turn: Nophaie has the ability to "understand"—maybe he does have the same mental abilities as "the white man"? Alas, it cannot be, because this dangerous challenge to the natural hierarchy of races is quickly resolved through his death. Bart Wilson, a white man who is respected by the Indians, is hired as the new agent. This move emphasizes that it's irrelevant who the agent is, because the natural hierarchy of the races and the authority of the U.S. government will ultimately prevail.

In the last scene, Nophaie's body is carried off and the screen reads: "—for the races of men come—and go. But the mighty stage remains." The final shot shows an empty landscape and then a shadowed "end of the trail" silhouette. As promised in the title, the Indians vanish. The landscape remains and is under control of the "white man" or the U.S. government. What's the difference? Sigh, "The End."

DEAR DIARY:

This is our last silent picture, and thank heaven for that. I was bored witless by those deaf and dumb Indians. From now on it's gonna be "shoot 'em up, wipe 'em out" with noisy Gatling guns ablazing as we conquer the West, Vitaphone-style.

Ya-ta-hey everybody!

HOLLYWOOD

Redskin

CRISTINA STANCIU

Enthusiasts of the Washington Redskins and other mascot worshippers will be disappointed in this early silent feature film from 1929. It's not about sports—well, not entirely—although the Indian protagonist, white actor Richard Dix, is briefly recruited with an athletic scholarship to a fictional Thorpe University on the East Coast. Thorpe University is a nod to the famous Sac and Fox Jim Thorpe, winner of the 1912 Olympic Games decathlon and pentathlon competitions. Students of film may be surprised to learn that American Indians appeared in films before *Dances with Wolves* (1990). As early as the beginning of what would become "Hollywood," there were Indian directors and actors, such as Winnebago actors James Youngdeer and his wife, Lillian St. Cyr (aka Princess Redwing), long before the John Wayne Westerns took hold of the market and audience imagination. Yet, in the first decade of the twentieth century, silent Indian-themed films were in high demand, and their subjects ranged from failed Indian-white relations, cross-racial romances, or indictments of white civilization. Although many Indian actors worked for Hollywood, the filmmakers' assumption was that anybody could play Indian.

Redskin, one of Paramount's last silent films, has a predominantly white cast. Richard Dix plays the leading role, Navajo Wing Foot or Yat-tay, and Gladys Belmont plays his Pueblo love interest, Corn Blossom. Jane Novak appears in the role of the white teacher named Judith Stearns, and a thin-mustached Larry Steers plays the boarding-school disciplinarian, John Walton. Because of its fascinating look at American frontier racism, the National Film Preservation Foundation reissued *Redskin* in 2007 as part of volume 4 in its "Social Issues in American Film, 1900–1934" collection.

The sentimental plot line follows Wing Foot from his peaceful childhood on the Navajo reservation as Chief Notani's son, to his boarding-school days at the U.S. Indian Boarding School on the Chaco reservation. Later, we follow Wing Foot to the U.S. Albuquerque Indian College and Thorpe University, until his return home. "Go with the white man! But come to me—an Indian," his father urges him reluctantly as the son is taken to boarding school by force. In the process, Wing Foot meets Corn Blossom, his Acoma Pueblo love interest, and love does blossom.

Corn Blossom is called back home before the romance can really get going. Things fall apart for the two lovers: he is banished from his own tribe for defying his elders, for refusing the honor of becoming the new medicine man, and for criticizing his tribe for "dying through ignorance." Wing Foot has a heavy heart, as this is a difficult episode in his life, but the film's narrative doesn't develop his character through backstory. Banished from both worlds, he returns "to his only refuge, the wilderness of burning sand and thirst-stricken mountains," as the intertitle informs us. It seems for Wing Foot you really can go home again. He discovers oil on his land claim, shares half of it with the Pueblos (thus ending the long-standing feud between the tribes), and weds Corn Blossom in a brief traditional ceremony. Wing Foot orchestrates a reconciliation between the tribes, which brings forth "the greatest gift of heaven—tolerance," as the last intertitle reads. "Indian problem" solved.

The film is based on a novel written by a Navajo enthusiast, Elizabeth Pickett. Initially titled *Navajo*, the novel was published as *Redskin* shortly after the film's premiere in 1929, with illustrations from the film, perhaps fulfilling larger marketing agendas than its author had anticipated. Pickett also wrote the screenplay for the film, her last script for Hollywood, following a series of documentaries about the Pueblos she did in 1925. The studio employed hundreds of Native people as extras to give the film its aura of authenticity, and to render the sense of rivalry between Navajos and Pueblos. Although almost completely silent throughout this silent film, the voicelessness of the Native people in their casual or ceremonial dress speaks volumes through their body language and inquisitive glances at the camera, perhaps eschewing directorial instructions. Filmed in both black-and-white and two-color Technicolor, *Redskin* combines the black-and-white scenes (in the white man's world) with the two-color scenes filmed on tribal lands (mostly in Arizona and New Mexico). Produced by Paramount and directed by a Paramount house name, Victor Schertzinger, *Redskin* arguably falls into the category of other Hollywood racist films—or, films with racist titles like *Justice of the Redskin* (1908), *Romantic Redskins* (1910), *The Trapper and the Redskins* (1910). Unlike these earlier films, *Redskin* wants to be more sympathetic to Indian representation, and is really "pretty"; as early reviews of the film in major national newspapers put it, *Redskin* is a "triumph of color!" In other words, racism—but in Technicolor!

There are reasons both to love and hate this film, and then love to hate it, and often with similar intensity. First, there's the racist title. Some linguists argue that the term "redskin" has been around since the seventeenth century, when it served as a conventional reference to North American Indians, used by European colonial powers and indigenous peoples alike. At least the records produced by nonindigenous people supported this theory. During treaty negotiations, the word "redskin" first saw print around 1815, reaching an unparalleled popularity with James Fenimore Cooper's novel *The Pioneers* (1823) as "redskin," "red skin," or "Red-skin." Then there's Pickett's screenplay, an attempt to rectify misrepresentations of Indians on the silver screen during one of Hollywood's tamest periods in terms of Indian representation, marked by pseudo-sympathy for Native people in a decade of intense criticism of federal Indian policy in the 1920s. Like its predecessor *The Vanishing American* (see the review in this chapter), Zane Grey's cinematic tribute to the noble but nonetheless vanishing Indian, *Redskin*'s progressive impulse succumbs to a racist logic reinforced by characters, acting, script, intertitles, music score, plot, themes, and the cinematic enterprise as a whole.

The initial screenings of the film were accompanied by a "Redskin" theme song setting the mood and tone for audience identification. Early enthusiastic reviews of the film usually raved about the theme song, which was itself a radio hit. The song captured Pickett's and the country's fascination with an imagined Indian male, masculine yet infantile, and thus posing no threat to American manhood and presumed racial superiority:

Redskin, Redskin, boy of my dreams
Take me back to silvery streams

. . .

With happy hearts we'll go roaming,
I'll whisper in the gloaming,
I love you, Redskin, love you.

The song also sets the tone for a potential interracial romance between Wing Foot and the white college flapper, attracted to the mysterious Navajo. As she glances at his athletic body on the track field from her reserved box seat, she commands her chubby white boyfriend: "You must invite that Redskin to the dance tonight. He ought to be a new thrill—in the Ballroom!" In the meantime, Corn Blossom cheers for Wing Foot from an upper stadium tier, "Come on, you Navajo!" Wing Foot does his best to navigate these competing gazes, speeds up, and wins the race.

Later at the ball, the flapper asks her boyfriend, "Where's my Redskin?" as everybody awaits the triumphant appearance of the Indian track champion. "Say! What's the idea—getting all steamed up over an Indian?" asks her plump beau. Unable to control his jealousy, he provokes Wing Foot to a fistfight just as his girlfriend provoked him to a whooping dance only minutes before. Wing Foot ends up surrounded by white students dancing and whooping around him—"Well, if you can't dance my way, I'll dance yours!" But Wing Foot's humiliations are just beginning; he's punched in the face and told he's tolerated only because he is needed on the track team. Shamed, he passively withdraws and returns to his college room, only to find out that "he sure acted white—for a Redskin!" The roommate's sympathy is the last straw and triggers Wing Foot's radical gesture of separation from a world where he is branded a "redskin." In a scene full of pathos (and perhaps too much makeup), Wing Foot decides to return home. Sobbing, clutching Corn Blossom's portrait to his heart, he declares his pride in being a "redskin" in a scene memorable for its internalized racism: "After what I saw tonight, I'm proud to be a Redskin. My mistake was in thinking I ever had a chance among you whites! I'm going back to my own people where I belong!"

Throughout the film, Wing Foot navigates between several identities, names, landscapes, and (presumably) languages that make any kind of belonging tentative. I am uncertain about Wing Foot's linguistic navigation since English dominates this silent film's intertitles—even when he speaks with his grandmother Yina, played by Augustina Lopez—a slip that exposes the assumption about the film's main audience in 1929. (In fact, *Redskin* was one of Hollywood's last silents, although the silent era technically ended in 1927 with the first sound feature film, *The Jazz Singer*.) In Pickett's book, the linguistic nuances are more apparent, and the Indian characters are said to speak specific Indian "dialects."

Taken to boarding school by force at the age of nine, Wing Foot rebels against the confines of the regulatory institution and its Americanization practices, which include saluting the U.S. flag. His refusal costs him not only a major whipping and failure of his first Americanization lesson, but also a shameful name his Indian fellow students give him: "Do-Atin," or "The Whipped One." We don't know how much the director assumed that the white audiences knew about corporal punishment in Indian communities, but the writer makes clear in her book that "The Whipped One" or "The Tamed One" was a shameful phrase the Navajos used to refer to a broken mustang. Wing Foot's own father, Chief Notani, calls him "Do-Atin" after he refuses the honor of becoming the tribe's medicine man. As a student of medicine in the white man's world, Wing Foot comes to disdain traditional medicinal ways: "Your witchcraft killed my mother [who died in childbirth]—it is killing my grandmother [who is going blind]—and now you want me to preach such nonsense!" Wing Foot concludes bitterly, commenting on his education: "I am neither Indian nor White Man. Just . . . Redskin."

Next—location, location, location. Many other Indian-themed silents before *Redskin* were invested in capturing "authentic" landscapes for the screen. *Redskin* was a big studio film (with a budget of $ 400,000) and it was shot on location in Arizona and New Mexico. The commissioner of Indian Affairs at the time, Charles H. Burke, gave Paramount his blessing to make this film—as long as it provided "wholesome and instructive entertainment to the public," especially concerning the government attitude toward Indians. We don't really know how Navajos or Pueblos may have felt about the filming. And so, in 1928, Paramount carved a road, which is still functional today, of about three hundred feet to carry the heavy equipment up the mesa of Acoma Pueblo. At the beginning of the movie, Wing Foot lives in Arizona, in Canyon de Chelly, and Corn Blossom lives on the mesa of Acoma Pueblo in New Mexico. The boarding-school scenes, in black-and-white, were filmed at the Chinle Indian Boarding School in Arizona, and at the Sherman Indian Institute in Riverside, California. I am ambivalent about this choice of locations. On the one hand, it's admirable that the studio went the extra mile(s) to set the story on Navajo and Pueblo lands in an attempt to portray the inhumanity of the boarding school experience and the failure of assimilation policies. On the other hand, by praising the location and glossing over the film's other artistic choices, we miss an important opportunity to question the film's larger ideological and political implications. For example, one of the film's early reviews bombastically described it as "one of the most complete historical moving pictures ever made." Clearly an overstatement for 1929, or even 2012. Even contemporary viewers and reviewers, who are aware of concepts like "decolonization" or "decolonizing viewing relations," still consider it one of the most "authentic" Hollywood films about American Indians, thus privileging the film's artistic accomplishments and medium (the beautiful photography, with seductive scenery and wonderful shades of the red and green desert) over *Redskin*'s message and subject matter. Indeed, one of the film's early reviews completely ignored the fact that the film was about Pueblos and Navajos, and focused instead on the film's sound effects, music, and Richard Dix.

And indeed there's handsome Richard Dix . . . He embodies a determined and almost heroic Wing Foot only four years after he played a dying Navajo in George B. Seitz's melodramatic *The Vanishing American* (1925). Did Dix accept the role of Wing Foot to redeem his star image that was tarnished by the melodramatic caricature of the Navajo man in his previous film, or was he, in fact, interested in a more sympathetic representation. It's hard to tell. But it wasn't the story of Indian boarding schools, alcoholism, government neglect, violent disciplinarians, silent Indian women, flappers, dying mothers and grandmothers that sold the film; it was Richard Dix. It was Richard Dix who became the "redskin" audiences were waiting to see. The "boy of their dreams," Dix, could carry his spectators to safer places than any Indian actor in the 1920s. Dix embodied a collective national fantasy in an "authentic" setting, answering a pressing question of early American cinema publics—"Where's my redskin?"

CHAPTER 2

John Ford and "The Duke" on the Warpath

DEAR DIARY:

I don't know why everyone on the Mohawk reservation is upset with Drums. *They're so tiresome in New York. Must be the East Coast weather and cold, overcast skies. Didn't Hank Fonda say, "Oh, I don't think we'll have any trouble with the Indians! We've always treated them fair." Lands o' Goshen. It's either we're too red or too blue! You can't please everyone.*

Love ya babe,

HOLLYWOOD

Drums along the Mohawk

JOSEPH BAUERKEMPER

In an August 28, 2008, speech when he accepted the Democratic Party's nomination for the presidency of the United States, President-elect Barack Obama explicitly positioned the aspirations of his campaign within the dominant and intertwined narratives of American exceptionalism and Manifest Destiny. Celebrating the unparalleled wealth and military might of the United States, and assuredly asserting that "our culture" is "the envy of the world," Obama ultimately located the exceptional character of the United States in something he calls the "American spirit":

> It is that American spirit—that American promise—that pushes us forward even when the path is uncertain; that binds us together in spite of our differences; that makes us fix our eye not on what is seen, but what is unseen, that better place around the bend. That promise is our greatest inheritance. It's a promise I make to my daughters when I tuck them in at night, and a promise that you make to yours—a promise that has led immigrants to cross oceans and pioneers to travel west.

While I am thoroughly disappointed with Obama's embrace of Manifest Destiny, I reluctantly acknowledge the political expediency of a presidential candidate allying himself with this fundamental aspect of the U.S. national narrative. I cannot help but agree with Obama's assessment that the blind and terminal pursuit of progress by way of colonial expansion is that which defines America. However, I cannot help but reject his endorsement of this narrative. It is, after all, a narrative premised upon the ongoing removal and dispossession of the indigenous peoples of North America, and upon the ongoing violence of American imperialist practices beyond the continent.

Even with its thoroughly unsavory history of colonization and its ongoing perpetration of relentless injustice, the U.S. national narrative of exceptionalism and Manifest Destiny that now President Obama heartily endorses continues to be legitimized, I think, through a matrix of cultural, social, political, and economic factors. In his book *The End of Victory Culture*, cultural critic Tom Engelhardt explores and attempts to explain the absurd illogic underpinning this legitimizing matrix. Offering critical considerations of captivity narratives, Hollywood films, government propaganda, comics, and children's toys, Engelhardt identifies a core subnarrative of U.S. nationalism and terms it "the American war story." In each of its iterations, the American war story begins with a thoroughly naturalized, peaceful, and purposeful community of Euro-Americans living idyllically at home in North America. The presence of Euro-Americans in North America is cast simply as the result of natural and unquestioned developments of human history. The war story thus forecloses critical engagement with European invasion and colonization of North America.

According to Engelhardt's framework, the naturalized Euro-American community is victimized by a horrendously violent and shamefully unwarranted attack carried out by savage Indian invaders. While devastating, the core of the Euro-American community involved survives the ordeal, and the attack comes to serve as a "mobilizing prelude to victory." Universalized imperatives of moral justice and the necessity of maintaining the security of the Euro-American community demand the pursuit of vengeance. The subsequent heroic mission of revenge, while fraught with requisite risk and peril, is preordained by the infallible nobility of the Euro-American cause—freedom's inexorable progress—to successfully culminate in the righteous annihilation of uncivilized evil. With the despicable Indians dispatched, the ever-endangered, yet ever-invincible Euro-American community embraces a future even rosier than the idyllic good ol' days preceding the Indians' initial ambush.

With the addition of various embellishments that serve to reinforce the core cultural logic of U.S. nationalism, John Ford's 1939 film *Drums along the Mohawk*—a text that Engelhardt does not address in his book—employs the American war story as its guiding narrative template. Based on Walter D. Edmonds's 1936 historical novel of the same name, the story was adapted for the screen by Lamar Trotti and Sonya Levien, with uncredited contributions from William Faulkner—yes, *that* William Faulkner—and Bess Meredyth. *Drums along the Mohawk* offers a fictionalized, though historically grounded account of the American Revolution as experienced by white settlers in central New York's Mohawk River Valley. The film opens in 1776 in the Albany home of the well-to-do Borst family. Lana Borst, played by Claudette Colbert, is marrying frontier farmer Gil Martin, played by Henry Fonda. Immediately after the two are pronounced husband and wife, Gil and Lana Martin embark on the two-day trek from Albany to their remote farm near the settlement and frontier fort at "German Flats." As they travel across the open lands of central New York's Mohawk River Valley, Lana revels in her first glimpses of the unrivaled beauty of the soon-to-be national landscape of the United States. Perched in front of their covered wagon with Gil at the reins, the newlyweds are the twentieth-century ideal of Revolutionary-era America. He in his handsomely simple blue frock coat, and she in a bold blue dress. With viewers fully aware that this is a story of the American Revolution, this blue theme—which permeates the entire film via costumes and lighting—is put to extensive use, distinguishing the good Americans from red-donning Tories and their sanguinary Seneca allies.

During their stopover at the Kings Road tavern, the Martins meet a suspicious eye-patch-wearing character played by John Carradine. He boldly asks Gil what political party is most prevalent around the German Flats area. Gil informs him that the American Party is favored, and that he knows of no Tories in the area. Carradine's character tells Gil and Lana of rumors swirling that the Indians (Haudenosaunee in this case, though in the film they're simply "Indians") are expected to ally with the British against the American insurgency. While seeming a shade unnerved by this suggestion, Gil reassures Lana that neither the Tories nor the Indians are anything to worry about.

The following day, Gil and Lana arrive at their farm during a torrential downpour. While Gil is outside tending to the horse and wagon, Lana warms herself at their humble cabin hearth. We hear the cabin door open, and Lana, bathed in blue moonlight, turns, expecting to see Gil. Just as a thunderclap crashes, the camera cuts quickly to reveal the foreboding figure of an Indian (a character named Blue Back, portrayed by Seneca actor Chief John Big Tree) standing in the doorway, his face eerily illuminated from below by the flickering firelight. Fearing for her life, Lana goes into a screaming fit and cowers in the corner of the room. Hearing this, Gil runs back into the cabin. He recognizes the intruder as a friend, and resorts to slapping Lana to rouse her from her dreadful panic. (Of course, he apologizes and explains that he "had to do it.") As Lana's screams quickly fade into muffled sobs, Gil greets Blue Back and explains that Lana's fearful fit was due to the storm and to her weariness after the long trip from Albany. In a conversation serving to make clear to Lana—and to the film's audience—that Blue Back is a good and helpful Indian, Blue Back employs the predictable monosyllabic grunt-speak of the early twentieth-century Hollywood Indian. He explains that he has stopped by to offer Gil and Lana a wedding gift consisting of a half deer he has hung outside, and he further asserts that he is a "good Christian" and a "fine friend" to Gil and the Euro-American community surrounding German Flats. Blue Back also provides Gil with a war club and some related matrimonial advice, saying, "You got a fine woman, but you young man. You use this on her. Lick her good! Make fine woman." Even though we have just seen Gil strike his spouse and sternly dictate that she is to "do as [he] say[s] from now on," Gil and Lana chuckle at the ridiculousness of Blue Back's suggestion, indicating that domestic violence is the primitive and peculiar cultural practice of Indians.

Regardless of his attitude toward marriage, Blue Back fills the role of a frequent and familiar accouterment of the American war story: the Noble Indian Savage. Like any worthwhile Indian helper-character, Blue Back will time and again prove his steadfast loyalty by warning Gil and Lana of an imminent Indian attack on their farmstead, and fighting alongside them in defense of the Euro-American community at German Flats. Indeed, Blue Back's very name serves to differentiate him from the Tories and their allies. British soldiers, after all, were commonly referred to as "bloody backs" by derisive American insurgents.

After a successful harvest season, the Martins make a largely social trip to the fort at German Flats, where Gil is required to check in and run through parade drills with General Nicholas Herkimer's Tryon County militia. Herkimer explains to his men that the Continental Army is unable to provide defense to the Mohawk River Valley, and that the residents of the area must be prepared to look after themselves. Herkimer asserts: "This is our home and our land, and I say it's worth fighting for." He goes on to explain that the Indians have not yet allied with either side in the war, but that the Tories are aggressively courting Indian alliances. Unconcerned, Gil confidently responds: "Oh, I don't think we'll have any trouble with the Indians. We've always treated them fair." (Of course one wonders what is meant by fair.) Other militia members affirm Gil's assessment. Gil's absurd yet important remark establishes a circumstance in which any actions taken by Indians in defense of their lands, governance practices, and resources will be seen as unwarranted.

In the subsequent scene, families from across the German Flats area have convened at the Martin farmstead for the communal work of clearing land. While they are harmoniously going about their labor, a gunshot rings out, and an out-of-breath Blue Back comes running out of the surrounding forest. He informs Gil and the others that one hundred Senecas in war paint, and eight Tories—the leader of whom turns out to be the notorious William Caldwell, the eye-patch-wearing stranger that Gil and Lana met at the inn on their wedding night—are on the warpath and approaching the farm. Blue Back warns Gil that everyone must leave the area and head to the fort because the Senecas are especially brutal. This is the only moment in the film that the Indians are referred to with a tribally specific name. (Perhaps even more interesting to some, Chief John Big Tree, the actor who portrays Blue Back, was himself a member of the Seneca Nation.) As the colonists scramble to flee, the invading Indians set fire to Gil and Lana's drying hay and burn down their cabin. The Tryon County militia convenes at the fort and immediately engages the Indians in an off-screen battle, after which it is clear that the Indians and their Tory leaders have been easily repelled. Left with neither home nor harvest, Gil and Lana turn to the feisty widow Mrs. Barnabas McKlennar, who offers them a place to live and payment for running her farm.

The Tory/Indian attack on the Martin farm serves as the galvanizing event that inaugurates the film's elaborate retelling of the American war story. The savage, irrational, and purposeless Indians unleash an unwarranted attack on the peaceful and harmonious Euro-American community. (There is, of course, no mention in the film of the Proclamation of 1763 or any of the myriad other reasons that the Haudenosaunee tended to ally with the British against the American insurgency.) With this unprovoked depredation, the Indians have courted the colonists' violent revenge. Upon learning that the Tories and Indians have regrouped, expanded their ranks, and are marching toward another attack on the Mohawk Valley settlements, General Herkimer gathers the militia once again and marches them into yet another off-screen battle: the film's heavily revised version of the August 1777 Battle of Oriskany. After enduring an Indian ambush and more than three hundred casualties, the weary militia return from battle with a hard-fought victory, a mortally wounded General Herkimer, and ubiquitous thousand-yard stares. While not significantly wounded, Gil has been profoundly affected by the carnage he witnessed during the fighting. As Lana is tending to his superficial wounds, a shell-shocked Gil performs a monologue recounting in detail the deaths of his fellow soldiers in the battle, and the deaths of the Indians and Tories he himself has killed. Finally, Gil enters a deep slumber. Upon waking, he has returned to his familiar demeanor, and he assures Lana that the Indians will not be bothering their community anymore. Relieved, Lana informs Gil that they are expecting a child.

Things go well for the colonists in the months following the Battle of Oriskany, and it comes time for Lana to give birth. A healthy baby boy is born to her and Gil. With the new child, a bountiful harvest, and a wedding in the community, the residents of the German Flats area have much to celebrate, and they gather to do so at the McKlennar farmstead. During the wonderfully ideal evening, Gil slips away to check on his son as he sleeps peacefully in his cradle. Lana follows after Gil, and seeing him in loving awe of their child, she says a private prayer: "Please God. Please let it go on like this forever." Lana's oh-so-American yearning for the culmination of freedom's progress in an enduring and idyllic state—in the end of history—is not yet ready to be satisfied. It requires a final test . . .

In the next bizarre scene, two drunken Indians carrying a torch and a jug of liquor enter the McKlennar house and set it on fire. Rather than being frightened, Mrs. McKlennar is indignant. She orders the Indians to move her bed away from the flames. For whatever (un)reason, they comply before running away. Gil, Lana, and Mrs. McKlennar then learn that Caldwell has amassed a force of over a thousand Indians, who are wreaking havoc across the valley as they head toward an assault on the fort at German Flats.

The colonists race to the fort and brace for the coming onslaught. The men take defensive positions along the fort's walls, while the women stand by to reload rifles. Caldwell sounds the order for the Indians to charge the fort. The advance is easily repelled, and Caldwell orders his officers to "call the filthy beggars back." Before this initial offensive is over, however, Mrs. McKlennar is mortally wounded by an Indian's arrow. As she lies dying, she bequeaths her home and farm to Gil and Lana, and tells them of a sizeable cache of gold pieces stashed under her porch that should be distributed to community members.

With a lull in the fighting, the men of German Flats assess their situation. As long as supplies hold up, they can hold off the Indians. Yet they are running low on ammunition, so someone must go for reinforcements. The first man to attempt to sneak through, a character named Joe Boleo played by John Ford's older brother Francis Ford, is captured and bound to a wagon of dry hay that the Indians set ablaze. Appearing to be crucified amid the flames, Joe is mercifully shot by the parson from the fort before he feels the pain of the fire. (After the battle is over, the parson has a thousand-yard stare and mumbles, "I killed a man." Of course, he has killed several Indians during the battle, but only Joe counts as "a man.")

The American insurgents need another volunteer to make an attempt to get help. Gil steps up to the challenge, reassuring Lana that if he "can get in the clear, there isn't an Indian living that can catch [him]." Gil's stealthy departure from the fort initiates a lengthy high-speed chase as he is trailed by three Indians. Hatchet in hand, Gil runs and runs and runs (and runs and runs) to the neighboring Fort Dayton. With superior running speed and a righteous cause enabling him to prevail in the footrace, Gil's pursuers eventually tire and give up the chase.

The rebels hold the Indians off as best they can, but eventually the walls of the fort are breached. Just as the hundreds and hundreds of Indians swarm the American insurgents, Gil arrives with reinforcements from Fort Dayton to save the day. In yet another example of the film's thorough resonance with the conventions of the American war story, the cavalry swoops in to the rescue at the last moment, slaughtering the Indians and letting freedom live another day. As he surveys the battle's aftermath, an officer from Fort Dayton asks if anyone knows the whereabouts of Caldwell. One of the stammering insurgents points up to the pulpit of the fort's chapel, where Blue Back stands, wearing Caldwell's eye patch—the implication being that he has heroically dispatched the dishonorable Tory leader.

As the post-battle cleanup and reconstruction of the fort continues, a company of regulars from the Continental Army pass through the area. Their commanding officer informs the German Flats community that the Revolutionary War is over and that the Americans have emerged victorious. Shouting with glee and proudly informing the regulars that they "did a little fightin' around here [them]selves," the patriots at German Flats borrow the company's American flag and hoist it to the top of the fort. Envisioning a pluralist patriotism—yet one with clear racial and class hierarchies—the film moves from a shot of the late Mrs. McKlennar's black slave Daisy as she looks upon the flag with emotional reverence, to the image of a white blacksmith as he does the same, and then to Blue Back as he salutes the flag. With an orchestral version of "My Country 'Tis of Thee" playing in the background, Gil joins Daisy, the blacksmith, and Blue Back in admiring the flag, and offers the film's closing line: "Well I reckon we better be gettin' back to work. There's gonna be a heap to do from now on."

Culminating in a forward-looking statement, *Drums along the Mohawk* dramatizes a national narrative that focuses on a narrow future while selectively remembering and strategically forgetting the past. The film is certainly neither the earliest nor the most recent rendition of the American war story inserted into popular consciousness. Yet as a text that incorporates so many aspects of U.S. national mythology in its retelling of the birth of the nation, the film aggressively asserts the war-story narrative as integral to U.S. national identity.

Produced in the summer months of 1939 and premiering in the fall of that year—just as World War II was flaring up considerably in Europe—Gil's final line would quickly prove prescient. Looking back upon the film and its historical contexts, one can easily recognize its relevance for Americans as they learned of and responded to the December 1941 attack on Pearl Harbor. Here was a real-life twentieth-century version of the American war story. As devastating, deadly, and destructive as Pearl Harbor was, Americans could take heart in the assurance that this ambush would prove to be a preamble to absolute American victory. According to Engelhardt, "The Japanese attack on Pearl Harbor fit the lineaments of this story well. At the country's periphery, a savage, nonwhite enemy had launched a barbaric attack on Americans going about their lives early on Sunday morning, and that enemy would be repaid in brutal combat on distant jungle islands in a modern version of 'Indian fighting.'" A revisionist and ideological historical template, the American war story has authored and continues to reinforce U.S. nationalism. Tales of Indian "depredations" remain embedded in the American national consciousness and constitute a lens through which the U.S. populace continues to perceive and respond to threats—both imagined and otherwise—to national security.

While World War II provided a modern American war story that would anoint America's "greatest generation," this unified narrative would weaken as the second half of the twentieth century came to pass. The anticlimactic thawing of the Cold War, the catastrophe of U.S. military intervention in Indochina, the unfinished business of the first Gulf War, and, more generally, the increasing visibility of the world's complexity left the American war story looking more like a vestigial narrative no longer capable of maintaining a coherent national ethos. After the fall of the Soviet Union and the slick success of the seemingly made-for-TV Gulf War, the United

States found itself without an identifiable enemy worthy of serving as a foil to the righteous greatness of the American spirit. America needs enemies, after all; its guiding narrative—the American war story—is a fundamentally reactionary enterprise.

On September 11, 2001, Mohammed Atta, Osama bin Laden, and their al-Qaeda associates came seemingly out of nowhere—in true war-story fashion—to more than fill this void. Violently jolted from its dull, restless, and willfully ignorant slumber, the United States found itself back on a familiar terrain of moral simplicity where there are unmistakably righteous heroes and undeniably heinous evildoers. The post-9/11 world offered an errand into the wilderness; a crucible by means of which the American spirit could be reforged and renewed. By making invisible the motives of al-Qaeda, and instead attributing terrorism to backward Islamofascists that hate freedom, the terrorist attacks of 9/11 are cast as an irrational, unprovoked assault on the American way of life that continues to motivate and authorize the current wars in Afghanistan, Syria, Pakistan, and Iraq.

In order to position the terrorist attacks of 9/11 as an event that would galvanize support for an invasion of Iraq, United States government officials have repeatedly, falsely, and deceptively linked Saddam Hussein's regime to al-Qaeda. Countless press reports and numerous leaks of classified government "intelligence" indicate the Bush administration's deceptive and relentless efforts to legitimize the invasion. The fabrication of evidence indicating that Iraq held weapons of mass destruction, and the fraudulent, yet relentless assertion that the war in Iraq is a central component of the "war on terror"—a fiction that is itself a version of the American war story, replete with references to enemy-controlled territory as "Indian country"—reveal that the reactionary character of militant American nationalism has now escalated to a preemptive character. The United States no longer even requires an identifiable offense to rationalize revenge on whomever it decides to target; the mere possibility of an attack on Americans—even if improbable, impossible, or completely invented—will suffice. This hubris is proving that the American war story is ultimately a tragedy—a tragedy without catharsis.

The American war story as conveyed by *Drums along the Mohawk* reinforces the destructive and intertwined narratives of American exceptionalism and Manifest Destiny. As long as these narratives continue to authorize cultural tendencies and political policies that react to crises with violent revenge, enduring resolution to conflict will remain out of reach. Yet, this can change. By knowing and recounting the unsavory stories of unfreedom that have enabled the birth of the American nation, and by critically engaging with the profound deception underlying the war in Iraq—and so many other instances of imperial and military adventurism—we might find the wisdom and humility to elaborate an alternative to the American war story, a narrative of narratives that informs communities of justice. This effort, of course, will not be easy. It seems, then, that we might consider relevant Gil Martin's words at the close of *Drums along the Mohawk*: "I reckon we better be gettin' back to work. There's gonna be a heap to do from now on."

Dear Diary:

My heart soars like an eagle every time I see "The Duke" on horseback, prancing across wide, open spaces. And how I use to love little Miss Shirley Temple in The Good Ship Lollipop. *Call me sentimental, but I wish John Ford could have found a place for her to tap dance up and down the fort's steps with Mr. Bojangles. Too bad there were only Indians on the set. They have no natural rhythm.*

A bientôt, mon chéri,

Hollywood

Fort Apache

Matthew Sakiestewa Gilbert

The old black-and-white films take me back to my childhood. As a child living in northeastern Arizona, I remember spending Saturday afternoons with my dad watching John Wayne movies. My dad never referred to him as "John Wayne," but always "The Duke." In a time span of fifteen or so years, I must have watched every John Wayne film at least twice. We cheered when the Indians defeated or killed government troops, and became depressed when the opposite occurred. In our minds, the Indians never truly lost a battle in a fair and square way. Government troops had vast supplies of guns and access to myriads of horses, and often surprised the Indians in an attack. In our family, John Wayne's character was neither a complete villain nor a hero. "The Duke" seemed to understand and respect Indian people and served as a mediator between the Native and white world. But this did not mean that we always looked favorably upon his character.

When I set out to review *Fort Apache*, I originally planned to write a scathing commentary on the racist ways the film depicted American Indian people. Instead, I decided to watch the film with my oldest daughter, Hannah, and attempt to understand the film from her perspective as an American Indian child. "Hannah, today you and I are going to watch a movie called *Fort Apache.*" "Oh," she said. "Is it a cartoon?" "No," I replied, "it's an old black-and-white movie that Daddy used to watch when he was a kid." She seemed utterly disappointed that *Fort Apache* was not an animated show, but I told her that if she watched the movie with me, I would make her popcorn and she could have a few cookies. I don't recall my dad having to bribe me with popcorn and cookies to watch a John Wayne film, but four-year-old girls seem more interested in movies about princesses and ponies than in black-and-white Westerns.

With popcorn and cookies in hand, I started the movie, and Hannah said, "Honey, what is this movie about?" Since Hannah could talk, she has referred to me as "Honey" and rarely uses the name "Daddy." My wife calls me "Honey," and Hannah just assumed that was my name. Even my two-year-old daughter calls me "Honey," and I have no doubt that my youngest daughter will do the same. When Hannah asked "Honey" to explain the movie, I paused for a moment, and then endeavored to give her a brief synopsis of the film in a way that she could understand. But explaining a John Wayne Western to a four-year-old proved a challenge.

I told Hannah that the film was about a Civil War veteran named Lieutenant Colonel Owen Thursday (Henry Fonda) who was stationed in a remote military fort in Arizona called Fort Apache. I mentioned to Hannah that Thursday graduated from a very special school named West Point, and that he was not happy to be working and living in Arizona. "Why was he not happy?" Hannah asked. "Because he did not like Indians," I answered, "and he did not like it when people such as Captain Kirby York (John Wayne) told him that the Indians (Apaches) threatened the safety of their fort." I also told Hannah that Thursday had a daughter named Philadelphia (Shirley Temple) who lived with him at Fort Apache. "Philadelphia was very pretty," I said to Hannah, "and she fell in love with a young soldier named Second Lieutenant Michael Shannon O'Rourke [John Agar]." "Was he a prince?" asked Hannah. "No, but Philadelphia and Second Lieutenant O'Rourke were very close friends and they cared about each other a lot," I told her. "They were married in real life."

I then told Hannah that the people at Fort Apache did not like the Indians, especially the Indian leader named Cochise. "Why didn't they like Cochise?" Hannah asked. "Because he was a brave man," I replied, "and he did not allow Philadelphia's father to tell him what to do." "Like when you tell me to go to bed and I throw a fit?" Hannah asked. "Or when I want you to buy chocolate milk at the store, and you say 'no!' and then I get very upset and cry and I get a time-out when we get home?" "Yeeesss," I replied slowly, processing her assessment, "except that Cochise did not cry and throw a fit. He stayed true to what he believed and what was right." I even explained to Hannah that the film's director, John Ford, made the film to glorify the U.S. government and dehumanize American Indian people. I told her that *Fort Apache* was the first of Ford's "Cavalry Trilogy," which was based on James Warner Bellah's *Massacre,* a book that praises and honors Custer's Last Stand. Of course, my daughter was not interested in the film's background. She was happy and content with her popcorn, cookies, and having her father by her side. But she wanted me to stop talking so that we could watch the "show."

The film begins with a one-carriage convoy racing through Monument Valley in Utah. Hannah pointed at the screen and said with much excitement, "Look, Hopi!" "You're right, Hannah," I said to her, "that certainly looks like Hopi." Hannah sees Hopi in everything. Shortly after we moved to the Midwest, we passed by a Methodist church and Hannah called our attention to a Hopi-looking design on the church building. Since that day she has referred to the church as the "Hopi church." Hannah's comment made me contemplate my father's enjoyment of watching John Wayne films. Part of me thinks that it was because the films' images reminded him of home. For a brief ninety minutes on Saturday afternoons, he escaped the stress of work and was taken to a familiar place—a place that reminded him of growing up on the Hopi and Navajo reservations. As the buttes of Monument Valley dashed across the screen, Hannah saw the landscape of the Southwest and also made the connection to home.

Although the producers include a brief scene of a Navajo woman weaving a rug near the beginning of the film, the Apaches do not make their appearance until one hour of the movie has passed. When I asked Hannah to point out the Indians in the film, she asked me, "What is an Indian?" I replied, "You are an Indian; you are a Hopi Indian." In our home, we seldom use the term "Indian" to refer to ourselves or other people. We are Hopi or Hopitu-Shinumu, and our Native friends are Chickasaw, Choctaw, Diné, Nambé Pueblo, Osage, Creek, Maricopa, and Chamorro. My daughter understands what it means to be Hopi. She can tell you about the Hopi mesas in northeastern Arizona, she knows the significance of corn and the butterfly in Hopi culture, and she uses some Hopi words in her everyday speech. But it took a John Wayne movie for her to realize that she is an "Indian."

I have a responsibility to show Hannah that she and other Native peoples are not like the ones depicted in the film. At several places in the movie, government troops use the word "savage" to describe the Apaches. I told Hannah that people once referred to Hopis as "savage Indians" just like in the movie, and that this term was intended to harm our people. "Like being not nice to us?" Hannah replied. "Yes, not nice and very mean," I said to her. It was difficult for me to talk about the term "savage" with my daughter. In our culture, fathers have always considered their young daughters to be corn sprouts. Just as a Hopi farmer protects his sprouts from the wind, sun, and animals, so Hopi fathers are similarly called to care for and protect their daughters. As a father, I know that my daughter will encounter the term "savage" again in life, and she will feel the cruelty behind racial stereotypes. But while we sat eating popcorn and cookies, I chose to shelter her from this conversation until my corn sprout was a little taller, a little older. Instead, we talked about the many beautiful horses in the film, and which ones were her favorites. We talked about how pretty the dresses were that the women wore, and Hannah especially liked it when the military men and their wives danced at the fort.

After we finished the movie, I asked Hannah if she liked the film. "Yes," she replied, "but I didn't like it when the people fell off their horses." "Maybe we could watch another black-and-white movie together one of these days," I said. "Maybe," she replied, "but I think I would rather watch one of my princess shows."

Dear Diary:

Note to Self: Next time get the Spanish to play the Indians. Some sweetface like Antonio, or Penelope, or even Selma. No, scratch that. Selma is Mexican. Casting is such a bitch these days. How I yearn for those happy days of yesteryear when Jeff Chandler and Anthony Quinn would jump at the chance to put on the feathers. Must think about new locations for Westerns. Maybe Romania. No one protests there, do they? Must check with Nici Ceauşescu. He once gave me good tips on cheap hotels.

Kissy, kissy,

Hollywood

She Wore a Yellow Ribbon

Gwen N. Westerman

Along with *Fort Apache* (1948) and *Rio Grande* (1950), John Ford's renowned Cavalry Trilogy includes *She Wore a Yellow Ribbon* (1949), which the *Classic Film Guide* calls an "essential Western." There's just something about an "essential" John Ford Western. It's a wonderfully romantic vision of the place that became the United States: breathtaking landscapes reminiscent of Remington paintings; epic battles brewing under ominous skies; virtuous women in need of rescue; and hostile Indians to be subdued.

Ford has taken some heat about his representations of Indians throughout his career, which spanned more than fifty years. Critics object to "savage" portrayals in *The Searchers* (see the following review) and *Stagecoach*, while supporters hold up the "sympathetic" images in *Cheyenne Autumn*, says Angela Aleiss in "A Race Divided: The Indian Westerns of John Ford."[1] Aleiss goes on to say that Ford's Westerns "show Native American characters holding firmly to a distinct identity and culture (although not necessarily an accurate one) and never fully embracing white society." But *She Wore a Yellow Ribbon* is not a movie about Indians holding onto their culture or their autonomy. It's a movie filled with romanticized images of an aging Civil War veteran relinquishing command to a new generation of soldiers just after the

Battle on the Greasy Grass. Indians—in composite stereotypes and as literary backdrops—just happen to be in the way.

One of the most recognized landscapes in Hollywood depictions of the American frontier is that of Monument Valley. Filmed in Utah, *She Wore a Yellow Ribbon* capitalizes on romanticized images of not only these sweeping plateaus and vast formations, but also approaching thunderstorms and spectacular sunsets. After all, every Western hero must be able to ride off into the sunset or through a vast herd of buffalo. Yes, there are large numbers of buffalo roaming free in Monument Valley in 1876. Captain Nathan Brittles, played by John Wayne, tells a young soldier in his company, "First time the herd's been this far north since the summer of '68. You never saw a buffalo, Mr. Pennell [Harry Carey Jr.]? Before your time." Never mind that buffalo hunting as a business and a sport had decimated the American bison population between 1871 and 1874, and the southern buffalo herd consisted of only small, scattered bands by the beginning of 1875.

Captain Brittles is happy, happy, happy because he is retiring from the U.S. Cavalry in six days. Like God, he will finish his work just in time for a day of "rest." He commands a group of clean, well-outfitted soldiers at Fort Stark, far out in Indian country, half a day's ride from the nearest stagecoach stop. Despite the isolation and harsh desert conditions, the soldiers look as if they are on their way to sit for another of Remington's paintings, complete with yellow neckerchiefs (which were not part of regulation Army uniforms, but immortalized by Remington's keen eye for color). Within the fort there is a saloon and a "sutler," Mr. Rynders, who also serves conveniently as the Indian agent and is secretly negotiating an arms deal with a renegade band of Southern Cheyennes.

The men of Company C have bonded in their quest to subdue the hostile Indians, especially in the wake of Custer's defeat. They come from back east and down south and have left behind all remnants of hostility caused by the Civil War. Southern boy Sergeant Travis Tyree (Ben Johnson), immensely knowledgeable about Indian customs, finds a military cap with a feather in the band and proclaims, "Cheyennes. The same ones that killed Custer." When the paymaster's wagon is attacked, Tyree and his patrol bring the dead paymaster back to the fort. Captain Brittles, a Yankee, pulls an arrow from the side of the wagon and examines its yellow, red, and white bands. "This arrow is not Kiowa, Comanche, or Arapaho either," Brittles observes. "See that clan mark? Sign of the dog," says Tyree. "Dog soldiers of the Southern Cheyenne." Tyree and Brittles share an easy camaraderie, and when Brittles receives word that he has been endorsed by Philip Sheridan, William Tecumseh Sherman, and Ulysses S. Grant for an appointment as chief of scouts, Tyree replies, "Kinda wish you'd a been holdin' a full hand, sir. Robert E. Lee, sir." Against a blazing sunset, Brittles replies, "Oh. Ha! Wouldn'a been bad. Let's go!" And they ride off together, Yankee and Rebel, to subdue the hostiles.

Captain Brittles is not the usual cavalry officer hardened by war. His first revealing conversation is with his beloved wife and two daughters, who died in June 1867 and were buried in the Fort Stark cemetery. Kneeling beside the grave, watering flowers, he tells her spirit he's finally retiring. "We got some sad news, Mary. George Custer was killed and his whole command. Cheyennes are out. Time to drive them back north."

She Wore a Yellow Ribbon was adapted from two short stories by James Warner Bellah that appeared in the *Saturday Evening Post*: "The Big Hunt" (1947) and "The War Party" (1948). A romantic subplot was added to the screenplay, as well as some softening of Brittles's character. In "The War Party," Captain Brittles attacks a Northern Cheyenne camp in 1868, stampedes nine hundred horses off a cliff, and then marches a thousand Cheyenne people to Wind River. In the movie adaptation, Brittles stampedes the horses off into the desert, and few shots find their marks among the Indians of the camp: "No casualties. No Indian war. No court-martial," he proclaims proudly. He then issues orders to his men: "Walkin' hurts their pride. Follow the hostiles back to the reservation. If you're watchin' it'll hurt 'em worse." It appears that the Southern Cheyenne "hostiles" will pack up willingly and walk somewhere without their horses, and it is left to the imagination whether that will be to Indian Territory or to Wind River. But a reservation is a reservation is a reservation, no matter where it is.

Relocation brings up another element of "essential" Westerns—the Indian. As a postwar movie—filmed in 1949, post–World War II, about a group of romantic post–Civil War cavalry soldiers—it would not be complete without composite Indians. Inside and outside the fort, faceless, voiceless, and stationary Indians are seen and not heard. Indians with blankets pulled up over their shoulders. Men with black ten-gallon Stetson hats covering their eyes. A group of them have set up camp within a few feet of the fort walls, erecting tipis adorned with Navajo rugs and Southwestern-style baskets, and tripods with iron pots over cooking fires. Women with scarves that hide their faces sit in a line near clay ovens and a grazing paint pony. A few men, their backs to the camera, "eagle" feathers fluttering in the wind, face the fort.

No sooner does Company C roll out of the fort to take Commander Allshard's wife and niece, Miss Olivia Dandridge (Joanne Dru), to the stage and away from impending Indian peril, than ominous music swells along with the dust from a procession of Indians off in the distance. Two local dogs lead the company, darting ahead and barking joyously, unafraid. Everyone knows that where there is ominous music, there are always Indians. "Are those really hostile Indians?" asks Miss Dandridge. "Are you going to fight them, Captain Brittles?" Burdened with the women and their safe delivery to the stage, Brittles sends Tyree to investigate. Arapahos are moving their whole village south—wagons, lodges, travois contraptions, bad wigs, headbands, spears, and all. Yelping, a band of red-shirted Arapahos attacks Tyree and his patrol, taunts them with spears, and rides away. Thirty of these angry young renegades join up with the Cheyenne Dog Soldiers to attack the stagecoach stop before Captain Brittles arrives. They want war. Menacing music surges again as the stagecoach and the small station burn. Although the Indians aren't shown attacking the stagecoach way station, the music confirms it.

The Southern Cheyennes and Arapahos were allied at this time with the Kiowas, Comanches, and Apaches, so at least the tribal identifications are correct in *She Wore a Yellow Ribbon*, even if the material culture is a composite of all things known to be "Indian" by filmmakers in 1949. Ford is known, however, for the use of indigenous languages in his films, particularly in *Cheyenne Autumn* (1964). When Brittles takes two young officers out on night patrol to discover what Mr. Rynders and the hostile renegades are up to, menacing drumbeats set the mood. Rynders wants to sell Winchester rifles for $50 to the Indians, dressed in beaded cuffs and quill roach headdresses. His interpreter tries to convince the group in the Lakota language (those Sioux are everywhere):

INTERPRETER: "Wašte, kola, wašte!" (It's good, friend, it's good.)
CHIEF: "Hiya! Šica! Wošica!" (No! It's bad! Evil!)
INTERPRETER TO TRADER: "$50 is not enough, he said."
INTERPRETER TO CHIEF: "Chimookiman machos camano! Lila šica! Wošica! Lakota šica!"

Okay, so the last line takes a little more work. "Chimookiman" is Ojibwe for "American," and "machos camano," sounds like Spanish, but appears meaningless. Then what incites a riot among the Cheyenne and Arapaho renegades, causing them to kill the trader and his men, is "Lila šica! Wošica! Lakota šica!" What he does is insult the Lakota people with "It's really bad! Evil! Lakota are bad!" Go figure. These are real Ojibwe and Lakota words, not gibberish. So, are the Cheyennes and Arapahos angry about the price of the guns, or because the interpreter insulted their Lakota comrades?

The next time Indians speak is when Brittles meets with the chief to prevent war between the United States and the renegades. Pony-That-Walks is played by Chief John Big Tree, a Seneca man who actually gets his name in the film credits. Brittles comes into their camp where women sit on blankets in scarves, once again faceless. Drums sound a threatening rhythm, and warriors ride horses with Navajo patterned blankets. Amid grand hand signals, the chief greets the captain in slurred, broken English.

> CHIEF: "Nay-tan! I am Christian! Hallelujah! Old friend me. Take salt. Smoke pipe."
> BRITTLES: "We must stop this war."
> CHIEF: "Yellow hair Custer dead. Great sign. Buffalo return. Great sign. Young men fight. We old men, Nay-tan."
> BATTLES: "I'm going far away."
> CHIEF: "Go in peace."

The men then place their right hands on each other's shoulders for a moment, another classic image that could have been painted by Remington. Brittles bids Pony-That-Walks farewell with "Nina wašte, kola." He mixes Dakota ("nina") and Lakota ("kola") dialects, but the chief gets the message because he is, after all, a composite Indian.

As with most Westerns, the Indians here are literary backdrops that help move along the plot. The theatrical trailer for *She Wore a Yellow Ribbon* pans the desert landscape, and a bright yellow banner flashes across the screen: "A Lusty Romance and Adventure of the Untamed West! Drama moves here! Raw. Violent. Real." Turns out Miss Dandridge is quite the busy woman, playing two young officers against each other as they compete for her affections. Second Lieutenant Ross Pennell is a Yankee blue blood with no desire to make a career in the army, and Lieutenant Flint Cohill (John Agar) is a common Southerner. Miss Dandridge ties a yellow ribbon in her hair, a symbol among the cavalry that she has a sweetheart, but she won't reveal who it is. The Indian "peril" creates a motive for the soldiers to protect her as they try to get her back to civilization and safety, and ultimately to win her hand.

Captain Brittles's final mission before he retires is to get her on the stage and shape up his company. On his last official duty day, he reviews his troops while the two local dogs sleep in the middle of the formation, impervious to what is going on around them. He appears to leave the fort after his retirement ceremony. However, because of the impending war with the renegade Indians, he leads the young officers and the men in their goal to subdue the hostiles because the day "don't end 'til midnight." The threat of Indian attack is ever present, and he makes sure that the young officers are ready to take over command. War drums beat as smoke signals rise; feathered war bonnets are silhouetted against the darkening sky. Even the Indian women are mad as they beat on hollow log drums with heavy sticks. Lieutenants Pennell and Cohill come through with flying colors as they stampede the horses out of the camp while the Indians shoot their arrows and guns randomly and never hit a mark.

While Company C must drive the hostiles back to the reservation, the threat has not ended there. In a voice-over at the beginning of the movie, the narrator foreshadows the continuing conflict:

> "Custer is dead. And around the bloody guidon of the immortal Seventh Cavalry lie 212 officers and men. . . . And from the Canadian border to the Rio Bravo, 10,000 Indians—Kiowa, Comanche, Arapahos, Sioux, and Apache under Sitting Bull and Crazy Horse, Gall and Crow King—are uniting in a common war against the United States Cavalry."

Brittles can't leave the frontier unprotected while the menace remains. As chief of scouts, he'll stay with the soldiers at Fort Stark as long as the grass grows, the rivers flow—even in the desert—and the Indians show up as backdrops.

She Wore a Yellow Ribbon is a "classic" American Western. To avenge Custer's death, the cavalry defeats the Indians and drives them back to the reservation where they belong. Order is restored, the women are safe, and the cavalry has come to the rescue. As the narrator makes clear while the sun sets in the west, "Wherever they rode and whatever they fought for, that place became the United States!" Given the conventions and attitudes of the time when this film was made, it is not a surprise that the story plays fast and loose with history and with its depictions of Indian peoples. Aleiss suggests that "Ford's Indians differ from those in other films of his time because they resist the loss of cultural identity and refuse to join the 'melting pot' of the dominant Anglo-American society."[2] It's difficult to see how being marched back to the reservation, horses lost, counts as "resisting," or how hanging around the fort expectantly means "refusal." However, the comical reservation dogs do add an element of authenticity to the story. While the Indian characters are flat stereotypes decked out in a combination of tribal styles, at least there is an effort to include a fair representation of Lakota language (with an Ojibwe word thrown in for good measure). Those Lakotas sure get around.

NOTES

1. Angela Aleiss, "A Race Divided: Indian Westerns of John Ford," *American Indian Culture and Research Journal* 18 (Summer 1994): 167–87.
2. Ibid., 184.

Dear Diary:

Why can't all Westerns be The Searchers*? (Oh wait, they are.) What won't The Duke be demanding after this? Attila the Hun, here we come. And speaking of hons, what can we do for Jeffrey Hunter? Note to Self: Get Ford on the horn and make him give Jeff the starring role in his next pic. Or, no more French lingerie for his friends. I mean it.*

Ta-ta, darlings,

Hollywood

The Searchers

Susan Stebbins

Despite the many ways it bothers me, *The Searchers* is a movie that I will watch time after time. Part of the film's appeal can be attributed to cinematographer Winton C. Hoch's keen eye for its dramatic imaging of Monument Valley. The landscape is not only beautiful and grand, but is used symbolically to illuminate the movie's underlying themes as well as to identify its genre. This is a Western, albeit an alternative Western.

Apropos, the opening scene of the film is shot through the opening door of a small cabin that simultaneously reveals and frames the stunning, quintessential Western landscape, but also shows a lone figure riding towards the viewer. Within this visual frame, the audience understands that outside of the cabin is the "Wild West." Yet, inside the frame of the door is a mythic "fine, good place" from which settlers are desperately trying to eke out a meager living in the harsh land.

The approaching rider is Ethan Edwards, played by John Wayne. Throughout the film he is a character forever caught between the open wilderness in which he is comfortable and the confines of the home that he desires but can never have. As Richard Slotkin has demonstrated in his trilogy *Regeneration through Violence: Mythology of the American West*, *Fatal Environment*, and *Gunfighter Nation*, America's psyche is tied to the mythic Old West. Boundaries such as the cabin door separate civilization from the wilderness, and establish a focal point for the motives and actions of the story of the American West.

The Searchers is widely recognized as one of John Ford's best films because he understood

Americans' need to identify with the imaginary Old West. What I want to concentrate on, though (and what was widely commented on at the time of the film's release), is Ford's treatment of racism toward Natives in *The Searchers.* It's my belief that John Ford was concerned about Native American mistreatment at the hands of Europeans and Euro-Americans, so he sought to address it (as he would in later films *Sergeant Rutledge*, 1960, and *Cheyenne Autumn*, 1964) in this hate-ridden odyssey of revenge. On the surface, Ford addresses racism by focusing the film's plot on Euro-American settlers and their interactions with the Comanches—or "the Comanch," as Ethan refers to them.

The first of many violent acts contained in the Frank S. Nugent and Alan LeMay script occurs during the opening fifteen minutes of the film with the massacre of the Edwards family. Ethan's brother Aaron Edwards (Walter Coy), his wife Martha (Dorothy Jordan), and their son (an apparently uncredited role) and their two daughters, Lucy (Pippa Scott) and Debbie (Natalie Wood), are all at home when the massacre takes place. In the attack, Aaron, Martha, and their son are killed and Lucy and Debbie are taken captive. The scene of the massacre is grim, yet breathtaking, set against the big sky of Monument Valley. The capture of young Debbie, clutching a doll and hiding behind a family gravestone as a shadow of a man towers over her, is particularly haunting. Of course, viewers understand within minutes that the killers of the Edwards family are Comanche warriors.

However, I argue that Ford's intent in making *The Searchers* was not simply to address racism against American Indians, but also mixed-race marriages as well, which were abhorrent to many moviegoers of the 1950s. Most urban moviegoers in the 1950s took for granted that they were never going to meet a "real" American Indian, much less marry one. Therefore, I present a different reading of *The Searchers*, based on several key elements of the plot that have, to date, not been adequately explored: the fears Euro-American moviegoers in the 1950s held concerning interracial marriages. In the American culture of the 1950s, the intermixing of the "races" was verboten.

First, let us consider Ethan's quest to find and kill Debbie in order to prevent her from bearing a mixed-breed child. For me, this part of the plot symbolizes widespread fears among the American public over interracial sexual relations between African Americans and whites. I grew up living in both northern and southern states in the 1950s and 1960s. I remember, after moving to the South, being confused by separate water fountains and bathrooms, and the controversies surrounding the integration of my high school. I also recall that when I saw the occasional Western (which my parents had restricted me from seeing, and I suspect not just because of the gunfights) I was also confused, because the Indians in the movies and television shows were nothing like what I heard from my grandfathers and great-aunts and uncles about their youth. In college, I quickly realized that *Billy Jack* (see the review in chapter 9) had a lot more to do with troubled urban white kids than American Indians. So when I first saw *The Searchers* as a college student, I did so without the benefit of a historical context that included the processes of Manifest Destiny and the confiscation of Native lands. As a result, the movie I saw was one in which the lead character had some troubling issues with "the mixing of the races"—the very social problem that had dominated my youth.

The plot element of women or girls being stolen by American Indians links *The Searchers* to the genre of "captivity narratives": fictional and nonfictional accounts of the capture of white women and children by American Indians. What is symbolically at stake in many captivity narratives is the racial integrity of their white literary and film heroines. From colonial times to the dime novels of the nineteenth century to movies of the twentieth century, rape by a nonwhite man is considered a "fate worse than death" and an attack on the moral integrity of the white community.

Two specific scenes in *The Searchers* illustrate the fate of women or girls, like Lucy and Debbie, captured by the Indians. In the first, Ethan returns from scouting an area, looking for the two girls. He appears ill, and Martin Pawley (Aaron and Martha Edwardses' adopted son, played by Jeffery Hunter) comments he is missing his Confederate coat. Eventually Ethan tells Martin and Brad Jorgensen (Lucy's fiancé, played by Harry Carey Jr.) that he found Lucy's mutilated body in the hills and buried her in his coat. But an air of mystery surrounds Ethan's rendition of the event: did Ethan find Lucy alive and kill her with the very knife he's later seen digging with in the dirt to clean off blood?

In the second scene, Ethan and Martin come to a fort to look for Debbie among women and children rescued by the army. The women cry, moan, and speak gibberish as they sit on the floor, showing that their mental capacities have been diminished. One woman cradles a doll while gently rocking. The implication is that this is what happens to white women when they've been held captive too long by Indians. Ethan tells a cavalry officer that they are no longer white, but "Comanch." But what truly accounts for the behavior of the women: their treatment by the Comanches or their treatment by the army? In many captivity narratives, such as *The Diary of Mary Jemison*, or *The Unredeemed Captive*, the captured women don't want to leave their American Indian families. Could the women in *The Searchers* be grieving for the children and families left behind? The theme of Euro-American settlers forsaking their outposts for an uncivilized way of life is one that continued to haunt captivity narratives up through the mid-twentieth century, when *The Searchers* was made. Or is this just an over-the top scene by the writers to show the audience the dangers of close contact and sexual intermixing between the two races?

There are conflicting fears here: one, that the captives will be killed, the other that they won't be killed. The action of this nearly three-hour movie focuses on the efforts of Ethan and Martin to find Lucy and Debbie. Ethan's motive, unknown to Martin (but clear to the viewer as the film unfolds), is that he intends to kill both his nieces when he finds them, because they have been defiled by the "young bucks" (Ethan's slang for Comanche braves). Ethan's intent here is like that of Muslims and others who kill their sisters and daughters if they have been "defiled" before marriage. Did Ethan actually find Lucy dead and mutilated in the mountains? or did he "defend" the honor of his family and race by killing her?

The distinctions between Christian Euro-Americans and "heathen" Indians are depicted in many parts of the movie—from the slaughter of the Edwards family at the beginning of the movie, to the unkempt filthiness of the Comanche women and children and the rescued white captives, to battle scenes in which their own women and children are killed by the Comanches. Freud would call this the "narcissism of minor differences." That is the emphasis, often false, of differences between peoples to justify the subordination of those thought to be inferior. In the early encounters between the indigenous peoples of the Americas and the Europeans, religion, language, clothing, food, and the roles of women were highlighted to demonstrate the difference and therefore inferiority of the Native peoples. These elements are demonstrated in an earlier Ford movie, *Drums along the Mohawk* (1939; see the review in chapter 2).

In *The Searchers*, it is acts of violence that initiate and drive the plot. Another of the film's themes is the importance of family obligations. Three years after the end of the Civil War, Ethan returns to Texas to visit his brother and his family. He uses his kinship obligations as an uncle as a rationale for undertaking his search for Lucy and Debbie. In similar fashion, the Edwardses' adopted son, Martin, is motivated by kinship obligations to join in the search for his sisters, despite Ethan's constant refusal to accept him as kin. Throughout Martin's relationship with Ethan, he must constantly justify his identity as kin to the Edwards family.

Scar (Cicatriz), played by Henry Brandon, the Comanche chief who led the raid against the Edwards family, also has kinship obligations. When Ethan and Scar finally confront each other, Scar tells Ethan he has taken many scalps to avenge the deaths of his sons at the hands of white settlers. It is a brief moment; the possibility that the Comanches might have reasons for attacking white settlements is never developed. The screenwriters only consider the interests of "civilized" Americans worthy of attention, and thus reinforce the audiences' taken-for-granted assumption that peace and prosperity can only be achieved when the nation has been cleared of difference. The concept that the Comanches might have reasons for attacking white settlements is buried in this one brief, visually interesting scene. Being the same height, both men face each other eye-to-eye. Scar speaks to Ethan in English, with Ethan telling him that he speaks "pretty good English." Then the situation is reversed, with Ethan speaking to Scar in Comanche and Scar telling him that he speaks "pretty good Comanch." The scene is a very powerful standoff between two men who understand each other very well.

Interestingly, in this same scene, the now adult Debbie holds Scar's scalp-decorated war lance for Ethan to see. It is Debbie who has brought these two enemies together. Each man has a dark side. While he may be a grieving father, it was Scar who led the raid at the Edwardses' farm that resulted in the death and mutilation of Aaron, Martha, and their son. Ethan has a mysterious past. Where has he been in the three years since the end of the Civil War? When he rides up to his brother's farm, he still has his sword and is dressed in Confederate gray. He carries a bag of Mexican coins. The Reverend/Captain Clayton (Ward Bond) wants to "bring him in" for some unspecified crime. While it is Martin who ultimately kills Scar, Ethan scalps him. In an earlier scene, Ethan shoots out the eyes of a Comanche he has killed. He states that this is to prevent him from finding his way to "the happy hunting ground." Indeed, and how is it that Ethan has learned so much "Comanch," as he calls it. Ethan and Scar mirror each other in their acts of violence. Both act upon the duties they feel toward their families, but both have committed acts of atrocity. These acts place both men outside the bounds of civilization.

As Slotkin has pointed out in his aforementioned trilogy, much of the ideology promoted in Westerns is that Native Americans no longer had a place in the American landscape. It doesn't matter why Scar or any other Native American attacked a white settlement. They are obstacles to the development of American civilization; the motives for their actions don't matter. The West will be a safe place for women and children: a peaceful place of farmers and ranchers, and towns with schools and churches. This concept is clearly stated by Mrs. Jorgensen, played by Olive Carey, one of the Edwardses' neighbors, whose son Brad was killed trying to rescue Lucy and Debbie. Flanked by Ethan and her husband, Mrs. Jorgensen responds to the death of her son by saying, "We be Texans. A Texan ain't nothing but a man out on a limb. This year and the next, maybe for a hundred more. Won't be forever. Someday this country is going to be a fine, good place. Maybe it needs our bones in the ground before that day can come."

The West as portrayed in *The Searchers* is still a wild and violent place, but thanks to the sacrifices of settlers like the Edwardses and Jorgensens, it will be tamed. On the other hand, men like Ethan and Scar will have no place in this "fine, good place." They must make way for the settlements with schools and churches, women and children. On a broad level *The Searchers* is about the loss of the "Wild West" and all it entails in the American mythos. At the end of the movie, Ethan does not even enter the Jorgensen farmhouse with Debbie. He returns to his horse and rides out into the wilderness, again framed by the door of the cabin. Ethan's acts of violence dictate that he, like Scar, must leave civilization to the civilized. In many ways this is the heart of a typical Western, though Ford has represented it better than most.

The Searchers presented John Ford with the opportunity to examine the roles of Manifest Destiny and nationalism in the American Dream, and I believe he does just that. Ford was an Irish immigrant to the United States. His films demonstrate both an immigrant's pride in his adopted homeland, and the immigrant's insight as an outsider. At his best, Ford's images of the West encapsulate these two perspectives. Some critics have pointed out that Ford's vision of the American Dream was tempered by his experiences as a documentary filmmaker during World War II. Regardless, his later films (such as *Cheyenne Autumn*, 1964, and *Sergeant Rutledge*, 1960) demonstrate this disillusionment.

It has long been acknowledged that American films with Native themes are often not about American Indians, or issues that concern them. Instead, when Indians appear in films, they're usually shown to depict the problems Euro-Americans had in conquering "the West." The most obvious example of this type of usage is *Little Big Man* (see the review in chapter 5), which satirizes the myth of the American West. In like fashion, a film about miscegenation between African Americans and whites in America might not have been made in the mid-1950s. Therefore, I suggest that Ford used *The Searchers* to examine Euro-American fears about encounters with people and societies different from themselves—people socially construed as a different race. In a surprising twist of cinematic irony, American Indians in *The Searchers* stand in for African Americans.

In the 1950s it would have been difficult for any movie director to approach Euro-American/African American interactions and relationships directly, especially sexual relations. At this time the Motion Picture Production Code (better known as the Hayes Code of 1930) still controlled what could be seen and heard in American movies. Though the Hayes Code is usually remembered for restricting sexuality in movies, it also affirmed racial integrity by banning the depiction of interracial unions. "Miscegenation" is a term first used in 1863 in laws that forbade sexual relations between Euro-Americans and African Americans, although much older laws (1691 in Virginia and 1692 in Maryland) also criminalized such behavior. By 1915, twenty-eight states had laws prohibiting or invalidating marriages between Euro-Americans and African Americans. After World War II, white segregationists accused those in the civil rights movement of being part of a communist plot to destroy the white race through miscegenation. One year after the release of *The Searchers*, a court in the state of Virginia in *Loving v. The Commonwealth of Virginia* sentenced Mildred Jeter Loving (an African American woman) and Richard Loving (a white man) to a year in jail for violating the Racial Integrity Law (1924). The Lovings' sentence was suspended on the condition they leave Virginia and not return for twenty-five years. The Virginia Supreme Court twice upheld the conviction. It was not until 1967 that the United States Supreme Court unanimously struck down the Racial Integrity Act and similar laws in fifteen other states.

I suggest that in *The Searchers*, John Ford might have been grappling with issues of race that will be more fully and successfully examined in his later film *Sergeant Rutledge.* The Buffalo Soldier Rutledge is accused of a rape and double murder of which he is innocent. The whole plot of the movie is centered on attempts to preserve the racial integrity of the women of the settlement. In the end it is neither the Buffalo Soldier nor an Indian who is guilty of the crime, but one of the white settlers.

Sergeant Rutledge, like *The Searchers*, begins with murder. But unlike that film, in *The Searchers* there's never any doubt about who committed these crimes. Rather, it is taken for granted that the Comanches are to blame. The anxiety and fear of interracial relations, of any kind, are illustrated in the film by the impossibility of accommodation between the settler-colonials and the Comanches. This is reinforced by the near absence in the film of any exploration of the Comanches' and Scar's motives for behaving as they do. Because of this, they appear to lack any humanity. It is instructive to contrast this with the subtle exploration of how racial tensions influence the character of Martin.

In LeMay's book that *The Searchers* is based on, the character of Martin is white, but the film goes to extremes to identity him as a "half-breed." Our first image of Martin is of him riding a horse bareback to the cabin, with his shirt open to reveal his dark skin. Ethan's first words to him are, "I could have mistook you for a breed." Martin responds that he's one-eighth Cherokee. I doubt it's an accident that Martin is identified as Cherokee, one of the "Five Civilized Tribes" forced west on the Trail of Tears, or that his family is killed in a Comanche raid. On the one hand, his "half-breed" status explains Ethan's refusal to accept Martin as a nephew. It also allows the odd plot maneuvers, such as Martin disguising himself as a Comanche to rescue Debbie. (Comanches, it seems, can't tell the difference between Cherokees and themselves.)

In another pivotal scene, Martin shoots and kills a Comanche warrior. At first he hesitates, then shoots and lowers his gun with a look of grief, but finally raises the gun again and continues firing. Many critics have taken this scene to illustrate that Martin, representing "civilized Indians," has made a decision about which society he will align himself with. I'm not so sure I agree with this conclusion. Could it be that this is the first time the young Martin has killed anyone, and the grief we see reflects his humanity?

The whole issue of Martin's racial identity is very problematic. He barely remembers his parents, much less any cultural or linguistic identity as a Cherokee. Ethan speaks Comanche, but in his five years of traveling with him, searching for Debbie, Martin never learns a word of Comanche, or Cherokee for that matter. Being part Indian doesn't prevent Martin from courting the Jorgensen's daughter Laurie (Vera Miles). From the beginning of the movie Martin is shown to be part Indian: one of the "good, civilized Cherokees" as opposed to the "bad" Comanches and Scar—but Indian nonetheless. Why?

It is in the character of Martin that we see Ford trying to wrestle with issues of race he would more fully and successfully examine in *Sergeant Rutledge.* This could account for the contradictory elements of the movie. For example, why is no one except Ethan the least bit concerned that Martin is part Cherokee? It is the "half-breed" Martin who is the truly heroic character in this film. It is he who rescues Debbie and kills Scar. Unlike Ethan, Martin never engages in needless violence. Martin will be part of the new civilization being built in the West.

At the end of the movie, Martin enters the Jorgensen's farmhouse with their daughter. He will be a welcome participant in "the fine good place" the settlers are establishing. At the beginning of the movie, both Ethan and Martin are outside the boundary of the cabin door. In the end Martin passes through that boundary, but Ethan does not. I think Ford has a message here, however muddled it may be. In my read of the film, it's not skin color but behavior that should determine an individual's place in the world. However, in the 1950s people's private fears about interracial love, sex, and marriage made their depiction a taboo subject. Thus, the issues of race, whether red and white, or white and black, are hidden behind this beautiful and rich symbolic scenery of *The Searchers.*

CHAPTER 3

The Disney Version

Dear Diary:

What did make the Red Man red? Was it the war paint, or the sun, or some kind of strange illness? Who can say that far back what happened? But I love the cross-dressing in the stage performance, don't you? Mary Martin was a hottie as a man. I secretly wanted her to kiss Wendy, but it never happened. But what if we wanted to redo it today?!

Note to Self: Make Peter Pan *with an all-girl cast. Throw out the G rating, those pesky Indians, and that sexless crocodile. Have the gecko's agent contact our people.*

Goodnight and sweet dreams,

Hollywood

Peter Pan

David Martínez

What made the Red Man Red?
When did he first say, "Ugh!"
When did he first say, "Ugh!"
In the Injun book it say,
When the first brave married squaw
He gave out with a big ugh
When he saw his Mother-in-Law

What made the red man red?
What made the red man red?
Let's go back a million years
To the very first Injun prince
He kissed a maid and start to blush
And we've all been blushin' since

You've got it from the headman
The real true story of the red man

No matter what's been written or said
Now you know why the red man's red!
—as performed by Candy Candido

My jaw hit the ground when I heard this song and saw these "redskins" hopping around and making fools of themselves. Granted, it was only a cartoon, but it was one in which the animators took the liberty of demeaning an entire race in the name of entertainment. Led by a "chief" who spoke with an "Injun" accent that was thicker than Tonto's, the Indians in Disney's *Peter Pan* were nothing less than buffoonish. While many Indians do not fail to pay back the favor by subjecting white people to their own sense of parody and satire, nevertheless, Indians have never had the advantage of a mega-corporation capable of worldwide distribution, which is further empowered by being a part of the world's dominant economy, the United States. I guess attaining the goals of westward expansion and Manifest Destiny weren't enough, as many American institutions, especially movie studios, still feel a compulsion to reproduce the kind of propaganda that drove American settlers, railroads, and troops westward in the first place. At the same time, as I watched the appalling images of the Indian Chief and Tiger Lily dance across the screen, I couldn't but think that the reasons behind this so-called tradition had to do with something less simplistic than "Indian hating." What I slowly began to realize was that the Indian stereotypes in *Peter Pan* weren't so much meant to be representations of "real Indians," but instead were symptomatic of Americans' own ongoing search for a distinct identity, rooted in the American soil. The Indian Chief and Tiger Lily weren't Indians, as you and I know them; they were really white people trying to *become* Indians.

During the summer of 2005 a former student of mine, a Minnesotan of non-Indian descent, who also happened to be a former Disney Store employee, expressed her dismay upon hearing about the Indian stereotypes in *Peter Pan.* It wasn't that she was surprised that such things appear in an old Disney film from 1953, but rather, having grown up with the film, she honestly didn't recall the way in which Indians were portrayed. As a matter of fact, she said that the only things that came up when she discussed *Peter Pan* with her Disney Store coworkers and customers were the children flying and the pirates. The "redskins" only get as much screen time as the mermaids, which also didn't come up much in my student's Disney Store experience. This begs the question, what do people think when they encounter, or re-encounter, the "redskins" today, especially those people who thought of *Peter Pan* as one of their favorite films from childhood?

According to a Netflix customer, identified only as "TAT," "The sometime politically incorrect scenes were refreshing in a world that has become too afraid to say anything for fear of offending anyone. My fractional Indian heritage was not at all put off by this movie. On the contrary, I was rolling on the floor laughing at the song 'What Makes the Red Man Red.'" Still another customer, a self-described "Film School Graduate/Punk/Long-Time Disney Cast Member" writing under the name "JRawkSteady" emphatically states, "The Native American population of America loves Peter Pan too! Unfortunately PC people don't realize that the only people they're trying to please are themselves!" Most customers, however, chose not to say anything about the "redskins," evoking instead their nostalgia for their childhood. The latter scenario is repeated by customers at Amazon.com, particularly the nostalgia.

In fact, virtually everyone who liked *Peter Pan*, and who felt compelled to say something about the film's portrayal of Indians, inevitably made defensive remarks against "political correctness," similar to the two customers quoted above. "Politically correct," it seems, has become one of those terms, like "liberal" or "commie," that is bandied about by those who want a quick and easy way of dismissing such opinions, as opposed to dealing with them seriously. Ultimately, I would argue, the purpose of this rhetorical device is to make it sound as if the "non–politically correct" person is the true victim here, or at least the potential victim unless political correctness is stopped. From the non-PC point of view, the assertion that "Indians are demeaned in *Peter Pan*" is comparable to when Russian Communists proclaimed that the "American worker was exploited"—less of a real concern and more of a pretense for seizing power. In the final analysis, the non-PC person is doing nothing more than defending home and country from the latest ideological threat to American society.

At this point, it may look as if I'm blowing things way out of proportion; after all, we're only talking about a children's animated movie. In response, I would remind the reader that although we may be considering a children's film, we are far from dealing with children. Disney, a major American studio, produced Peter Pan at a time when American Indian communities had very little political power. That power was poised to shrink even further due to the termination policy that the federal government began inflicting on American Indian tribes. Moreover, while termination was being perpetrated, most Anglo-Americans learned about Indians only through what they gleaned from a John Ford Western, radio shows like the *Lone Ranger*, Zane Grey novels, or comic books like *Scalphunter.* Indeed, ever since William F. Cody created the "Wild West show," Indians have had to contend with an insatiable thirst on the part of non-Indians for "savages." What has gone on just as long, though, is the Indian criticism of such portrayals.

From Luther Standing Bear to Philip Deloria, American Indian intellectuals have challenged the historical and cultural accuracy of Indian images in the mass media, not to mention the ethical appropriateness of concocting such stereotypes in the first place. In *My People, the Sioux*, Standing Bear observed in 1928:

> I have seen probably all of the pictures, which are supposed to depict Indian life, and not one of them is correctly made. There is not an Indian play on the stage that is put on as it should be. I have gone personally to directors and stage managers and playwrights and explained this to them, telling them that their actors do not play the part as it should be played, and do not even know how to put on an Indian costume and get it right; but the answer is always the same, "The public don't know the difference, and we should worry!"

Nearly eighty years later, let alone 1953, the public by and large still does not know the difference. Why is this the case? One would think that after more than a generation of sympathetic works about the American Indians, from *Bury My Heart at Wounded Knee* to *Dances with Wolves*, in addition to a variety of American Indian/Native American Studies programs throughout a range of colleges and universities, we could finally move beyond the problem of stereotypes. Instead, Indian attempts at promoting authenticity on their own terms has been met with Americans conjuring newer stereotypes, such as the ethnic fraud (e.g., Ward Churchill) and the Casino Indian. The last "real Indians" apparently died when Kevin Costner couldn't protect them anymore. What are our white neighbors up to? Perhaps the answer to this conundrum lies in *Peter Pan* itself.

Despite the fact that *Peter Pan* was the invention of British playwright J. M. Barrie, the people at Disney, most specifically Walt Disney himself, did not refrain from *re*-presenting the story of the boy who refused to grow up in their own way. Bosley Crowther, a *New York Times* critic often quoted in this volume, stated in 1953:

> Mr. Disney's animated cartoon of the widely loved children's fantasy is frankly and boldly created in what may best be described as "Disney style." The characters are drawn and animated in such a way that they readily recall not only the appearance, but the behavior of familiars in other Disney films.

Unsurprisingly, Crowther is far from taken aback by the Indian stereotypes, as he finds the whole sequence during the song "What Makes the Red Man Red" to "rollick with gleeful vitality." What bothers Crowther instead is the omission from the original play of the climactic scene in which Tinker Bell is near death and the audience is asked if they "believe in faeries." If the audience says "yes," (and they always do) then Tinker Bell will be saved. Crowther then speculates that the reasons why Disney eliminated this vital turn in the original story is that Disney assumed that "present day adults and children are more literal than they were in Barrie's time," when the play was produced in 1904. Crowther also wondered sardonically whether the missing Tinker Bell scene was "due to some anxiety that the mention of pixiness in the modern American movie theatre might provoke some embarrassment." Perhaps, indeed. It may be worth noting that in 1953 the infamous *Sexual Behavior in the Human Male* by Alfred Kinsey was published, in which homosexuality, among other types of sexuality, was suddenly brought out of the shadows into the light of public discourse. The fact that the "Kinsey report" became a national bestseller automatically made it a part of Americana. In such an atmosphere, from Disney's perspective, maybe it would be better—that is, safer—to focus on Indians rather than faeries. Anglo-Americans, to be sure, have been "playing Indian" for generations without any threat to their sexual identities. The implication here is that believing in faeries is more of a "British thing," anyway.

According to Herbert Brenon, a British film director who made a very popular silent version of *Peter Pan*, it was Barrie's idea to place a girl in the staged version of *Peter Pan*, which he thought appropriate because Peter exhibited "a gentleness associated with femininity that no boy actor ever could have." This tradition would be duplicated in the United States, and wouldn't be broken until Bobby Driscoll played the role in Disney's *Peter Pan*. Nevertheless, Gladwin Hill of the *New York Times* recounted that Brenon "enjoyed the Disney 'Peter Pan' in some respects, and took a dim view of it in others. Like some other commentators, [Brenon] felt there was more Disney than Barrie in the new treatment." From this perspective, what we begin to see is that Disney, at least ostensibly, is more concerned with "Americanizing" *Peter Pan* than it is with the sexual implications of believing in faeries. I say this in spite of the fact that Disney's rendition of this story still takes place in London before moving on to "Neverland." In fact, integral to the Disneyfication, if you will, of any story—be it myth, history, or fantasy—is to make all the characters appear and act like people you might meet on the streets of New York, at least in their idealized, antiseptic form, in which everyone, even "white" characters, is a stereotype.

In the end, Disney's animated films, including *Peter Pan*, reflect the "melting pot" mentality that remains surprisingly resilient in American society. The idea that becoming American ineluctably entails divesting oneself of ethnic distinction is an idea that persists precisely because it's a uniquely American ideal. America is supposedly where people can leave their ethnic strife behind, pursuing the American Dream instead. Disney's Magic Kingdom epitomizes this ethos, above all, in the notion that "It's a Small World, After All." The magic kingdom is what Walt Disney's ancestors sought as well when they settled in Kansas during the nineteenth century as "Irish" immigrants (the D'Isigny family was actually of ancient Breton descent). Like his predecessors, Walt Disney became a self-made man, attaining a level of success that his "sod farming" grandparents could only dream of. Unfortunately, in a country that places a priority on money, power, and technical innovation over history and culture, Disney's vision is also reflective of a society that is still in denial of its Indian past, not to mention its Indian present and future. Until that vision matures—which it has done dubiously with *Pocahontas* (oh dear), I can console myself with the fact that in both the Barrie and Disney versions of *Peter Pan*, even the pirates were afraid of the Indians. *Hey Ya!*

Dear Diary:

I hate Disney. That horrible little mouse with his creepy mouseketeers is ruining my tranquility by insisting on making movies with animals in them. Singing no less. This year, it's Lady and the Tramp *and* Davy Crockett: King of the Wild Frontier. *Who wants to see a bunch of cartoon dogs eating spaghetti? And seriously, who ever thought a coonskin hat was a good idea? Talk about fashion don'ts! If any studio mogul is going to suspend the disbelief of worldwide audiences, it's going to be me. We're so-o-o-o headed for a showdown at the famous "Hollywood" sign if Disney keeps this up.*

Note to Walt: Remember the Alamo? What audiences are going to remember is Donald, Goofy, and Mickey skinned for my hat. Mark my words!

There will be blood,

Hollywood

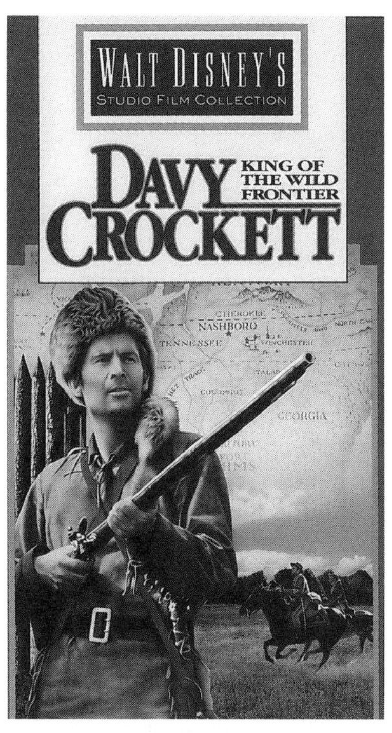

Davy Crockett, King of the Wild Frontier

Clifford E. Trafzer

Walt Disney's landmark television production *Davy Crockett, King of the Wild Frontier* is a challenging film to review. Natives appear on-screen for much of the movie, a compilation of the first three stories from the 1950s television series *Davy Crockett Indian Fighter*, broadcast December 15, 1954; *Davy Crockett Goes to Congress*, broadcast January 26, 1955; and *Davy Crockett at the Alamo*, broadcast February 23, 1955. Throughout the three productions, characters such as Crockett, Andrew Jackson, and others make frequent and nonsensical references to Indians. The portrayals of Indians by actors of Native and non-Native heritage all work to tell the story of the conflict between Indians and the expanding American nation-state. I must say up front it's a mixed bag, with inaccurate stereotypes and derogatory language existing alongside a genuine effort at authenticity.

Fess Parker stars as Davy Crockett, a role that was to catapult him from playing stock characters into stardom. Buddy Ebsen, a song-and-dance man from Hollywood's 1930s era, plays Davy's sidekick, George Russel. This mid-century version of the Crockett saga caught the American public by storm. "Crockett mania" spread throughout the Western world, and retailers responded by stocking their shelves with coonskin caps, flintlock guns, and a host of other toys. From school lunch boxes, dinner plates, and cereal bowls it seems everyone in America went Crockett. The impact of the series was, in retrospect, staggering, affecting an entire generation's perceptions of Indians, Davy Crockett, and the future of American expansionism. America was going places in the 1950s. Having just tamed Japan with an atom bomb, we were about to set our gun sights on Vietnam.

As interpreters of American folk history, Disney writer Tom Blackburn, director Norman Foster, and cinematographer Charles P. Boyle got it right as often as they embraced mythic lore and stereotypes. However, in both respects audiences came to know many American historical figures, as well as early American history through the eyes of corporate America, *er-r-r-r*, I mean Disney.

The concept of living on a perpetual frontier, central to the Davy Crockett story, invigorated a generation that was born decades after the American frontier was declared closed, contributing to John F. Kennedy's drive for a "New Frontier" in Southeast Asia. But other messages came through that were less positive and uplifting: a tendency toward arrogant confidence in your own position, seen through the policies of American administrations; a justification for taking what rightfully belongs to less technologically advanced peoples; and the contradictory ideology underlying noble savage vs. ruthless savage. The subtext in *Davy Crockett, King of the Wild Frontier* is clear: all can be co-opted, trained, and assimilated in an "honorable" fashion.

The film opens during the War of 1812 with President Andrew Jackson, played by Basil Ruysdaereal, leading American soldiers and volunteers against the Creeks, who are fighting to keep their lands from settlers, and preserve their way of life. Only a small portion of the Creeks, headed by the real-life charismatic leader Hildis Harjo, whom Disney renames Chief Red Stick after the historical name of the warring Creek faction, receive any screen time. While Jackson plans his invasion of Creek lands against the leadership of Chief Red Stick, played by Pat Hogan, Davy Crockett pursues the more mundane matter of hunting bear for food with his faithful sidekick and chronicler, George Russel. In characteristic Disney style, the scene symbolizes more than just the action that follows; it's meant to emphasize Crockett's heroic qualities as well as larger themes explored throughout the film. Crockett opts to tame a bear, rather than shoot him, by utilizing a technique of grinning at the animal—the same technique that he'd previously used to sway a raccoon. An army major interrupts him, and the angry bear attacks poor Davy, who is tossed from the brush where he was standing. Our hero charges back in to kill the bear the old-fashioned way, with his hunting knife—rather than with his rifle from a safe distance. After finishing off the bear, Crockett returns to camp victoriously with his kill, ready to meet Jackson, who instructs him to use his hunting skills to track the Creeks. It's not difficult to make the leap from Crockett's interaction with the bear—initially seeking to cajole the animal into compliance, but willing to use deadly force if necessary to maintain his safety and that of his fellow Americans. This identification of Natives with a wild animal deliberately classifies them as savage.

Throughout *Davy Crockett*, white characters consistently refer to Indians as "redskins" and

"Injuns," alluding to their role as natural enemies to civilized folk. This must be the work of writer Blackburn and director Norman Foster. Disney and company also portray most Indians as hostile aliens, the uncivilized and barbaric impediment to white progress and civilization. However, Disney does present one family, Crockett's neighbors, the Two Shirts, as Noble Savages who want to live in a civilized world just as the Crocketts do. Charlie Two Shirts, played by Jeff Thompson, is the "good Indian," whose attempts to adapt to white civilization are foiled by unscrupulous white men. By making Charlie Two Shirts both amenable to white culture and its victim, any threat he or similar American Indians might pose to the dominant culture is neutralized. And what reason would Charlie Two Shirts have for not wishing to participate in the American way of life? Discounting any loyalty to one's ancestors, homelands, and upbringing, the movie presents little reason for Two Shirts and other Indians to forget their traditional lifeways and adapt to the civilized "American way." In the *Davy Crockett* universe, the United States government is honorable in its dealings with Indians, allowing Davy to assure Chief Red Stick that American leaders will abide by treaty promises and allow the Creeks to live in their own homelands, according to their own ways.

Unlike Charlie Two Shirts, a common family man, Chief Red Stick and his warriors are presented in the film as bloodthirsty savages. In one scene we see warriors performing a frenzied dance around a roaring fire in the middle of the day. However, whether portrayed as savages or domesticated animals, Indians appear to be not very bright. Thus, both Chief Red Stick and Charlie Two Shirts are depicted as being simpler than the average white man. In fact, at one point in the movie, Crockett and Russel outsmart a group of Creek warriors that have attacked an army patrol. With the threat of total annihilation facing them, the army retreats into the rocks to fight for their lives. Serendipitously, Davy and Russel arrive on the scene to save the army, and miraculously convince the foolish warriors that Jackson's entire army is present. Then, with speed and precision, Davy and George kill several Indians, and the entire scene looks like the shooting gallery at Disneyland: one, two, three, four, etc., Indians fall to their deaths. After the Indians' defeat, Davy and George report to the major as "Company A" and "Company B" of Jackson's army.

After Crockett's wife, Polly, dies, he moves west to "paradise." Disney portrays the westward movement and Manifest Destiny as positive events in American history. And it was for white Americans, but not for Indians. Crockett and Russel both make claims on former Indian lands, but they're committed to living in peace with Charlie Two Shirts—the noble savage—forever being mistreated by greedy whites. This romantic portrayal of the frontier completely ignores the heartbreak of the Battle of Horseshoe Bend, the theft of Indian homelands through treaties, or the cry for Indian removal during the decades of the 1820s and 1830s. Most contemporary non-Natives believed that the coming of state and local governments to the frontier signaled a change from primitive to civilized. But for tribal nations, American federalism posed a great threat to tribal sovereignty and culture. Since Indians were not U.S. citizens, laws that protected citizens didn't apply to them. Governments at all levels used their authority and power to steal Native homelands so they might appropriate all resources that once belonged to Natives. And they drove Indian peoples from their homelands in mass removals known as the Trail of Tears.

In real life, Davy Crockett was a great hunter and accomplished storyteller. Purportedly, by his own self-promotion he killed, skinned, salted, and ate Creek Indians.[1] Yet, while Disney makes the most out of Crockett's hunting prowess, the business about cannibalism is left out. After all, this was for television-audience consumption. Crockett served as a member of the United States

House of Representatives and took Washington, D.C., by storm, wearing his buckskin clothing and entertaining his colleagues with stories that included, we are told, his appetites for human flesh. While serving in the House, Crockett proved to be no lackey of President Jackson and openly disagreed with him on the Indian Removal Bill of 1830. Disney is careful to refer to the act by the innocuous term the "Indian Bill," never alluding to the forced removal it imposed on Indian tribes from the eastern and southern portions of the United States to the "Great American Desert" west of the Mississippi River. The entire issue appears as a political falling-out of two heroes, rather than a national tragedy that still casts a dark shadow on American history.

Davy's opposition to Jackson's Indian policy ended up costing him his seat in the House of Representatives. Given Crockett's true nature, he likely had had enough of Washington, D.C. (and Washingtonites likely had enough of his nasty, vulgar stories of cannibalism), national politics, and the proper protocol of government officials. Whatever the case, the movie finds Davy next racing off to Texas with Russel and a gambler they pick up along the way, in order to help Americans fight for "freedom, liberty, and the American way."

As they ride through Texas, the trio witnesses plenty of signs of Indians. Smoke signals rise over the mountains (actually located in California instead of Texas), and Davy suggests they are a sign of the Comanche. Apparently Davy views the Comanches as another warlike tribe, so the group decides to move quickly out of harm's way. They eventually reach a spot where they hear and feel the earth rumble. Abandoning their horses, they climb a steep grade from whose peak they witness a herd of buffalo being chased by a lone Comanche hunter with a lance. When the hunter is thrown by his horse, Davy rushes to his aid and learns that he has been exiled from the tribe because he is a failure as a warrior and hunter. This particular Comanche, who remains nameless, decides to join Davy and the others and show them the way to San Antonio and the Alamo.

As it turns out, the party reaches the Alamo as the battle is about to erupt, and the rest is history (so to speak). There they find William Travis, portrayed by Don Megowan; Jim Bowie, played by Kenneth Tobey; and a host of other frontiersmen—Anglos and Mexicans—standing firm against Santa Anna. Though the situation is dire, all the men at the Alamo agree to fight to the death.

Disney was never one to allow history to get in the way of a good story, so in this version, many Americans, and Texans whom we all know and love, live on. And the finale is inspiring, with all the Texans fighting gallantly to the finish—especially Davy Crockett, who is seen brandishing his trusted rifle "Betsy." Disney does not allow viewers to see the hero die, because as we all know, "Davy never really died." He lives on in the hearts and minds of millions of viewers everywhere, and Fess Parker's portrayal of Crockett competes with that of John Wayne's Crockett in the 1960 film epic *The Alamo.* (Wayne directed that film.)

Though Disney's view of Davy Crockett and the American frontier was wrong, it is what most American viewers commonly believe. Throughout the three films, Crockett is portrayed as treating fairly with Indians. The movie's creators are short on fact and long on mythmaking. Disney filmmakers helped perpetuate the view that America's frontier experience was benign and positive for all participants, including Indians. But freedom, liberty, and opportunity for white settlers, represented through Davy's television character, did not reflect the reality of nineteenth-century Indians. In fact, the actions of the United States were based on an ideology of Indian genocide and ethnic cleansing. In the end, Disney's films greatly enhanced the reputation of Davy Crockett, but missed the mark when it came to Natives.

NOTE

1. For a fuller description of Crockett's escapades, see Catherine L. Albanese's *Nature Religion in America: From the Algonkian Indians to the New Age* (Chicago: University of Chicago Press, 1991), and Thomas A. Tweed, ed., *Retelling U.S. Religious History* (Berkeley: University of California Press, 1997).

Dear Diary:

Again I ask, what would the Indians do without us? Disney's Peter Pan *solved the mystery of what made the Indians red? And now Disney has once again come through with* Pocahontas. *What a babe! And even AIM guy Russell Means has said* Pocahontas *is the best movie about Indians ever made. What a pal!*

Hey Diary, I see Mattel is making a Pocahontas "Barbie," complete with patented big boobs and tiny waist.

Note to Self: Send assistant to buy Pocbie. I'll dress her as stewardess, fashion model, or . . . candy stripper. Yum. What's for din-din?

Love ya loads,

Hollywood

Pocahontas

Jeff Berglund

I would like to title my review "Pocahontas Disneyfied, or: How I Learned to Stop Worrying and Love and Ignore Genocide." The subtitle is a deliberate nod to Stanley Kubrick's *Dr. Strangelove*, one of the twentieth century's preeminent films, an absurdist critique of nuclear buildup and our nationalist tendencies toward annihilation of others in the name of freedom and progress. These tendencies are supported by the rhetoric of freedom and democracy, which is further sustained by our national amnesia, a nationalist failure to recognize and "own" our serial history of genocidal tendencies, foremost of which is the bloody legacy of conquest of indigenous peoples in the name of Manifest Destiny and "civilization."

Whoa. What does all of this have to do with Disney's 1995 blockbuster Pocahontas? *This all sounds pretty serious. This is a Disney princess movie, after all. Are you sure that's what's really going on?*

Truth be told, it's the question I keep turning over in my mind, though I know the answer—this *is* what is going on. See, we're all vulnerable to Disney magic, even those of us who know history, even those of us who know the legacy of conquest in the Americas. Wait a second, was *Pocahontas* about genocide and conquest? Well, directly, no. But, ultimately, yes, it's all about genocide and the processes by which we're lulled into ignorance and complacency about the truth of the past.

The millions who watched *Pocahontas*, and continue to watch it on DVD, have been lured into thinking they're watching a love story, a multicultural adventure story set during the time of this nation's founding in seventeenth-century Virginia. The fact that you and practically everyone else were, and are, reeled in by the love story and the mesmerizing beauty and spunk of the heroine and her suitor means that you likely give in and drink Disney's magic Kool-Aid. Well, okay, not exactly Kool-Aid, but the film *is* a sugary concoction, filled with pretty images, a motherless heroine, cute animal sidekicks, comic relief, a raving mad villain, gorgeous vistas, catchy, inspiring songs (the recipient of four Academy Awards for music), a vision of multicultural harmony and friendship, and on the surface, somewhat positive and corrective portraits of Native peoples, particularly when you compare them to Disney's vision of Indian peoples in 1953's *Peter Pan* and its horrifying musical number "What Makes the Red Man Red?" (See the review in this chapter.)

While *Peter Pan* traded in racist, minstrel-style stereotypes, it never purported to "bring an American legend to life," a first for Disney in 1995 just as their growing Princess franchise was being deliberately cultivated. Much was made of their effort to tell a story rooted in history, rather than in the archives of primarily European fairy tales. American history has always given a prominent position to the story of Pocahontas, for the story as it's been rendered by mainstream accounts is one of an intracultural broker, particularly as a figure for the New World's recognition of the value of the explorer-colonizers. The story of Pocahontas has functioned as an example of early cultural intermarriage, on two different levels: first, for her intervention in the execution of Captain Smith (the subject of the Disney film), and then later, through her marriage to John Rolfe (detailed in Disney's sequel with a catchy title, *Pocahontas II*). While I am not interested in examining the myriad critiques of the flattening of the complexity of the historical figure—Paula Gunn Allen's *Pocahontas: Medicine Woman, Spy, Entrepreneur, Diplomat* does all of this very effectively—I do want to draw attention to the way that Disney exploits this historical basis as a means of authorizing its version of history. These claims to legitimacy through a basis in historical fact are one central ingredient of Disney's nutrition-deficient confectionary. By now I hope you know that after consuming sugary *Pocahontas* you need to mentally floss, rinse well with antiseptic truth-telling cleaner, and fortify with the knowledge equivalent of fluoride.

Now, let me indecorously shift metaphoric gears, so to speak: I want to concentrate on Disney's magic. That's a frequent slogan of the studio, I'm sure you recognize. The voice actress for Pocahontas, the talented Native actress Irene Bedard, even said as much in the bonus features included on the DVD for the film: about the complexities of production of an animated film, Bedard notes, "Watching a Disney animated film is like watching a magic trick!" While I'm certain that the studio didn't mean it quite this way, I say, *exactly*, and that's what is troubling. The magic trick performed by Disney in *Pocahontas* is a disappearing act. Add the right elements, create distractions, play into the audience's needs, and "poof," genocide and the enduring trauma of conquest vanishes.

While I am no magician, I'm pretty good at figuring out some of the primary elements that structure Disney's trick in this movie. Any good magic trick requires some distractions to divert the audience's attention from central deceptions (or what appear in narrative as tensions). The movie's animal sidekicks—Meeko, a raccoon; Flit, a hummingbird; and Percy, an English pug—all provide these distractions. Meeko and Flit, the yin-and-yang response to Pocahontas's burgeoning romance with John Smith, provide comic relief in their continuing battles with one another. Percy's initial disdain for the "dirtiness" of the New World eventually gives way to an assimilation of sorts. Just as Pocahontas eventually saves Smith, so does Meeko "rescue" Percy and join him in a sort of minstrelized marriage: Percy dons "Native" garb and Meeko dresses like a colonist, and then the two are joined together in their cultural reversals. Flit's cranky criticism of John Smith is counterbalanced by the humorous actions of Meeko; ultimately his good will brings the two animal worlds together, which precedes the emotional if not physical joining of Pocahontas and John Smith. Viewers of Disney are familiar with animal friends, but in this context they serve to emphasize Pocahontas's bond with the natural world. While they function in this way, they also undercut the emotional heft of numerous scenes, diverting attention from serious issues, such as the killing of Kocoum, the only Native person, and the only person at all to die during the film's eighty-eight minutes.

A good magician must gain the confidence of his or her audience. In this regard, Disney magic gains the confidence of the audience by its claim to authenticity, particularly in terms of the indigenous aspects of the film: it's rooted in the historical story, and was supposedly meticulously researched, resulting in deliberate choices about representing clothing, language, and the culture of the Powhatan people. Somehow, despite this meticulous research, Pocahontas is morphed from a girl of twelve into a fully developed woman, scantily clad in clothing reminiscent of a Barbarella, and the male characters resemble Rambo or *Jersey Shore* meatheads with long hair. Strategic casting decisions also served to strengthen this aura of authenticity. Central Native characters were voiced by well-known Native actors: Irene Bedard for Pocahontas, Michelle St. John for Nakoma, James Fall for Kocoum, and Russell Means for Chief Powhatan. If only Hollywood had been so conscientious in previous generations: casting Native people in Native roles. But wait a minute: we're talking about voice work. Well, let's not debate this issue, and just go with the premise that more authentic characters were created through the informed perspectives of voice actors.

That would be fine if it ended there, but I become suspicious about these casting decisions when I see them being used to validate and promote the film. The very fact that Native actors were involved—earning a living using their talents—is a great thing, but is co-opted by Disney as a validating, and thus market-minded, move. Therefore, any comment offered by these actors becomes an implicit endorsement of the film's narrative about indigenous history. Irene Bedard can be found on DVD extras saying, for example, seemingly innocently, "I think the story of Pocahontas is one of the most beautiful love stories ever told." How can you argue against that, especially as it's a view offered to us by a Native actress? The most significant "authenticating" endorsement of the film comes from Russell Means, former leader of AIM, whose foray into Hollywood has come with its share of criticism, to put it mildly. In describing his role he says, "I looked to my own ancestors and their spirits and identify with Powhatan; it's easy to relate to him because he's my role model." In other publicity work, Means notes with no degree of irony, "This is the best movie ever done about Indian people in the history of Hollywood." These factors create a susceptible mood necessary for the magician to lure the audience. If the film was carefully researched, involved Native people, and was endorsed by a Native activist (now turned actor), then something authentic must be going on here. Right?

In addition to authenticity, Disney's magic trick depends on a feeling of balance and fairness in the depiction of historical figures. Balance is a gesture at authenticity, but it also serves as a diversion, keeping us from seeing what values, what story, anchor the plot. Both the colonizers and Powhatans are subjected to our critical scrutiny. Or so it seems. The jaunty opening number reminds us that members of the Virginia Company were led to believe that "the New World is like heaven, and we'll all be rich and free, or so we're told by the Virginia Company!" The innocence of individuals, who have been sold a bill of goods, is maintained, and the wrongmindedness of conquest is reserved to one maniacally evil character, Governor Ratcliffe, whose name as well as physiognomy and body shape all iconographically convey Disney's prototype of evil. Thus, what starts out as balance is anything but that. The European mindset of explore-destroy-conquer-exploit-rule is condensed within one character alone. A narcissistic character, selfish and ruthless at the core, is to blame for the Virginia Company's plot once they've landed at Jamestown. Mocking criticism of Ratcliffe is whispered by Wiggins, his foppish (read effeminately gay) manservant, though these asides are just that, dismissed as comic interludes—for example, RATCLIFFE: "Why do you think the heathens don't like us?" WIGGINS: "We invaded their land, cut down their trees, dug up their earth?" Ultimately, in Disney's hands, Ratcliffe's genocidal and acquisition-driven efforts acquire the status of personality disorder rather than systemic political and economic regimes.

The appearance of balance is also struck in the portrayal of Native culture. The opening sequences of the movie show a pristine, Edenic world, with the Powhatan people living in harmony with nature. The illusion of a balanced view is conveyed visually, and later, through song, orally. How could viewers not embrace this vision of utopia, untainted by conquest? Pocahontas's father, Chief Powhatan, is a proud leader who listens to his elders, a medicine man who warns of coming violence. While he is reasonable leader, he is a stern, caring father interested in protecting his daughter, assigning her hand in marriage to a brave but serious warrior, Kocoum.

This sense of balance is maintained through turnabout parallelism, as evidenced in the scene when Pocahontas first "schools" Captain John Smith about who is really a "savage"; in perfectly balanced multicultural rhetoric, in the couple's first duet, she sings: "You think I'm an ignorant savage.... If I'm the savage one, how can there be so much that you don't know; you think you own whatever land you land on. / The earth is just a dead thing you can claim." Before we know it, John Smith has been swept into Pocahontas's reverie, and the two are caught in a swirl of colorful leaves, as they tumble in meadows of sunflowers, swim in rivers, run through forests, and witness the flight of their eagle counterparts. We learn, via the breakout song "The Colors of the Wind," that "For whether we are white or copper skinned / We need to sing with all the voices of the mountains / We need to paint with all the colors of the wind / You can own the Earth and still / All you'll own is Earth until / You can paint with all the colors of the wind."

This sense of balance is nowhere more clear than in the epic rendition of "Savages," a song sung in two parts by the men of the Virginia Company and the Powhatan men after Kocoum has been shot by Thomas, a man compelled by Governor Ratcliffe to prove his masculinity by getting a "savage." Chief Powhatan is portrayed as full of anger; it is rage that fuels his drive toward war, not injustice, not the need to protect his land and his way of life. The same lyrics are sung by each side, suggesting, as Pocahontas earlier claimed, that anyone who is different is labeled a "savage." In this song's logic, then, it's an equal sum game. This leveling of the playing field blatantly ignores an obvious factor: the Virginia Company had no claim to the land originally inhabited by the Powhatans. Meant to reverse and critique the Eurocentric stereotype of "savage" Indian, the dueling lyrics possess all of the force of the childish taunt, "I know you are, but what am I?"—an endless tautological circle that avoids the truth of power imbalance in this situation.

In addition to a false sense of balance and authenticity, Disney plays into our national fascination with the freedom of choice. Pocahontas's "spirit" mentor and mother substitute, Grandmother Willow—absurd and comical taken out of context—encourages her to follow her own path. Initially this encouragement of personal choice is meant to embolden her to resist her father's design that she marry Kocoum; Grandmother Willow tells her she "must find her path" by "listening to her heart"; and, while her path lies yet out of reach, recognition, or realization, it is "just around the riverbend." We see that Pocahontas's choice, her personal freedom to find her way, is paramount—a value supported by Disney's narrative vision for its heroines, but often simultaneously undermined by the homogenizing force of its standards of womanhood. That Pocahontas is encouraged by a spirit mentor, Grandmother Willow, further stresses to audiences that her choice is sanctioned by her cultural values and cosmology. Put another way, Grandmother Willow functions to remind us that Pocahontas isn't a sell-out—after all, even "streams must join the river."

When Pocahontas and John Smith first meet, the musical score swells with a prelude to "All the Colors of the Wind," and the two are wrapped in a swirl of leaves. Each time their romance is tested and then found to be triumphant because of their individual choices to follow "their path," the same music resumes, followed by a swirl of leaves. These issues are crucial in the final wrap-up of the film's narrative when Pocahontas makes a succession of important choices. She convinces her father to save John Smith's life. This favor is paid back within moments when Smith dives to push Chief Powhatan out of harm's way of Ratcliffe's gun. Rather than join the incarcerated Ratcliffe (his men heroically—and I might add, ahistorically—recognize his insanity) and the injured Smith on their journey back to England, Pocahontas makes a choice to remain behind, though the colorful leaves and reprise of "All the Colors of the Wind" remind us that her heart is pulled along with her lover. As Ratcliffe, and all the violence he embodies, sails back to England, Disney suggests that Pocahontas and her people may return to their Edenic life. One person, Kocoum, has died, but all the rest have survived and will continue on. Through the triumph of personal choice, Pocahontas has eliminated graver threats.

Grandmother Willow forgets to tell Pocahontas what is ultimately really around the river bend: more and more Ratcliffes—in other words, death and destruction. *Pocahontas II* ignores this too, as our heroine escapes death once again, even as she travels to England. Does it surprise you that *Pocahontas III: The Final Chapter* has never been made? Not sure audiences would buy that disappearing trick—the erasure of genocide—one more time.

CHAPTER 4

Mixed-Bloods in Distress

Dear Diary:

Overheard on the set today: "Mr. O. eats directors for breakfast?" (He's such a meanie.) What about wives, I asked? Anyway, Diary, all I can say is that we better fall to our knees and thank darling Howard Hughes for designing the push-up bra three years before we'd need it for our Pearl on Duel in the Sun. *Otherwise Jenny J. would have nothing to heave at the cameras.*

Note to Self: Invite Miss Jones to din-din tonight. Exclude Mr. O; that producer-husband of hers would make it an awkward threesome.

Love ya loads,

Hollywood

Duel in the Sun

Gary Harrington

A Brady Bunch station wagon pulls up in front of the Sandia Army Base Theater in Albuquerque, New Mexico. Five brothers, ranging in age from teenager to toddler, pile out. Regulation army haircuts, patched jeans, and collared, polyester short-sleeved shirts buttoned to the top. Although we are all Comanche/white, I'm the only dark one, smack dab in the middle of the birth order, wearing the dependent-personnel military-issue glasses and looking like Ernie Douglas's twin from the TV show *My Three Sons.* The station wagon pulls off, and we go inside to watch old Westerns and second-run movies while my mother and sister get groceries at the base commissary and my dad fights for all of us in Da Nang. It's 1969.

Duel in the Sun (1946) is one of those typical movies we would have seen at a Saturday matinee over forty years ago. David O. Selznick was trying to repeat the epic magic he'd conjured up for *Gone with the Wind* (1939). A top-notch cast of big stars, a musical score that would later be released on vinyl (a first), and a modern marketing campaign comprised of wide and early distribution assured that the movie would be a blockbuster. Selznick even wrote the adapted screenplay himself. However, *Duel in the Sun* suffered the same fate as *Avatar* (2009) would some sixty years later: kowtowing to a megalomaniac control freak may make for heaps of money in the short term, but it doesn't often make for great movies that stand the test of time. Although *Duel in the Sun* was a financial success, Selznick's attempt to pander to the baser, prurient desires of the movie-going public earned the movie the nickname of "Lust in the Dust," and a place on the matinee playbill of backwater army bases in the late 1960s.

The movie opens with a musical prelude and overture by Dimitri Tiomkin played over a still-frame image of the Old West. Tiomkin would later win an Oscar for his score in *High Noon* (1952). An Orson Welles voice-over narration of a supposed local legend about a flower is interjected. When the live action starts, Pearl Chavez (Jennifer Jones), the child of a Native American dancehall girl and down-on-his-luck poker player Scott Chavez (Herbert Marshall), is dancing to the delight of lovely little Mexican children costumed in sombreros and greasy hair. Pearl's dancing is simple and unspoiled, but we hear the primitive, throbbing tom-toms beating inside the dancehall. At this point, if the movie had been shot today, I could easily imagine a Scorsese-style tracking shot through a seedy strip club, starting from the low-life barker outside the door, dollying through the corpulent and sweaty clientele, and up to a bored and skanky over-the-hill woman sliding down her stripper pole. But, this is the golden age of cinema, where bigger-than-life and grimeless depictions of the Old West were commonplace, so instead we're treated to a flashy representative (a totem, if you will) pole dance by Pearl's Native American mother (played in heavy brown makeup by Tilly Losch, better known for her earlier portrayal of a Chinese woman in the 1937 film *The Good Earth*). Losch's full-blooded, unbridled, savage performance goads the hundreds of leering cowboys and card players into a very Freudian, pistol-shooting frenzy.

As Pearl's mother is flashing her dance panties, Pearl's father is tucked into a corner of the dancehall playing cards when he suddenly realizes that his wife is a slut. After her dance, Pearl's mother slips off with a customer, but Chavez tracks them down and kills them both. He's hanged for the killings, even though in Texas at the time (1880s), a cuckold killing his wife and her lover "in the act" ranked right up there with jaywalking as to the seriousness of the offense. For the sake of full disclosure, I should mention that in the early 1900s, my great-grandfather was caught "hiking the Appalachian trail" near Lawton, Oklahoma, with a woman not his wife, and suffered a similar fate at the hand, or gun, of her husband. The husband got off free and clear. Of course, that could be attributed to the law's lack of interest in pursuing red-on-red violence.

During his march to the gallows, Pearl promises her father that "she'll be a good girl" and not behave like her mother. Pearl then goes to live with her father's second cousin, Laura Belle McCanles (Lillian Gish), on the McCanleses' sprawling Spanish Bit Ranch. Pearl is met at the stagecoach by Jesse McCanles (Joseph Cotten), the son of Laura Belle and once larger-than-life Senator McCanles (Lionel Barrymore), who is now confined to a wheelchair. By this time in his career, Lionel Barrymore was actually wheelchair-bound due to arthritis, and may best be remembered as playing another wheelchair-bound character, the irascible Mr. Potter, in *It's a Wonderful Life* (1946), produced the same year as *Duel.*

As Pearl and Jesse are approaching the Spanish Bit, the audience is treated to magnificent Technicolor establishing exterior shots. This was the beginning of Hollywood's tinkering with new technology—Vistavision, Panavision, Cinemascope, etc.—in order to entice consumers into coming out to the cinema rather than staying at home watching television, much like the rediscovery of 3D technology is supposed to entice consumers back into theaters today. Director King Vidor, of silent movie fame, seems a tad uneasy with the new technology. Right after all these gorgeous shots, he inserts a rear projection two-shot of Pearl and Jesse. This type of shot was a staple of movies up through the late 1930s, when black-and-white rear projection only demanded a close lighting match to get a satisfactory result. However, in the 1940s, with the advent of color cinematography and better film stock, a precise color match between the rear projection image and front action was simply impossible, resulting in hokey, low-budget-looking shots like the one described above.

Duel also suffers from being produced during a transition in acting style as well. Although both Jennifer Jones and Lillian Gish were nominated for Academy Awards for their performances, Jennifer Jones's acting, in particular, is full of silent-movie poses, pouts, and hair pulling. The tried and true techniques that had worked so well in cinema up to this time were quickly giving way to more relaxed and nuanced acting styles that would be epitomized by actors such as Marlon Brando just a few years down the road.

Even with the technological and directorial strikes against it, *Duel*'s examination of "good and bad" does warrant a tip of the hat. After arriving at the Spanish Bit, Pearl is conflicted between her white, civilized side, symbolized by the good McCanles son Jesse, and her Native American, savage side, symbolized by the bad McCanles son Lewt (Gregory Peck). Pearl rejects Lewt's advances, and her civilized side seems to be winning out through the tutelage of Laura Belle and an itinerant preacher nicknamed "Sin Killer" (Walter Huston). Good son Jesse has even fallen in love with her. However, Jesse is exiled from the Spanish Bit after siding against his father in a land dispute with the railroad. As Jesse is getting ready to leave, Lewt, knowing that Jesse has feelings for Pearl, goes to her room and rapes her. In 1946, that was too much for the censors, who demanded that the scene be reedited so that Pearl, after initial resistance, is overcome by Lewt's charms. Jesse shows up at Pearl's room and is let in by a smirking Lewt, and it doesn't take much for Jesse to put two and two together. Jesse confesses his love for Pearl, but now that she's been spoiled, he doesn't want anything to do with her. Of course, he says it in a nice way, since he's the good son:

JESSE: I might as well say it. I loved you. Somehow you touched me.

PEARL: You, you loved me?

JESSE: I thought of what you'd be like when you grew up a little.

PEARL: Oh, I didn't know. Why didn't you tell me, Jesse?

JESSE: I didn't think it would be fair to tell ya. I was a fool. I came to your room to say goodbye, to tell you that someday I'd be back for you. That I'd think about you and I'd write. I'll write to you, Pearl.

PEARL: You will, Jesse, you will?

JESSE: If you need me, I'll come back, senator or no senator.

PEARL: And you'll forget about, about tonight, won't you? You'll forget it?

JESSE: No, I don't think I'll forget. I don't think I'll ever be able to. I shouldn't have told you the way I felt. It wasn't fair. There I go again. Gotta be fair.

PEARL: (*sobbing*) Trash. Trash, trash, trash, trash, trash.

So, what's a trashy girl to do at this point? Pearl turns her affections towards Lewt, who is happy to accept, considering he's getting the milk without having to buy the cow. Lewt promises to marry her, but when Pearl forces the issue and demands he announce their engagement, he refuses. Again, Pearl tries to pick up the pieces and gets engaged to an older man, Sam Pierce (Charles Bickford), whom Lewt promptly guns down, claiming that Pearl is his girl. Lewt is now on the run from the law, and Senator McCanles blames Pearl for Lewt's behavior, insisting that she be banished from the ranch; but Laura Belle says that Pearl will stay as long as she has a breath left in her body. Following this vow, Laura Belle gives a little cough, and you can guess the rest.

Jesse returns to Spanish Bit to see his dying mother, but he's too late. He does offer Pearl a new life with him and his very white fiancée, Helen Langford (Joan Tetzel), and Pearl takes him up on it. Unfortunately, Lewt gets wind of the arrangement and goes gunning after Jesse as well. Jesse confronts Lewt unarmed, but Lewt shoots him anyway. Jesse is only wounded, and Pearl nurses him back to health until Helen arrives. Helen reiterates the offer to Pearl to come live with them and become civilized, but Pearl knows that Lewt is still a threat, and decides to go gunning for Lewt. She meets up with him at Squaw's Head Rock and wounds him with a rifle shot. He shoots her and wounds her in the chest; she fires back and mortally wounds him. As Lewt is dying, he calls out to her that he's always loved her. She crawls to him, and they die in each other's arms. Even today, this sadomasochistic ending leaves me feeling queasy.

Pearl's "half-breed" status is merely a plot device to highlight the duel between civilized and savage behavior. The only person who seems to have a problem with Pearl's Native American heritage is Senator McCanles, and we find out late in the movie that his animosity towards Pearl is due to his jealousy of Pearl's father rather than her biracial status. However, the senator does have one of the best lines of the movie: "I rode through the night like a drunken Comanche." Having ridden once or twice myself through the night *as* a drunken Comanche, I could tell you a few stories that would have made much more entertaining movies than this one.

Duel is a classic Saturday-afternoon matinee movie—a big, forgettable production meant to kill time before your mom gets back from the commissary. What makes the movie worth watching is that it's a prime example of a production caught in the transition between pre- and post–World War II filmmaking.

Dear Diary:

John Huston is a big baby. Night after night I listened to his tiresome stories about tracking and hunting "big game" until I near went deaf. Now he's pitched a fit because we won't use his ad copy to market Unforgiven. *It read, "A splintered chronicle of sexual desire between a brother and sister, and a Kiowa Indian." Kinky, John, but we want to make some money, here. Sigh. It seems playing nice doesn't cut any ice with this haughty auteur. Oooo, that rhymed.*

Note to Self: Must write poetic screenplay. Call Larry Olivier's agent.

Frustrated,

Hollywood

The Unforgiven

LeAnne Howe

Picture this: I'm fourteen years old. It's 10:30 p.m. Saturday night, after the news. Feature-film time. My dog Ginger and I are plopped on the living room couch waiting for the weekend feature film to begin. Oh great, it's got Audrey Hepburn in it, she's one of my favorite actresses, and Burt Lancaster—loved him in *The Birdman of Alcatraz.* And look, there's Audie Murphy. *Wow*, he's a stud in this movie. (Yes, I used that word, but I didn't really think of "stud" in any particular way. I was emulating my older and wiser high school friends. Maybe it's the mustache and long sideburns he grew for the role that makes him seem so sexy to me. After all, this is the late '60s.) Everyone in our family is proud of Audie Murphy's heroism during World War II. Each time he appears in a late-night movie, someone says, "He won the Medal of Honor, the highest military honor given by our country."

However, I'm fourteen years old, petting my dog and thinking about making some popcorn when this strange, icky music (by Dimitri Tiomkin) plays over the film credits. I can tell the movie is going to be a Western. Audrey Hepburn (Rachel Zachary) is on a horse. She's wearing a wig, long brownish-black hair. In the distance, she spies an old Confederate-looking soldier, Abe Kelsey (Joseph Wiseman). He talks to Audrey like he's some kind of biblical prophet. His voice is shaky with an oratory vibrato of doom, and I think he sounds as creepy as the music. Already I'm scared, but still anxious to see what happens next.

In general, I'm not a fan of Westerns, because I always cheer for the Indians (I am one), and I wish that we could be the heroes in the movies instead of John Wayne and his band of Indian killers. But I hang in there. Burt Lancaster (Ben Zachary) makes his first appearance as Rachel's brother. I can tell that Rachel loves him, but not exactly like a brother. As they are paired in a scene to establish their relationship, Rachel tells Ben that since she's a foundling, and adopted by the Zacharys, it wouldn't be improper for them to marry. This is where things get, well, a little yucky, at least for the fourteen-year-old me. I'm adopted but can't imagine marrying my adopted brother. (He eats onion sandwiches and his room is an absolute pit.) But I let that go and trot off to the kitchen to make a skillet of popcorn for me and Ginger.

By the time I return to the TV, it's clear that the Kiowas have come looking for Rachel, their long-lost tribal member. "So, she's Kiowa," I say to Ginger. "They always wear such cool outfits."

The Zacharys, the white settler family that has adopted Rachel, are Manifest Destiny personified. In the film they stand in for all settler colonials running Indians off their lands out West. The whites are shown as honest, hard-working, nation-building patriots who have to deal with pesky Plains Indians, the barriers to progress, Jackson Turner–style. Ben is the family's eldest son of the Zachary clan; Audie Murphy is the middle brother, Cash; and Doug McClure is Andy, the youngest brother. Lillian Gish is their widowed mother, Mattilda. The family is torn apart when Kelsey reveals the truth about Rachel's Kiowa identity. The Zacharys must suddenly come to grips not only with the fact that they've been living with a savage, but the very savages that killed Pa Zachary, the head of their family. Needless to say, Cash goes a little nuts. Since their father's murder by the Kiowas, Cash hates *all* Indians. Ben doesn't like the way Cash is acting toward Rachel and tells him to "Pack up, and leave."

Now this is where the movie takes a sharp turn for me, causing me to lose faith in the storyline. Upon hearing she is an Indian, Rachel goes into her bedroom in the "old soddy"—a dugout carved out of the side of a hill, which is emblematic of settler homesteads, but I do not know this yet. She pulls her blouse out so she can look down at her breasts (apparently she'd never looked at her skin before) and discovers that she is indeed a Kiowa. From the look on her face, she wants to die. But instead, she takes a bit of burned charcoal and rubs a black mark across her forehead to reinforce that she is indeed a savage living among her very civilized adopted family. If you pretend you're French and say "*sauvage*" like the French, as I often do, it's a lot of fun when applying the term to oneself.

But, back to the movie.

Even as a teenager, this is the one scene that really ticked me off. What kind of girl, or woman, has never seen her breasts before? And, excuse me, Audrey/Rachel, what's wrong with being a Kiowa? The scene is well directed by John Huston, but to my fourteen-year-old sensibilities it seemed cruel, not only to her character, but to all Indians. "We're Indians, Audrey, I mean, Rachel. And there's nothing wrong with that!"

Or is there?

The Unforgiven is a film about racism in the nineteenth century, yet the subtext is the racism of the 1960s, when the film was produced. John Huston wanted Rachel's character to have to come to grips with her identity—and then what?—kill her biological brother as she does in the last scene to vanquish, sever, her Native identity and tribal roots? Maybe if

Huston had remained in the editing booth, we might have had a different resolution, or at least a more nuanced one.

Another minor flaw in the film is the role of John Saxon's character (Johnny Portugal), a half-breed who is harassed by Zachary's hired hands, and is set up to be a foil for Ben's deeply hidden sexual desire for Rachel. And Rachel does give Johnny the eye. Of course Ben (presumably jealous of his sister's affections) beats the crap out of the half-breed Johnny. The incest thing isn't really incest, but it's a bit weird. Ben and Rachel, Burt and Audrey do have strong chemistry onscreen, and I also love their interactions as actors onscreen. But normally in America, we don't marry our brothers.

So let me see if I can get this straight. She's Kiowa. She's been passing for white in West Texas. She kills lots of Kiowas in the final shootout, even as the old soddy, her home, burns. Her Kiowa brother makes it through the smoking soddy, and she shoots him point-blank in the belly, just as he holds his hand outstretched, saying, "Sister." Then she immediately kisses her adopted brother Ben flush on the lips, the brother whom she has lived with all her life. Have I left anything out? Oh yes, Ben tells Andy (he doesn't ask) that "we're all going to have a wedding." This is Ben's way of informing Rachel that she will marry him. Congratulations Sweetie! By murdering your Kiowa brother you have proven yourself civilized enough to wed your white brother Ben. (Murdering Indians pays off!) I should also mention that Cash returns during that final shootout at the soddy and kills all the Kiowas he can, thereby satiating his appetite to avenge his father. The new hybrid settler family stands around the burning ashes of their soddy; some geese fly overhead, signaling that there will be brighter days ahead. End credits—the icky music swells.

Having an Indian passing for white in West Texas or Indian Territory loomed large in the imagination of writers like Alan Le May, author of the screenplay and the novel. Incidentally, Le May also wrote the script for John Ford's *The Searchers* (see the review in chapter 2). Hint: Le May is obsessed with racial purity. However, his film script of *The Unforgiven* cannot decide where it stands on the issue of whites adopting and raising an Indian girl as their own. Lillian Gish gives one of her most moving screen performances, capturing the love of a mother toward her adopted child, one who is not of your own blood. As a fourteen-year-old, Gish's performance brought me to tears, and still does as an adult, because it hits so close to home. My adoptive mother was Cherokee, and I could not help equating Gish's love for Rachel with the love my adoptive mother had for me. My Cherokee mom wanted children, but she was unable to have children so she adopted me and my brother. When she talked of what it meant to have adopted my brother and me, I always cried. I'm Choctaw, my birth mother was Choctaw, my adopted brother is white, but our adoptive mother is Cherokee. For these reasons watching *The Unforgiven* as a teenager gave me a great deal to think about race and identity. I still could not help but feel sorry for Rachel's Kiowa brother as he reaches out to her. They lock eyes sorrowfully; then, of course, she shoots him. Bitch! What a heartbreaker she is. But the message is clear: Natives must kill their own to be fully civilized human beings.

If it's true John Huston once said that a good story should have "excitement, color, spectacle and humor, adventure, high drama, tragedy, good conversation, truth and irony,"[1] *The Unforgiven* hits the mark. In it, Huston brings all the complexities of race, identity, and sexual desire together—but to my mind, mucks it up by siding with the colonizers whose solution to the "Indian problem" alternated between genocide and ethnocide. Anyone remember Pratt's motto? It was "Kill the Indian, Save the Man." Why is the American film narrative "Indians must die?"

The film's title refers to the attitude of Abe Kelsey (Joseph Wiseman—later to play Dr. No), a bearded half-crazy avenger who has tormented the family for many years, ever since his son was abducted by the Indians and Ben's father refused to trade Rachel for Abe's son. The twist is that only while Abe and Mattilde know that Rachel's biological parents were Indians, everyone else (including Rachel) believes that she was the only survivor of a massacred white settler family. Until that breast-exam scene.

Another scene that is absolutely spellbinding is Rachel comforting the mother (June Walker) of the boy she was to marry earlier in the film who was killed by Kiowas. Walker slowly looks up at Rachel and then suddenly goes absolutely ballistic, shouting, "Red-hide Nigger." Audrey Hepburn's stunned reaction is riveting.

When Ginger and I finished our bowl of popcorn that Saturday night all those years ago, we went to bed. I dreamed fitfully. As Americans have completed the first decade of the twenty-first century, I have to say that I still love to hate this movie. I've watched it many times. The story haunts me, and its underlying message is a theme I teach in American Indian Studies courses: Why must Indians die? Why must we be the vanished, the dispossessed past tense peoples? If we're able to fully interrogate that question, we're on our way to realizing that American Indians, indigenous people, are alive and well. Still . . .

NOTE

1. See *http://www.imdb.com/title/tt0054428/reviews.*

Dear Diary:

Time for my yearly meditation on what to do next. Just finished wrapping up the last of the lasts. Thank the Maker that Russell Means signed onto the project. It really does pay to hire real Indians. Keeps down the protests. I've learned my lesson: authenticity pays.

Woo-hoo,

Hollywood

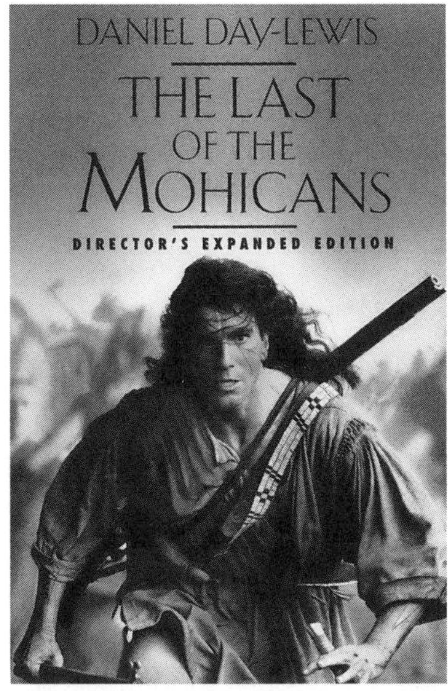

The Last of the Mohicans

Philip Deloria

Near the end of Michael Mann's *Last of the Mohicans*, the camera pulls back to reveal the white protagonists Cora (Madeline Stowe) and Hawkeye (Daniel Day-Lewis) standing together with the last Mohican, Chingachgook (Russell Means), mourning his son, the dead Uncas. As the ceremony ends, the camera moves again, this time dollying around to reveal a widening gap between what had initially seemed to be three people standing together. We see that in fact Cora and Hawkeye had been standing close together, with the Indian character somewhat apart. A gentle breeze lifts Cora's and Hawkeye's long black hair, and their locks fly together in beautiful unison as the camera frames them in profile, blurring the two figures together. The attentive viewer cannot help feeling a little bit sorry for Chingachgook, who had only an instant before been an equal partner in the scene.

The shot is only one of many stunning cinematographic moments in this lush and beautiful film. Part of the explosion of "Indian pictures" in the late 1980s and early 1990s, *Mohicans* features an excellent cast of familiar Native actors and extras, including Means, Eric Schweig (Uncas), Wes Studi (Magua), and Dennis Banks (Ongewasgone). Mann takes full advantage of a gorgeous landscape of cliffs, water, and mountains, making the stunning settings of North Carolina Cherokee country masquerade relatively successfully as Iroquois territory. The musical score evokes a kind of polished Scotch-Irish feel that, if not "authentic," gives a passable filmic sense of it. And Mann did not hesitate to edit James Fenimore Cooper's baroque tale into a tauter brand of drama; indeed, in interviews, Mann suggested that he paid little attention to Cooper, but worked his script around the 1934 version of *Mohicans*, one of four previous iterations of the story committed to film during the twentieth century.

All five *Mohicans* films depend upon Cooper's original plot and characters. In the 1826 book, the frontiersman Hawkeye and his Indian companions Chingachgook and Uncas rescue, protect, lose, and redeem two young women, Alice and Cora Munro, the daughters of a British commander who find themselves caught up in the violence of the French and Indian War. The daughters, and particularly Cora, are threatened by the heartless Magua, a French ally who seeks revenge against Munro for a previous humiliation. Against a narrative backdrop that centers on the burning of Fort William Henry, and the subsequent killing of British refugees, are played out a series of love stories involving the penultimate Mohican Uncas, on the one hand, and the dashing soldier Duncan Heyward, on the other. In the end, Uncas dies at the hands of Magua, leaving Chingachgook alone, the last of a vanishing race.

Michael Mann's script diverges from Cooper's book in significant ways. One suspects that most viewers do not know *Mohicans* well enough to notice Mann's changes (the book having been dropped from most literary canons long ago—replaced, if anything, by Mark Twain's satirical essay on Cooper). And yet, the transformations of the script are critical to understanding the ideologies that drive this film—and to making sense of that final scene, with its separation of Chingachgook from the flying black hair of its white protagonists. The scene's separation of Indian from Indian-inflected white people offers a fairly obvious visual cue, to be sure, but the scene is only a capstone to the structural narrative that underpins the film. To get at that narrative, however, it is necessary for us to revisit the structural relationships that characterized Cooper's original novel. Those relationships are built around a series of pairings: Cora/Alice, Uncas/Chingachgook, and Uncas/Magua, among others. Each of these twosomes is set in motion through the introduction of a third character, setting up a series of triangular tensions that are only resolved through complete reshufflings. The story ends with new pairings, which not only give the story its motion, but also explain Cooper's vision of America and its future.

The oppositional relation between sisters Cora and Alice Munroe lies at the heart of his story. Cooper explicitly racializes dark-haired, sensual, and durable Cora, hinting that her mother was "of color" and thus making her the subject (and, in relation to Magua's lust, the object) of race-crossing. Blond and delicate Alice—the child of a different mother—is figured as the essence of racial purity and civilized white femininity. The two are positioned as two sides of a number of different triangles. Place their father as the other side, and you have a familial drama of race and affection. Replace him with the officer Duncan Heyward, and you have a love triangle in which Cora functions as both a nurturing mother and a third wheel, destined only to bring together racially pure lovers. Place Uncas as the third side, and you have an alternative love relationship, one well-suited for Cora—though made possible only by Uncas's exceptional, almost transcendent Indian nobility. Replace him with Hawkeye or Chingachgook, and you have asexual uncles or grandparents, every bit as invested as Cora and her father in making the match between Duncan and Alice. And indeed, Cooper ends *Mohicans* not only with Uncas's death, but with the reproductive marital union of Duncan and Alice, who return to England briefly, then make their way back to America. The message is clear: the national future rests in the hands of racially pure, upper-class British elites, whose children will populate and rule the new world.

Uncas and Chingachgook make up a second pairing, and they too can be placed in relation to other characters. Put Hawkeye with the duo and one has the book's celebrated "rescue group," an eighteenth-century trio of commandos whose impressive skills will open the way for civilized folk, but who will themselves never marry, propagate, or have a future. Place Cora on the other side of the triangle. One immediately sees a desperate effort to keep Uncas alive in order to propagate and thus ensure an Indian future. Likely Indian partners are nowhere to be found in the book, so Cooper's "one-drop-rule Cora" offers a chance to imagine a "sort of" Indian-white future. (Note that it is a future that functions quite differently from the Indian woman/white man Pocahontas fantasy). Place Magua on the other side, and one perceives the threats to a Mohican future. He would, and does, destroy that future by killing Uncas. Indeed, the other critical triangle in the novel is the one linking "good Indian" Uncas, "bad Indian" Magua, and their mutual object of desire, Cora. Though Cooper tantalizes readers with the possibility that Uncas and Cora might actually enjoy a future, in the end they are both killed by Magua or (in Cora's case) his henchmen. The deaths of the three of them power the book's action and its conclusions. No white man is responsible for the Indian disappearance that is sealed by the death of the couple. The possibility of Indian-white love is deferred to the afterlife, a ghost story that will perhaps haunt America, but that will always be impossible in the here and now.

By the end of the book, earlier pairings have been resolved and reshuffled. The old dualities (Alice and her father; Alice and Cora) and the new possibilities (Cora and Uncas; Cora and Magua) are displaced by Alice and Duncan, the most powerful new pairing to emerge from the story's bloody climax. Chingachgook/Uncas, a pairing that began the book with a veneer of hope, has been broken: slow decay for the father, rapid death for the son. Chingachgook and Hawkeye emerge as a new partnership, confirmed as two variations on a dying breed, never to reproduce, and destined to disappear into the receding West. In these pairings, Cooper's sense of an American future becomes apparent: No race-crossing allowed. Thanks to those on the frontier, but please keep moving. Patrician elites ought to, and will, rule.

With Cooper's structure in mind, one can immediately see how Michael Mann's *Mohicans* works in an entirely different way. The stain of miscegenation is removed from Cora, who becomes simply a durable wilderness woman. Alice (Jodhi May) becomes even more pale and pathetic. The two love triangles become more explicit and better balanced. Dark Cora, not Alice, is the central object of desire, and her suitors are Duncan Heyward and Hawkeye, who, in the form of Daniel Day-Lewis, is anything but the asexual wilderness gentleman found in Cooper. The love triangle Mann uses to set the plot in motion—Duncan, Cora, Hawkeye—is more explicit and intense than any of the prudish colonial dramas surrounding Cooper's genteel Alice. If more compelling, however, the triangle almost inevitably telegraphs its conclusion. Mann's Duncan is a fop, and Cora rejects him repeatedly. It will come as no surprise that Cora and Hawkeye end up together at the end of the film, hair blowing in unison. And so it is the *second* love triangle, the one built around pale Alice, that actually drives Mann's storyline. Alice stands in for Cooper's Cora, for both Uncas and Magua desire her. If Cooper did no more than dangle a distant possibility, Mann seems quite willing to allow blond Alice to link up with the Indian hero.

The resulting drama—captures, negotiations, sacrifices, and fights—leads to the film's climax. Duncan sacrifices himself in order to free the Munro women, dying well at last, but destroying Cooper's vision of an American future built around English social elites. Indeed,

British sacrificial death by fire allows America to rise, phoenix-like, from the ashes. Magua kills the noble Uncas and is in turn killed by Chingachgook. Before this can happen, however, Alice escapes Magua's grasp and leaps to the edge of a precipice. In the film's critical moment, Magua gestures for her to return from the rocks, to choose life with him over death. Alice's blank stare moves between Uncas's broken body on the rocks below and the gesturing Magua. Here, Studi's face is magnificent and complex, a mix of wonderment, impatience, and desire. (Indeed, through sheer dramatic skill, Studi consistently makes a stereotypical evildoer into an unexpectedly complicated character). Alice hesitates, then slowly falls backward to her death. Was she a suicide joining her love, the dead Uncas? Or was she fleeing the live Magua, who seemed, even in the midst of it all, to hold out a promise of something resembling affection?

The different structural pairings created by Michael Mann completely erase and overwrite Cooper's argument and ideologies. The American future will not be owned by civilized, lily-white European elites. For Mann, the Brits are gritty enough when put to the test, but all too fragile in everyday life. Rather, the future will belong to bold Cora and Hawkeye. Sturdy pioneers, darkly touched by the Indian continent, they will tame the wild, produce the next generation, and build the nation. One cannot help but hear echoes of a Ronald Reagan inaugural in this white frontier tale of new mornings and bold forays westward. In order to make this new argument, however, Mann leaves intact Cooper's ideological understanding of Indian futures. As in Cooper, there will be no cross-race romance. And if Cooper lumped Indians and frontiersmen together as those without a future, Mann denies Chingachgook even the company of a Hawkeye-like frontiersman on the unspoken but inevitable flight to the west that will precede his eventual disappearance. Thus the subtle move of the camera in the final scene, which makes clear both the future for American pioneers and the lack of Indian possibility in that future. Read this way, *Mohicans*, in Mann's hands, offers the same message as Kevin Costner's *Dances with Wolves* (see the review in chapter 5): a white couple will learn from Indian people their true nature, and the nature of America. They will then pair up and ride off into the future, consigning Indian people to the past. The cavalry will surround the village, and Chingachgook will trudge away westward to the sea, the lonely last of the Mohicans.

Dear Diary:

I just loved the way Viggo juts out his chin as he rides across the finish line on that sweaty stud Hidalgo. Reminds me of Chuck Heston driving those four white stallions in Ben Hur*! Hubba-hubba. These blond guys sure have what it takes to play swarthy ethnic types. Yawn, Diary, I'm bushed. Time for my nappy-poo. "To sleep, perchance to dream" . . . to make shit up about cowboys and Indians.*

Note to Self: Must call Charlie Sheen and see if he's interested in playing Sitting Bull.

Yippe ki-yeah,

Hollywood

Hidalgo

Jim Wilson

A mustang pony and his Anglo/Lakota rider are lonely partners in Disney's 2004 film *Hidalgo*, where the two somehow manage to conquer the "Ocean of Fire," a three-thousand-mile race across the Arabian Desert.

Set in the late nineteenth century, *Hidalgo* stars Viggo Mortensen as Frank Hopkins; Omar Sharif as Sheikh Riyadh, an Arabian emir who owns the most beautiful and powerful horses in the world; and Zuleikha Robinson as Jazira—Sheikh Riyadh's headstrong daughter and Hopkins's love interest. The film panders to the myth of rugged American individualism in the story of "a man and his horse" set against the best stables and most dangerous terrain of Arabia. Talk about lack of teamwork—even *The Lone Ranger* fielded a bigger, more transnational team than *Hidalgo*.

Hidalgo veers off course right from the start with its opening caption: "Based on the life of Frank T. Hopkins." In the opening scene, Native flute music evocatively signals that "there be Indians." Next comes a montage of dead leaves, frozen water, and shots of a bitter cold wilderness. Presumably we're somewhere "out west," and as Hopkins whistles for his horse we're treated to a close-up of the magnificent mustang pony Hidalgo. The horse (who is refreshing himself at the frozen stream) immediately runs to Hopkins. "Come on Brother," says Frank, "checkout time," as he puts a saddle on Hidalgo's back. Hopkins's constant use of "Brother" reminds the audience of the close kinship between Indian and animal, and as the scene continues, we find out that our hero and horse are currently in a long-distance race against an Englishman on a thoroughbred. Of course, Hidalgo wins. Yet, before Hopkins can finish a celebratory shot of whiskey in a friendly saloon, he's asked to head over to a Lakota encampment and deliver a message to a Seventh Cavalry officer at Wounded Knee. *Uh-oh, not Wounded Knee and the Seventh Cavalry!* Everyone who's anyone knows this signals disaster for the Indians.

The film jump cuts to the next scene, eight months later: Hopkins perpetually drunk. He and Hidalgo are in a Wild West show, and it's clear the horse doesn't like it. In fact, he bucks Hopkins off into a crowd of white folks to demonstrate his displeasure. A couple of famous Injun fighters are depicted in this scene, including Buffalo Bill Cody (J. K. Simmons) and Annie Oakley (Elizabeth Berridge), who just wants her friend Frank Hopkins to sober up and ride. What we learn here is Frank's backstory. He's called "Blue Child" by his Lakota grannies and is haunted by his failure to prevent that slaughter of the innocents when the Seventh Cavalry massacred hundreds of Lakota men, women, and children near Wounded Knee, South Dakota, on December 29, 1890. Instead of staying to help his relatives, Frank had fled on Hidalgo, thereby saving himself and his horse for a brighter future as a trick rider in Buffalo Bill's Wild West Show (truly the Cirque du Soleil of its day).

Memories of Wounded Knee torture Hopkins—hence his drinking problem. *Hmmm.* And, the plot gets weirder when Frank has a fairly intense meeting with a couple of additional stereotypes: a fussy accountant with a bad accent, and a chunky Arab named Aziz dressed in a glitzy black galabiya, complete with long sword tucked into his sash. The two men tell Wild Bill and Frank about a great long-distance race in Arabia. They also say they're offended that Frank and Hidalgo are billed as the world's greatest endurance rider and horse, and they challenge the American upstarts to enter their great race in Arabia.

Segue. Another jump cut; we're back to Indians. Frank wakes up in his tent to find Chief Eagle Horn (Floyd Red Crow Westerman) at his bedside. Frank confesses that he delivered the message to the Seventh Cavalry and that he saw what they did to the Lakotas. Chief Eagle Horn replies, in so many words, that Frank is a "Far Rider," meaning that he rides far from himself. The chief passes him a Lakota symbol, a cross within a circle symbolizing the four directions. In the next scene, Frank is standing in front of Hidalgo, saying, "I don't know who Frank Hopkins is anymore"—a line reminiscent of John Dunbar's in *Dances with Wolves* (see the review in chapter 5). What's wrong with these guys? Do interactions with Indians make people say transcendently silly things like this? After Frank's confession to his horse, he and Hidalgo accept the challenge of a grueling horse race across the Arabian Desert.

The narrative speeds along with requisite epic shots of a steamship ride across the ocean, and we're even treated to a short scene in which Frank meets a rich English couple, Major Davenport (Malcolm McDowell) and his wife Lady Anne Davenport (Louise Lombard)—the really bad egg in the film. Lady Anne plots against everyone because she wants to breed her horse with the famous Arabian stallion owned by Sheikh Riyadh, whereby she schemes to make a fortune by breeding Arabians in England. After the great race begins, however, Frank rebuffs Lady Anne's sexual advances and becomes enamored of the sheikh's daughter instead. He confesses to Jazira that he's half Lakota, and their friendship grows because they discover they are both hiding behind veils.

When the film hit the big screen, an uprising of controversy arose over the real Hopkins and his veracity on everything from the Lakota Middle West to the Arabian Middle East. As such, the opening caption should have read: "Based on the *stories* of Frank T. Hopkins." By insisting that *Hidalgo* was based on actual events, director Joe Johnson and writer John Fusco simultaneously perpetuated Hopkins's colossal fabrications and missed an opportunity to take them in a smarter direction. They would have done better to emulate *Seabiscuit*'s dramatic premise of scattered characters (by class, nationality, and species) partnering to become champions. As it stands, the characters of Hopkins and Hidalgo primarily exist to thwart their rivals (British adventurers, Bedouin Arabs, competitor horses, etc.) rather than learn to partner through encounters. Absent from the film's story is the need to form surprising alliances. For diplomacy's sake, why not have Frank Hopkins's already bilingual character learn some Arabic? Or have Hidalgo befriend some of the Arabian horses to show the audience that friendship with non-American animals is okay?

Disney would have done better to tell viewers that *Hidalgo* was fictional, and then stake some claim to a greater dramatic truth. For example, why not have the part-Lakota man forsake America and all the tragedies that left him a loner, and have him form lasting ties with his Bedouin hosts in the great race across Arabia? Sheikh Riyadh and his precocious daughter Jazira develop an obvious affection for Hopkins and Hidalgo over the course of the film. How much sweeter if the lonely loner Hopkins had actually accepted their invitation to stay in the sheikh's house, to become Muslim, marry Jazira, breed Hidalgo to the sheikh's finest mares, and eventually become a sheikh himself?

In one of the sentimental final scenes in Arabia, Sheikh Riyadh invites Hopkins to "stay, be a guest in my house." If Hopkins and Hidalgo had stayed, they wouldn't be just American adventurers, but also transnational heroes who *find* something transcendent in going native with their new Arabian friends. As it stands, the return of Hopkins's character to the United States tells Americans that they are right to keep echoing Kipling with, "East is East, and West is West, and never the twain shall meet." There are demons Americans can exorcise in a film where hero and horse don't just conquer a new Middle Eastern place, but fall in love with what it contains as well.

There are precedents for Americans going to the Middle East for travel or work, only to stay and make their homes there. Whether coming as missionaries or doctors, educators or diplomats, merchants or soldiers, Americans have stayed on to establish institutions that have engaged generations of Arabs since the nineteenth century, when the Hopkins story is set. In higher education alone, two continuing legacies of such exchange in Lebanon and Egypt are the American University of Beirut (my alma mater) and the American University of Cairo. Such institutions show how American-Arab cultural symbiosis works in the Middle East. They could have served as signposts for a film—like *Hidalgo*—in search of a dramatic, original, and provocative storyline.

When I first began to study archaeology in 1980, my professor and academic advisor at the American University of Beirut (AUB) was Dr. William Ayers Ward. He was an American and an Egyptologist who had lived and taught in Lebanon since the late 1950s. In addition to his prodigious scholarship on ancient connections between Egypt and the Levant (in our first meeting, he informed me that he could read in twenty-six ancient and modern languages!), Dr. Ward had also married a Lebanese woman, raised a family, and loved his life in Beirut even given Lebanon's civil war. Perhaps such a blended American-Arab life isn't as simple to script as that of an American protagonist who comes for a season, makes war and peace, then leaves. But a story of blending nationalities is actually more hopeful. And as Dr. Ward would teach me, even ancient Egyptians could turn a story of cultural blending into a classic.

In "The Story of Sinuhe"[1] an official of the Egyptian Middle Kingdom flees regime change in roughly 1960 B.C. for exile among the Canaanite "Asiatics." As Sinuhe wanders lost through the Sinai borderlands, dying of thirst, he is found and saved by a "Sheikh among them, who had been in Egypt."[2] After spending a year and a half in various Canaanite towns, Sinuhe is taken in by another sheikh, who has also befriended expatriate Egyptians ("Thou wilt do well with me, and thou wilt hear the speech of Egypt"). The second sheikh eventually marries Sinuhe to his oldest daughter. Sinuhe stays in Canaan for years, has children who become tribal leaders themselves, and grows rich in livestock and influence. He even defeats the fearsome champion of a rival tribe in hand-to-hand combat. The story finishes with a homecoming as the elderly Sinuhe returns to Egypt—at home, but probably as lost as a post–Middle East T. E. Lawrence in Britain. Still, Sinuhe leaves behind an extraordinary story of an extended sojourn among the Canaanite Asiatics. It provides a precedent for more intriguing storytelling in which the foreign-born hero must make surprising symbiosis between himself and his Native hosts.

The Arabs Frank Hopkins encounters in *Hidalgo*, and the Lakotas he claims as kin, are *tribal* in community ties and in worldview. Extended-family logic permeates tribal cultures, whether Arab or American Indian. The film literally fails to marry the friendship that forms between Hopkins, Sheikh Riyadh, and Jazira. Rugged individualism may be an enduring American myth, but *Hidalgo*'s "go-it-alone" storyline resulted in a movie that lost a great opportunity. And it paid for it: while *Hidalgo* raced to cash in on the success of Universal Pictures's hit *Seabiscuit* (2003), it did poorly at the box office and among a plurality of critics. Hidalgo failed to imagine its own disparate characters coming together in more perfect union.

The film ends with a scene in which Hopkins returns to Indian Territory. He uses his winnings from the Arabian race to buy all the mustang ponies rounded up by ranchers and cavalry (just before they're about to be slaughtered), and sets them free in the Blackjack Mountains of Pushmataha County; not all that far from my home in southeastern Oklahoma. By the way, the Blackjack Mountains are only 1,243 feet high. *Uh-hum.* They look nothing like the images in the movie. In the end, Hopkins also sets Hidalgo free. Another strange turn in a story where the protagonists always win their race, but find no love and so must go it all alone. That's not American Indian. It's not Arab. And it's not good American filmmaking either.

NOTES

1. J. B. Pritchard, ed., *The Ancient Near East* (Princeton, NJ: Princeton University Press, 1958), 5–16.
2. Ibid., 7.

CHAPTER 5

You Mean, I'm a White Guy?

Dear Diary,

Wow, those Indians sure are a cranky lot. Ingrates, too. What we haven't done for them! I mean, really, where would they be without us? And so bitchy to the Johns. I'd like to see them make The Searchers. *Who would they cast as Ethan—Geronimo? That'll be the day. Ha! I slay me.*

Note to Self: we should make a movie of this: us talking to ourselves about Indians.

Hey, Diary, how do you make a hundred Indians say "shit?"

Answer: Yell BINGO!

No, I didn't write that myself, but who does in Hollywoodland? That's really not the point. The point is this: It seems like nowadays a hundred Indians yell even louder at the word "Western." Let me tell you a little story, Diary: We've been working our asses off trying to do right by them, and all we get is flack. You know how many crappy little towns want to be in the pictures? And there we are putting all of those Navajos up on the screen, and all they can do is say, "Uh, those aren't Comanches." Well, guess what, you didn't hear Texas complaining about Monument Valley not being in Texas. Or, that actor who played Mose in The Searchers *complain about not being crazy. You see where I'm coming from?*

And now there is Broken Arrow. *Slap my bottom and call me Debbie. What's next? "All along the Reservation"? "How Green Was My Pueblo"? "Citizen Sitting Bull"?*

Note to Self: look into Citizen Sitting Bull. See if Mitchum is available. Anyway, Diary, I am so sleepy. Good thing there is rest for the wicked! So glad we made Broken Arrow. Get them off my ass for a while.

More tomorrow!

Love, your best friend forever,

Hollywood

Broken Arrow

Dean Rader

Of all the movies in this book, *Broken Arrow* remains one of the most problematic. No one really knows what to do with it, how to read it, how to teach it, or even where it should sit among the pantheon of Westerns. Neither an Indian film nor a typical Western, it straddles the bucking

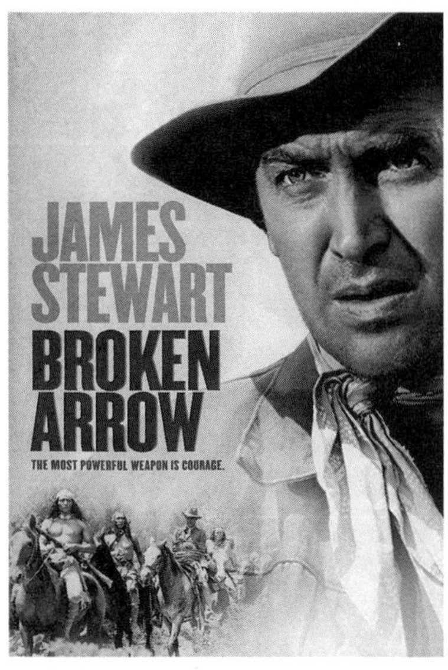

horse that is the un-PC movie. Will *Broken Arrow* get thrown off? Or, will it ride out its eight metaphorical seconds? And, if it does fall to the ground, what clowns will come to its rescue?

Along with the non-sympathetically titled *Redskin* (see the review in chapter 1), *Broken Arrow* is considered by most in the movie business to be a "sympathetic Western." This means it looks upon Indians with sympathy. *Sympathy*, from the Greek *sympathia*, means to "share a fellow feeling with" or, more accurately, "to suffer with." All indications are that Hollywood was pretty pleased with itself for *Broken Arrow*'s ability to suffer with Indians. The first of its kind in the post-studio 1950s, *Broken Arrow* is a project probably meant to make up for all of the other insulting Westerns that came before it, and also for all the ones Hollywood knew would come after it. This gesture is little bit like the scholarship to the Negro college the narrator of Ralph Ellison's *Invisible Man* receives after he's been forced to fight a bunch of other African American boys in a makeshift boxing ring to the delight of cigar-smoking, prostitute-fondling businessmen. Here you go, kid. No hard feelings, okay?

The synopsis: White people are taking Apache land in Arizona. Apaches don't like this. White people start killing Apaches. Apaches retaliate. White people *really* don't like this. They call in the U.S. Cavalry. But, the Apaches are smarter. Not just because they defeat the cavalry, but because blue wool uniforms are hot in Arizona. Plus, the whites are unorganized. The Apaches are organized. They're led by Cochise. He unites all the clans. Think: *finely tuned resistance machine.* Enter Jimmy Stewart, one actor who knows how to play a white man. He is a former military scout and sensitive kind of guy. He saves a wounded Apache boy shot by an insensitive white guy. In turn, the Apaches let Jimmy go free. Jimmy gets an idea. Let's make a deal with the Apaches. Ha ha! Funny sensitive white man. He nearly gets hanged. The insolence! The nerve! The very idea! Somehow, he convinces the military and the other white people to let him visit Cochise. He thinks Cochise might let the mail go through. Jimmy is ridiculed. He learns to speak Apache. He visits Cochise, who is played by a white man. They laugh. They talk. They bond, as two white men in movies often will. Jimmy gets his palm read by an Apache maiden named Sonseeahray or White Painted Lady. She is played by a white lady. They fall in love as white men and women often do in movies. Think: *Dances with Wolves.* (See the review in this chapter.) Cochise lets the white people's mail go through. White people rejoice. Jimmy is accused of being an Indian lover, as sensitive white men often are in movies. Jimmy and a general who loves Jesus decide to try to make a treaty with Cochise. They visit Cochise. Jimmy is still in love. He and the white Indian woman make out. Cochise meets with other Apache leaders. Most vote for the treaty. But not Geronimo! He defects. The Apaches approve the treaty. The white people approve the treaty. The treaty is ratified. Jimmy marries the white Indian woman. They "make love." Cochise's Apaches keep the treaty. Geronimo's Apaches do not. Insensitive white people also do not. They set a trap. They ambush the Apaches, Jimmy, and his new bride. They shoot Jimmy. They shoot his bride. She dies. Jimmy cries. Cochise stops him from revenge.

The Indian saves the white man! The Indian is the civilized one! The movie then opens up to chronicle the massacre at Sand Creek, the Trail of Tears, various examples of the Indian Removal Act, and detailed aftereffects of Termination policies.

Ha ha! That's a little joke.

The movie closes with viewers thinking that everything worked out okay, except for that Indian woman who was really a white woman dying and all. But, it was okay because both Jimmy and Cochise had sacrificed for "peace."

THE END.

In *Hollywood Genres*, Thomas Shatz keenly observes that during the glory days of the studio system, genre movies relied on visual indicators as early as possible in a film—even within the credits—to help set the celluloid stage for the movie itself. These indicators help viewers get into the right frame of mind. A baton might signify a musical; a pistol and bowler a gangster movie; a rose a romance. *Broken Arrow* could have relied on any number of icons for its clues—a tomahawk, a bow and arrow, a cowboy hat, a sheriff's badge. But those images, whether intentionally or not, connote aggression. They are combative signs, pointing to showdowns, shootouts, and scalpings. They reinforce stereotypical tensions between Anglos and Indians, and they inscribe the West as a contact zone of violence. Instead of these icons, *Broken Arrow* opens with its credits painted on a kind of winter count. A winter count is a Plains Indian mode of calendaring in which a hide, usually that of a buffalo, is stretched out in many directions and tied off on wooden poles to create a kind of papyrus. Members of the tribe or clan would draw pictograms each year to commemorate surviving that winter.

The choice of the winter count for *Broken Arrow*'s initial symbolic entrée intrigues. It's an attempt at authenticity. It hopes to lend the movie street cred. On one hand, it says, "Hey, we're a friendly Indian movie," but, on the other hand, because the Apaches didn't really do winter counts, it also says, "Hey, we still haven't gotten this right."

In fact, for all of director Delmar Daves's good intentions, there are quite a few things he didn't get quite right. *Broken Arrow* promoted its mimetic quality; it trafficked in the parlance of authenticity. But, there were problems. For one, there is that messy issue of casting. Both Cochise and Sonseeahray are played not by Indians but by white actors—Jeff Chandler in the case of Cochise, and Debra Paget as Sonseeahray. Interestingly, the main Anglo character, Tom Jeffords, happens to have been played by an Anglo, making the claim of authenticity at least one-third correct. A detail most people don't know, or remember, is that Paget went on to play an Indian princess in other films, so Daves was unusually prescient to recognize her innate Indianness for future roles.

The film's casting, though, is just part of its overall filter of whiteness. *Broken Arrow* wants to be pro-Indian, and thematically it probably is. It wants to promote an integrationist ethic; it longs to be seen as a progressive, recuperative text. But the entire film—including the Apache people and the Apache culture—is seen through the lens of hegemony. By this I mean that the movie's racial compass points directly at the values, experiences, references, and rituals of whites. In this way, *Broken Arrow* participates in what we might call mis-semiotics. Semiotics is the study of signs, and in particular the relationship between the signifier and the signified. Take a stop sign, for example. The signifier is the red octagon with the white letters S-T-O-P emblazoned on it; the signified is what Americans know to do—come to a complete halt—when they see that sign. Semiotic verisimilitude exists when the sign and signifier are in alignment. *Broken Arrow* trades on the visual iconography of semiotic verisimilitude, and its revisionist content helps make this point, but by casting Anglos as Indians, the movie undermines its authority. *Broken Arrow*'s mis-semiotics occurs when its signifiers are Indians but its signified is whiteness.

This is the case not simply because the two main Indian characters are played by white people—though, let's be honest, if Sidney Poitier's character in *Guess Who's Coming to Dinner* were played by Paul Newman, the film might have lost a bit of its punch—but because Indian identity is defined by its relation to whiteness. Or, put in the language of authenticity, *Broken Arrow* makes the argument that the Apaches are their truest Indian selves when we see in their Indianness stereotypical *whiteness.* The movie exchanges one type for another. Indian identity on its own, the filmmakers no doubt think, is of no interest to white viewers, but if Indians, at their most vulnerable, seem like white people, then they would be more *sympathetic.* For example, one of the richest scenes in the film is the "honeymoon" of Jeffords and Sonseeahray. Here, in their postcoital Garden of Eden, Jeffords tries to explain the etymology of "Ya Hoo!"

> SONSEEAHRAY: What does it mean? It is an American word?
> JEFFORDS: Uh huh. I think it was a word made by Adam when he opened his eyes and saw Eve.
> SONSEEAHRAY: Who are they?
> JEFFORDS: (*astonished*) Don't you know?
> SONSEEAHRAY: The world is big, and I know so little.

In her admission of her own Indian ignorance and her acknowledgment of American bigness, Sonseeahray subtly makes American—not Indian—points of reference her new canon. A similar moment of recognition occurs early in the film when Jeffords tells the audience in a voice-over that it strikes him as funny "that an Apache woman would cry over her son like any other woman." This instance reinforces Indians as *human*; whereas the scene with Sonseeahray reinforces the Indian as *longing for assimilation.* In both cases, sympathy occurs when the subaltern aligns with the hegemonic; or, put another way—it's easier to like them when they are more like us!

A true sympathetic Western allows the viewer to suffer with the Indian when the Indian gets to be an Indian on his own terms. When the Indian is a shadow white man, it's not sympathy—it's absorption.

Watch *Broken Arrow* for its campiness, its attempts at magnanimity, and its fine execution of benign reinscription. But don't watch it for its authenticity, its sympathy, or its humanity. That arrow don't fly straight!

Dear Diary:

Having cornered the market on the Western, it's time to give our horses a rest. Interweaving narratives of a crusty old Indian fighter has taken its toll. Surely this one will prove extremely popular among the voyeurs and sideburned mavericks of the world.

Note to Self: Must paint toenails "Indian Paintbrush Red" for the premier.

Ta-ta, darlings,

Hollywood

Little Big Man

Rebecca Kugel

Ever since I began teaching history almost twenty-five years ago, students on regular occasions have asked me, "What was it like to grow up in the '60s?" The question becomes more wistful with the passing of years and the students' distance from that storied and mythic decade. Sometimes they want their fantasies confirmed and yearn for tales of a time when the dope was cheap and the love was free, but mainly they are asking a much harder question: they want to know why the 1960s remain so hotly contested in American memory. Why is this decade so feared and vilified and at the same time so celebrated and beloved? This is a serious question and I've always tried to answer it seriously. And, while it may not seem like the film *Little Big Man* has anything to contribute to answering the question of why "the '60s" retain such a grip on Americans' collective psyche, in surprising ways it does.

If the decade of the 1960s (and, to be accurate, it spilled over into the 1970s, too) was about nothing else, it was about questions. People questioned whether the racism that disfigured the nation was so deeply rooted in American society that it could never be eradicated. People questioned whether the sexism, which exalted both maleness and heteronormativity, was so inextricably bound up with American capitalism that the entire system had to be dismantled. And people questioned the past. That is, they questioned the received stories, the interpretations of the past that had ignored or diminished the importance of racism, sexism, and economic and social injustice in the making of the United States. One important strand of that questioning involved how the dispossession of North America's Native peoples had been central to the process of American nation-building. Not just an unfortunate side issue, which was usually how it was treated—if it was mentioned in history books at all—but central, critical to the whole process.

As a young woman from a family of Native descent (and one deeply conflicted about that heritage), I had grown up with questions of my own concerning identity. I knew that the triumphal westward march of Euro-American progress did not reflect my family's past, and I knew that was part of the reason they didn't want to talk about it. Hoping for some insights, I sought out Native-themed films when I was a teen, only to feel a knot forming in my stomach as the predictable stereotypes unfolded: scenes of hideously painted Native warriors committing atrocities against innocent, clean-cut Anglos, who looked like my kindly next-door neighbors; Indian camp scenes of squalor and superstition and guttural grunting and nodding that supposedly showed Native cultures and languages for what they were. Even the few films that attempted sympathetic portrayals, such as *Broken Arrow* (see the review in this chapter), still featured heroic Anglo figures as the main characters. While Anglo actors played admirable Native characters, Native actors played the malevolent Native bad guys. Jay Silverheels was the evil Geronimo in *Broken Arrow*, after all, while Jeff Chandler (a white man) was given the role of the noble Cochise. But even worse than the Anglo actors playing Native roles, the Native characters speaking pidgin English ("Ugh!" or "How!") was supposed to explain that the defeat of Native peoples was necessary, yet inevitable, for the formation of America.

Needless to say, when I saw *Little Big Man* for the first time, I knew it was some different kind of movie. I think it was also the first film that I returned to see more than once. The film still knotted my stomach, but not for the usual reasons. It winked at me conspiratorially and satirized nearly all the "Indian movie" conventions. It was a comedy, of all things; most of the scenes were irreverent or ironic. The protagonist was the improbable 121-year-old Jack Crabb (Dustin Hoffman), who in the film's opening scene first described himself as the "only white survivor" of the Battle of the Little Bighorn. When the patronizing young academic who had come to interview him about bygone tribal lore made one galling, historically ignorant remark too many, Jack launched angrily into his life story, recounting what we would today perhaps call the counter-narrative of the West. His scratchy, aged voice shaking with indignation, Jack revealed the whole Anglo-American western migration as a far more complicated and unsavory tale than the young scholar (or the film's viewers) had ever dreamed of.

Jack's tale began with the fact that he and his sister Caroline were the orphaned, sole survivors of a westward-heading wagon train that was attacked by the Pawnees. They were rescued by the Cheyennes, neatly rendering probable a non-Native protagonist in a story that featured Native people. While Caroline escaped early in their stay, Jack remained to enjoy an idyllic youth among the Human Beings, as the Cheyennes called themselves. He was raised by an extended family of adoptive uncles, brothers, and an incomparable grandfather, Old Lodge Skins, played by Chief Dan George, who created the most believable Native character I had ever seen, a man rooted in a time and place, possessed of both a full range of human emotions and a thoroughly Native philosophical outlook. There were no cardboard, stoic, stereotyped Indians grunting "Ugh!" here. The Native characters spoke in complete sentences and articulated complex thoughts. They were complicated people, too. Young Jack befriended a youth named Little Horse who became a *hemane*, a third-gendered person whom the Cheyennes respected for his distinctive spiritual gifts. He also made a lifelong enemy of the ambitious and insecure

Younger Bear, a fact that gave rise to several neat twists of plot. While the Native female characters remained sadly two-dimensional, esteemed only as good cooks or good bedmates, the male characters revealed personal and cultural depth and accuracy. They were much like Native people I knew. They did things like offer you food when you came to visit, they paid attention to their dreams, they nonchalantly asked you questions about your sex life, and they understood family in expansive, encompassing terms. They were the first real Indians I felt I had ever seen in a film.

Jack's life as a Human Being was interrupted when he was forced to reveal himself as a "white captive" to American soldiers to avoid being killed. Returned to Anglo-American life, he was adopted by Mr. Pendrake, a stern, gluttonous preacher, and his lascivious wife, played by Faye Dunaway in a wonderful parody of chaste white womanhood, all fluttering eyelashes and barely contained lust. The beautiful Mrs. Pendrake was Jack's first schoolboy crush until he discovered that while he was supposed to be in the soda parlor drinking a sarsaparilla, she was downstairs in the basement storeroom boinking the proprietor. Disillusioned with God-fearing Anglo-American respectability, Jack turned his hand to several seedy professions, including snake-oil salesman and gunslinger, before once again attempting respectability by marrying a Swedish immigrant woman named Olga and opening a dry-goods store. Fleeced by his partner in the store, Jack stood helplessly with Olga watching their possessions auctioned off as General George Custer and his aide-de-camp rode down the quintessential dusty Western street. In voice-over, the aged Jack remarked that he would never forget his first sight of General George Armstrong Custer. As he rolled out the general's full name, the camera panned to the foppish blond officer, partially backlit by the sun so that, in a wicked visual joke, Jack's first view of the Civil War's Boy General was distorted and half sun-blinded. With this one shot, the film undermined the hero worship that was still the standard treatment of Custer in 1970. It was subtle, and a lot of people missed it (I learned this in post-film discussions in which I was involved); for me that one shot alone was worth the price of admission.

Custer's appearance in the film unleashed war and bloodshed. During a stagecoach robbery, Olga was abducted, and Jack searched unsuccessfully for her. He reconnected with his Cheyenne family only to witness horrific slaughter when army troops attacked their village. Ironically, he also found love and brief happiness with a Cheyenne woman named Sunshine, who survived this first massacre only to be gunned down a year later as she fled carrying their newborn son during the more horrific (and historically based) attack by Custer's men on the Cheyenne village on Washita Creek. Devastated, Jack attempted to lose himself in alcoholism and in the life of a hermit, but there was no escaping Custer; Jack remained bound to the egotistical officer as an unwilling witness. At the film's climactic Little Bighorn battle scene, Jack observed the general's complete collapse into babbling idiocy, offering a final blow to the heroic image of Custer left over from Errol Flynn days.

Thanks to his childhood rival Younger Bear, Jack survived the Battle of the Little Bighorn and was returned to the Cheyennes. Once again among the Human Beings, he participated in another of those scenes that subverted the expected message of the film. Old Lodge Skins, after singing his death song and attempting to depart from this world, determined that it was better to keep living than to die. If this penultimate scene suggested that the Cheyennes were assured of survival, the film's final conclusion was far less comforting. In the last scene, viewers were returned to the dismal present. The nameless young academic, chastened and mumbling,

"Mr. Crabb, I didn't know," packed up his recording equipment and crept away, while Jack sat exhausted from so much talk, alone in the bleak nursing home.

Thus *Little Big Man* inverted the typical Indian film one last time, leaving the audience feeling sorry for the Anglo protagonist, not the Native people. When last we saw Old Lodge Skins, he was anything but defeated. Descending the mountainside with his grandson's assistance, his interest in living rekindled, he talked of the joys of sex and food. Jack Crabb, by contrast, was alone and forgotten at the end of his life, living without relatives in the impersonal nursing home. For Native people, could there be a worse end?

If Jack's old age was particularly horrific from a Native perspective, it also profoundly questioned cherished Anglo-American beliefs about the West. According to the conventional wisdom, Jack should have prospered; he should have been a celebrated pioneer. Men like him were meant to have tamed the West, made their fortunes, and not ended their days poor, forgotten, and sad. But Jack's West was not the place where rugged individuals successfully tested their mettle; it was the place where con men preyed upon the unwary, and rogue army officers massacred Native women and their children.

And ultimately, this is why *Little Big Man* continues to disconcert and disrupt. It offers a profound challenge to an American view of itself as a land of endless opportunity and few problems. It asserts instead that America was built on economic rapacity justified in the name of white racial and male sexual hierarchy. This assertion was at the heart of the activist years we remember as "the '60s," too, and it presented a challenge profound enough that many white Americans would spend the next thirty years trying to deny its explanatory power. *Little Big Man* isn't a light-hearted or comfortable film, despite its comedy, but it was worth seeing then, and it is worth seeing now.

Dear Diary:

Just back from seeing A Man Called Horse. *Oh the way those ungrateful Lakotas treat Richard Harris made me so mad I could hardly finish my Milk Duds.*

Note to Self: remember to schedule those "copasetic-coping" classes my crystal gazer recommended so I can learn to walk a mile in another's Manolo Blahniks.

And imagine Dame Judith Anderson playing an old Lakota squaw! Really, what would Mrs. Danvers think!! She must have fallen on hard times, bless her heart. Well, at least she got to keep the designer deer-hide dresses.

Au revoir for now, my sweet.

Hollywood

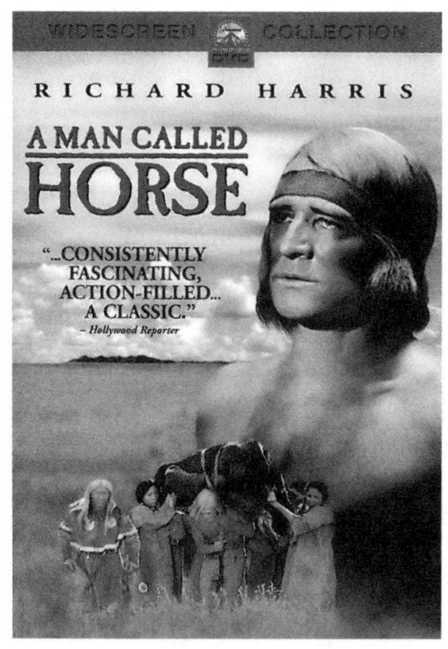

A Man Called Horse

Harvey Markowitz

It is late one night several months ago, and I'm lying in bed too wired to nod off, but too brain-dead to read. On the chance that some basic-cable trash—preferably on "E!"—might dumb me into sleep, I go on a scouting mission through the channels to find something . . . *anything!*

"I'm watching way too much television," I concede sheepishly. But just as I prepare to atone by heaving this newest source of angst onto my Mt. Everest of other anxieties, my attention is deflected by the American Indian music flooding the room. "Hey, that's a Lakota song," I mumble. And sure enough, as my retinas auto-recalibrate to bring the TV screen into focus, I realize that I am catching the opening credits of the 1970 Indian captivity epic *A Man Called Horse.*

Although I've not seen *Man/Horse* since it was first released nearly four decades ago, for some inexplicable reason I can still visualize many of the key moments in its plot with uncanny precision. "Hmmm, this seems strange," I say aloud. Yet, before I know it, my consciousness is canoeing down a stream of bizarre associations in search of the reason why so many of my few remaining brain cells have been assigned to this dubious film, rather than to something practical, like remembering where I've put my car keys. "Can it possibly be because the brain's major center for long-term memory, the hippocampus, is named for its resemblance to a horse?" Fearing that I'm just one association away from the crackerjack factory, my consciousness furiously paddles back upstream and I decide to just watch the damn movie.

And then I realize: hey, the screen credits have been replaced by a conversation between a dazzlingly golden-haired Lord John Morgan (Richard Harris) and Joe (Dub Tylor), the ringmaster of the Lord's trio of American booze-hound guides. Though I don't recall Richard Harris's hair being so retina-threatening bright, I do remember the gist of the uninspired dialogue: Lord Goldie Locks is traipsing around the early nineteenth-century American West in order to escape his meaningless, poor-little-rich-boy circumstances in England. However, quicker than you can say, "existence precedes essence," his inner Jean Paul Sartre grasps the absurdity of this attempt to find meaning by shooting unfamiliar critters.

"It just occurred to me," he muses to an understandably quizzical Joe, "I've traveled halfway around the world, at great expense, simply to kill a different kind of bird."

"Well, not exactly, your lordship," I snicker with shameless delight. "You've traveled all that way and spent all that money to be taken captive by the Lakotas." While Lord Morgan and Joe are philosophizing on the meaning of life, the audience has been cued that some sort of confrontation is about to take place by the film's director Eliot Silverstein, and editors Philip W. Anderson and Gene Fowler Jr.'s decision to splice footage of Lakota scouts stealing up on Lord Morgan's camp. However, before these braves can stage their attack, Morgan decides that it's time for his afternoon bath (pronounced *baath.*) Though the lord's decision defies nineteenth-century convention (the British were not known for being squeaky clean), I suddenly recall that this bath business is essential to the movie's narrative flow. First, it allows Morgan to be away when the Lakotas finally ambush the camp, and, second, it permits him to be photographed naked as a biscuit, sans gravy, when the Lakotas take him captive. The second point is noteworthy because Harris's nudity was the source of a lot of criticism directed at the movie's GP (today's PG) rating, and also because it prompted the administration of one unnamed institution of higher learning in western Nebraska to cancel the film's showing on campus. I know from where I speak concerning reason number two as I was one of a bunch of guys from the Rosebud Sioux Reservation who had traveled the 120 miles (one way) to see the movie, only to discover that school's mucky-mucks considered the sight of Richard Harris's naked rump too much of a threat to their students' purity to allow the show to go on.

Uh-hem, back to our story.

After changing into a red silk bathrobe whose appeal would seem limited to nineteenth-century English aristocrats and patrons of Frederick's of Hollywood, Morgan strolls down to a nearby river, much to the amusement of his guides and the concealed Lakotas. At first, the camera lingers lovingly on his apparently miraculous ability to work up lather in the river's hard, frigid water, but it then quickly cuts to the camp and a shot of Joe facing the camera. Suddenly we hear "zap, zap, zap," and realize that the old geezer is now wearing an arrow shirt, with the two other guides relieved of their lives, and scalps, moments later. One of the Lakotas is also killed in the attack. In an attempt to soften the horror of all this bloodshed (fairly graphic, even for the Sam Peckinpah/*Wild Bunch* era), the filmmakers have decided to toss in a smidgen of burlesque by showing the Lakotas' befuddlement at the bald pate of one of the soon-to-be scalpees. I suddenly find myself wishing that this were a Mel Brooks movie so that the scalpless guides and slain brave could return from the dead as a barbershop quartet performing some vulgar ditty like "Just a Little off the Top, Please." (Hey, I'm only thinking of the possibilities here!)

Meanwhile, down at the river, Morgan continues calmly with his toilette, unaware that his guides are already testifying at the great AA meeting in the sky. "Are his ears plugged with soap?" I grumble, "or were Lakotas of old able to convince their victims to take a vow of silence while being killed?" However, as we watch Morgan climb out of the water and onto a rock to sun-dry himself, we know that the halcyon days of his assault on the New World's "wingeds" and "four-leggeds" are about to end. All at once, a lasso, slung from off-screen, lands around his neck, and the Lakota braves proceed to drag him onto shore as if they were landing a flip-flopping fish. "Congratulations, your lordship," I snarl at the TV. "You've finally found your direction in life!"

Soon after Morgan's capture, the raiding party's leader, Yellow Hand (played by the late Fijian actor Manu Tupou), humiliates his exhausted prisoner because of his inability to pull himself up from his hands and knees. He thus informs the assembled warriors: "*Wicasa, wicasa sni*" (man, not a man). Then tapping a nearby horse and Morgan on their heads in quick succession, he advises the group, "*Sunkawakan, sunkawakan*" (horse, horse), placing a saddle blanket on Morgan's back to the delight of all (except Yellow Hand's new blond steed, understandably). To complete Morgan's transformation from man to beast, the chief marks his rump and that of one of the other captured horses with a yellow palm print, thus branding both as his own.

After a failed attempt to escape (again played for laughs), Lord Horse is led back to the Lakota village by the neck. Yellow Hand's mother, Buffalo Cow Head (Dame Judith Anderson, the great Australian actress whose choice for this role must have resulted from Casting's ingestion of some mind-altering substance), greets her son appropriately with the Lakota kinship term *micinksi* (my son). However, she promptly follows this welcome with the demand "*Taku mitawa*" (meant as "What's mine?"), which is not only ungrammatical, as it lacks the gender marker that makes it a question asked by a woman, but is also so impolite that no self-respecting Lakota would think of using it. Pointing to Morgan, Yellow Hand answers, "*sunkawakan.*" "*Sunkawakan?*" she repeats with puzzlement, and after checking the condition of her souvenir's teeth, walks away grumbling, "*Sunkawakan mitawa*" ("my horse"). Obviously "not looking a gift horse in the mouth" was a maxim old-time Lakotas chose to ignore.

Now, given the movie's use of Lakota up to this point (I won't dignify it with the term "dialogue"), one can be forgiven for suspecting that the speakers of that language, c.1820, were incapable of expressing complex thoughts. Rather, everything that they needed to say could apparently be communicated in one- to three-word phrases, coupled with lots of hand gestures and finger pointing. "Hmmm, finger pointing," I mumble, and reflect on why the actors' frequent use of their index fingers is gnawing at me. After all, pointing at people, places, and things certainly makes sense when none of your lead actors can actually speak the language of the characters they are portraying. But then I recall that lesson numero uno in the *Miss Manners Book of Lakota Etiquette* is that persons of breeding always point with their lips rather than their index fingers. While attending the Rosebud Reservation "finishing school," my tutors often illustrated this elemental of Lakota politesse by insisting that if an Indian had designed the Crazy Horse Monument, he would have depicted that great leader pointing to a spot in the Black Hills with—you guessed it—his lips rather than his index finger.

There are some additional smatterings of Lakota language as we are introduced to Yellow Hand's wife and his unmarried younger sister (Corinna Sopei, Miss Greece and Miss Universe,

1964, who is named in the film "Running Deer") and witness their tussle over a piece of booty (not the one exposed earlier by Lord Morgan). But, aside from a few times later in the film when Buffalo Cow Head and Yellow Hand are given more complicated Lakota lines (which, I understand, always bring hoots from Native speakers), and when a Lakota bit player prays to the spirits, the characters who do most of the chattering—in English—are Horse and a polyglot (Lakota, French, and English) mixed-blood captive named Batise (Jean Gascon). In fact, Batise's chief function in the movie is apparently to explain to his fellow abductee (and audience) what the Lakotas are doing and why. As if to atone for this clumsy narrative device, screenwriter Jack DeWitt has goosed up Batise's character so he comes off like a cross between a two-spirit male and a lunatic. Because of this, he is not a fellow to whom everyone takes a shine, especially Buffalo Cow Head who, in one scene, chases him away from Horse with a cane while shouting "*witko, witko*" ("crazy, crazy").

It finally occurs to me that I'm *witko* for deciding to watch *Man/Horse* instead of whatever black hole of intelligence was showing on "E!". So, I grab the remote once more and start searching for another program . . . this time, one guaranteed to bring me some shuteye. Now, this will take a few moments. So, while I am surfing the channels, allow me to present some of the key plot developments that lead to Horse's transformation from a beast of burden to the Lakota band's savior.

Morgan's ascent to social prominence begins simply enough when a blizzard forces him to do the unthinkable: to seek shelter in the Buffalo Cow Head family tipi. Though he manages to wake up all of its occupants, they nevertheless allow him to stay, perhaps out of pity for having proven himself such an inept "tipi-creeper." The next thing we know, winter is giving way to spring (depicted, as I recall, through a series of hokey nature tableaux). Finally, as our story resumes, there's a shot of Horse gathering berries with the women and putting the moves on Running Deer. But suddenly, in the midst of his gnarly attempts at courtship, he seizes the opportunity to prove that he is man rather than equine by singlehandedly killing two Shoshoni spies and taking one of their scalps. The Lakota men who witness his bravery lead Horse back to the camp in triumph, much to the delight of his beloved Running Deer. Striking while the fire is hot, Horse offers Yellow Hand the two ponies he has just captured from the Shoshonis to obtain permission to marry Running Deer. But, alas, as she's a true Indian princess, Horse must first prove that he's worthy of her hand by undergoing the grueling "Vow to the Sun" ceremony. As expected, he survives the ritual and the dewy-eyed lovers are allowed to wed.

Lest I be criticized for being a "spoiler," I will not divulge the details of how Horse eventually adds Yellow Hand's band to his realm, and whether he ultimately chooses to stay with his new people or return to merrie olde England. Let me just say, there are enough tears jerked in the film's final half hour to outsoak any vintage Hollywood melodrama.

As late-night basic cable has essentially become "paid-programming paradise,' and since there was nothing stupid enough on "E!" to warrant watching, I have chosen as my new video sleeping pill an infomercial for Presto's "Fry Daddy Deep Fryer," hoping that the sound of all that bubbling oil will have the same sedating effect as white noise. However, much to my surprise, the sizzling and popping act as cues for my consciousness to conjure up a vision of a gazillion triangles of golden-brown frybread tap dancing in Busby Berkeley fashion to powwow music. As delectable as this might sound, I soon discover that the mental distance between this high-cholesterol fantasy and *A Man Called Horse* can be measured in milliseconds, due perhaps to a shared Lakota wormhole connecting them. As a result, I'm back stewing over the forty-five minutes I squandered watching the movie.

However, as my anger recedes, I actually find myself a bit startled by the level of my hostility toward *Man/Horse*, especially when I remember how much I enjoyed it the first time around. Mind you, I am not suggesting that back in 1970 I considered it the best thing since commodity cheese. In fact, I had plenty of bones to pick with the movie, most of them related to the plot's domination by the conventions of the "classic" Hollywood love story. I recollect being especially annoyed by Ms. Sopei's portrayal of Running Deer as the Indian princess with "a Pepsodent smile." She has the most sparkling choppers since Debra Paget's Sonseeahray in *Broken Arrow* (see the review in this chapter). However, despite these and other issues, the fact remains that I generally liked the movie, as I believed that it presented an interesting departure from most Hollywood bow-and-arrow epics in a couple of ways. Its creators chose as the story's main locus Yellow Hand's Lakota camp instead of some fort or pioneer town. The filmmakers also attempted to fill this locus with ways of Indian thinking and acting different from those familiar to mainstream audiences. So we're saved from depictions of Yellow Hand's band as stereotypical Indians or noble savages. Since only Horse and Batise speak English, we are additionally spared from the typical Walt Whitman sampler of Indian poetics.

I began to puzzle over what factors during the last forty years were responsible for completely upending my response to *Man/Horse*. I quickly realized that tracking down all these conditions would be exceedingly difficult. Nevertheless, a couple of them, one autobiographical and the other historical, immediately come to mind.

In earlier parts of the review, I alluded to having lived on the Rosebud Sioux Reservation in South Dakota. From the mid-1970s to the late 1980s, I spent a total of twelve years on Rosebud, working on a doctoral dissertation in anthropology. During that time I was very fortunate to have been adopted by a family, the Horselookings, who taught me how to speak Lakota and allowed me to accompany them to most of the social and religious gatherings they attended. The education in Lakota history and culture that this family and other Rosebud Lakotas generously imparted to me became a permanent layer of my lens for viewing the world.

It was inevitable that upon revisiting *Man/Horse* this lens would drastically alter my thoughts and feelings regarding it. Thus, while I still find the love story that serves as one of the film's major subplots insipid, I have reversed my original positive reading of the way the movie uses Lakota traditions to buck mainstream attitudes and values. A good example of the change concerns the so-called "Vow to the Sun" ceremony. To its credit, the film does not explicitly depict this ritual as the traditional Lakota "Sundance." And yet, its creators rifle so many elements from the latter—songs, the piercing of and suspension by the pectoral muscles—that it takes on the appearance of a very close cousin. However, we are ultimately dealing here with a case of fictive kinship, since no such Lakota ceremony ever existed. Being unaware of this fact, many critics focused exclusively on the ritual's violence, again questioning the appropriateness of *Man/Horse*'s GP rating. Now, it's true that one could attempt to justify both the fabrication and the violence, as did the film's producer Sandy Howard, by insisting that they serve as a means to the end of "actually portraying the Indian's life as it really was, his emotion and sacrifice of pain." This turns out to be a pretty flimsy rationale since the movie totally ignores the ultimate reason *why* Lakotas were willing to undergo painful sacrifices, this being the value they placed on the needs and welfare of the group. Instead, what we get is a non-Indian showing that he can out-macho any Lakota in order to win the hand of his best girl. In the process, the audience is allowed to take comfort from the implicit message that the Lakotas "weren't so much different from us after all." Hooray for Hollywood.

Viewed from a historical perspective, *Man/Horse* occupies a fairly interesting place in the continuity and change of Hollywood's representation of Indians. At the time of its release, the movie received mixed reviews from critics and audiences alike. Thus, while Alex Keneas of *Newsweek* insisted that "for all the teepee truisms, its anthropological ancestor is Hollywood,"[1] Stephen Farber of *Film Quarterly* maintained that "the attention to carefully researched details of setting, costume, ceremony produces some extraordinarily beautiful images, a tableau of Indian life more striking than anything seen on the screen before."[2] More recently, however, the movie has witnessed a growth both in its popularity and its importance in film history. Modern critics, such as Richard Harland Smith, writing for *Turner Classic Movies*, frequently cite the film as an example of the subgenre of revisionist Westerns that emerged in the latter 1960s and continues to this day, and *Rotten Tomatoes*'s "T-Meter" reviewers (all contributing post-2000 ratings) collectively certify the movie with an impressive 86 percent of "freshness," making it eight points more fresh than *Dances with Wolves*!

Despite its growing reputation as "fresh" and "revisionist," I believe that a close examination of *Man/Horse* reveals that it is just another cloaked effort, along with Disney's *Pocahontas*, *Broken Arrow*, *Dances with Wolves* (see the reviews in chapters 3 and 5), to maintain the status quo in the film industry's representation of Indians. Far from being revisionist or fresh, *Man/Horse* fundamentally accepts the conventions of the Hollywood Indian, protesting "no" while nodding "yes." On the surface there certainly seems to be a lot of Indian "stuff" going on. However, although the movie's primary locus is Yellow Hand's camp (which impressed me forty years ago), its center of gravity is the story of Lord Morgan's transformative encounter with Lakotas. The Lakotas themselves are little more than satellites orbiting around his story, never exercising any significant pull in their own direction. It's no wonder these pathetic "savages" need a "civilized" Brit to save them.

Suddenly a light, other than that coming from the TV, catches my attention. As I look at the shadows of tree branches playing on my bedroom curtains, I realize that my sleepless night has given way to a new day. I manage to convince myself that there is still sufficient time for me to catch an hour or two of sleep before I have to get up and tackle writing a review for *Seeing Red*. My brain begins switching off its lights, and I sense myself sinking into unconsciousness, accompanied by some muffled music coming from the TV. "Hey wait!!" I hear myself screaming. "Isn't that the theme song from *Dances with Wolves*?"

NOTES

1. Alex Keneas, "Indian Pudding," *Newsweek* 25 (May 25, 1970): 32.
2. Stephen Farber, "Review of A Man Called Horse," *Film Quarterly* 24 (1970): 61.

Dear Diary:

What do you get when you feed a Lakota nothing but power bars and energy drinks for a week? Kevin Costner. Just kidding. But have I found a pot of gold in this one. I can just see the new properties flying onto the screen: "Dances with Wolves 2," "3," *and for the family-values crowd,* "Children of Dances with Wolves." *Picture this: Dances with Wolves's "first born," a male of course, returns to find Kicking Bird's daughter grown up. They marry and return to Washington, D.C., where he, "the son of," runs for U.S. senator, but poor Kicking Bird's daughter must return to the Rez. "She's just not fitten." Hummmm, that dialogue sounds familiar, but no matter. Onward. The script will practically write itself and make us bazillionaires. Must get Michael Blake on the horn.*

Hokahe,

Hollywood

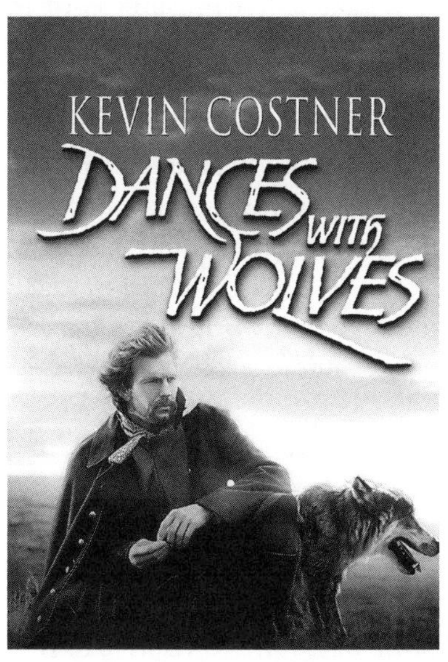

Dances with Wolves

James Riding In

Unfortunately, the movie industry seems to relish scripts that slander my people, the Pawnees. Take, for example, *Dances with Wolves*, whose plot may be summarized as follows for the few lonely souls who have not seen it in theaters, on DVD, or cable TV marathons:

> After proving himself a hero in the Civil War, U.S. army lieutenant John Dunbar requests a transfer to the western frontier so he can experience it "before it is gone."

Check out that "vanishing" theme in other films reviewed in this volume, such as *The Vanishing American*, *Last of the Mohicans*, *Little Big Man*, and many others. It's not just the wilderness that's disappearing. Though Dunbar's transfer is approved, he finds himself the sole occupant of a dilapidated military outpost. Clearing away the filth left behind by the fort's former occupants, it's not long before Dunbar becomes acquainted with some of his Plains neighbors: first, a wolf with whom he bonds, and then the members of a band of noble Lakotas (including

Graham Greene, Rodney Grant, and Floyd Red Crow Westerman). They all make friends with the lone white man; even the wolf eventually accepts him. One of the band's members, Stands With a Fist (Mary McDonnell), just happens to be a white woman whom the tribe saved and adopted years earlier after the dreaded Pawnees massacred her family. Ah, romance on the high plains. The more Dunbar embraces Lakota lifeways, the more he becomes alienated from and disdainful of white culture, represented at its worst by rapacious hunters who slaughter buffalo solely for their hides while leaving their meat to rot and the Lakotas to starve. However, the heroic Dunbar saves the day by leading his Indian friends to a buffalo herd. If this were not enough, he then rescues them from imminent destruction at the hands of the fiendish Pawnees by retrieving firearms he buried months earlier at the fort. Dunbar then teaches the Lakotas how to use the weapons against their Pawnee enemies, who, Dunbar observes, "have been very hard on these [Lakota] people." How did this hapless group of Lakotas manage to survive before Dunbar graced them with his presence?!

Even with the Pawnees out of the picture, the Lakotas' troubles are far from over. The new menace to arrive on the scene is a force of bellicose U.S. soldiers who arrest Dunbar for deserting his post and treason. The Lakotas, being a people who practice reciprocity, free Dunbar from captivity.

Alas, the future still looks dim for the survival of the Lakotas and their lifeways by the end of the film. In the final sequences of shots, Dunbar and Stands With a Fist watch as the U.S. soldiers and the dreadful Pawnee scouts chase the pitiful band of Lakotas into the snow-covered Black Hills. The implication is that the Lakotas are a vanishing people whose disappearance will leave their traditional homelands available for white American occupancy. End credits.

Not long after its release in the fall of 1990, *Dances with Wolves* was already being hailed as a groundbreaking, "revisionist" work that had finally succeeded in capturing the realities of Lakota historical experience and culture on film. Most moviegoers and critics were especially impressed by the movie's sensitive portrayal of Lakota history, culture, and relations with white Americans, and Pawnee Indians on the plains during the mid-1860s. This enthusiastic reception was reflected in *Wolves*'s box office receipts, which amounted to nearly $500 million in worldwide sales. The members of the Academy of Motion Pictures Arts and Sciences awarded the film seven Oscars, including best picture of the year.

However, to this Pawnee, *Wolves* deserves neither the praise nor the awards that have been heaped on it. It distorts the history and culture of mid-nineteenth-century Plains Indians' societies. It's therefore folly to think of the film as anything other than a more subtle spin on Hollywood's traditional Indian mythmaking. On the other hand, if you delight in movies that portray Pawnees as psychopathic killers, then *Wolves* is for you.

I should have known that this would be the case when late in 1990, Karen Swisher, a Lakota friend and colleague of mine at Arizona State University, told me that although *Dances with Wolves* captured the splendor of the northern plains landscape and rich elements of her people's culture, it presented an unflattering portrayal of Pawnees. Having seen Pawnees vilified in *Little Big Man* (1970), I felt no sense of urgency to see another movie of this sort, even though my work as a Pawnee scholar gave me a compelling reason to do so. Within a few months, though, I had to abandon my personal boycott and watch the film, as I had agreed to participate in a panel discussion about *Wolves* at North Dakota State University at Fargo. The year was 1991, and I saw my role as offering a meaningful critique of the film in the context of nineteenth-century Pawnee/Lakota relations.

I can honestly state that despite my predisposition to dislike the movie, I attempted to watch it with an open mind. And yet, try as I might, I grew more and more disheartened each time the audience reacted negatively both vocally and with body language to acts of Pawnee violence, while cheering when the white American protagonist, Lieutenant John J. Dunbar, orchestrated the Lakotas' successful defense of their encampment from a Pawnee attack. The audience's reaction confirmed the movie industry's ability to glorify one group of indigenous people while demonizing another. I left the theater feeling I had been culturally and historically violated. The film that had won so many awards did not represent the cinematic paradigm shift in Hollywood's representation of Indians that many had trumpeted it to be. I came away from the theater wondering if Hollywood could make a sympathetic film about one group of Indians without demonizing another. For example, Jack Crabb, played by Dustin Hoffman, offers yet another unflattering characterization of the bad Indians (my tribe) in *Little Big Man* (see the review in this chapter) when he says, "Pawnees was always sucking up to whites."

At any rate, having now endured the movie, I was ready to participate on the panel. On the morning the discussion was to take place, I sat in my hotel room in Fargo watching a national news program. Some coincidences we never forget. Who should appear as a guest but Michael Blake, the "brains" behind *Wolves.* He spoke passionately about his meteoric rise from an impoverished dishwasher to an accomplished novelist and screenwriter. He claimed the movie was historically and culturally accurate because of his exhaustive research. Blake's assertions about the rigor of his research troubled me. I especially wondered what sources he consulted to create the role of the Pawnees in the film, and the inaccuracies.

Mindful of Blake's interview, I left the hotel prepared to argue that the information contained in *Wolves* could not be relied upon for its historical and cultural accuracy. However, being the only person on the panel presenting a Pawnee perspective, I considered it a distinct possibility that most of the audience might reject my views. My sarcastic observation that the only scene in the movie that rang true was the one in which it took twenty-five Sioux to kill one Pawnee didn't help my cause. And yet, this comment was more than a failed attempt at stand-up comedy. Aided by humor, I was also attempting to inform the audience that in the 1860s Lakotas outnumbered Pawnees by about twenty-five to one. In the end, it seemed that few attending the discussion were prepared to reconsider the film's historical veracity.

Sometime afterwards, at a conference on Indian religious freedom, the late Floyd Westerman, a Dakota who gave an excellent performance in the role of Ten Bears, asked me what I thought of the film. I responded that the film was not only historically inaccurate, but it also demonized Pawnees. Floyd countered that he believed that film depicted Pawnees as proud and brave warriors. In our periodic meetings in the years that followed, neither of us spoke about the movie again. We shared common concerns about such matters as sacred sites protection, repatriation, and cultural survival that took precedence over our difference of opinion concerning one more example of Hollywood mythmaking.

Years after first seeing *Dances with Wolves* I want to talk about some of the "good" aspects of the film amidst its "bad" and "ugly" storylines. First the good: It features an impressive cast of authentic Native actors. The characters brought to life by Floyd Red Crow Westerman (Ten Bears), Tantoo Cardinal (Black Shawl), Graham Greene (Kicking Bird), Rodney A. Grant (Wind in His Hair), Doris Leader Charge (Pretty Shield), Wes Studi (the fierce Pawnee), and others make a mockery out of the pitiful performances given by generations of non-Indian imitators, including the likes of Chuck Conners (*Geronimo*, 1962), Anthony Quinn (*Flap*, 1970), and Sal Mineo (*Tonka*, 1958). The movie also uses spoken Indian languages with English subtitles, though I would be remiss if I didn't mention that the languages are often spoken imperfectly. In the case of the Lakota, a language with gender distinctions, the male actors often used ways of talking normally reserved for women. Some Lakota speakers found this aspect of the movie amusing if not offensive.

The movie is also one of those rare films that allow the actors portraying Lakotas to perform as believable human beings who act and react with intelligence, even humor. Although the writers and directors fail to present Pawnees as multidimensional characters, some of my people, including my aunt, have told me that they closely identify with the on-screen Lakota characters who gave wonderful performances.

Additionally, *Dances with Wolves* contains important lessons on the dangers of prejudice and ecocide. Some of the non-Indian characters' attitudes accurately reflect the deep-seated hatred that many nineteenth-century white Americans held for Indians and their lifeways. However, in his role as a cultural broker, Dunbar both admires his new people and shows the audience that he's disgusted by the former soldiers at his post who had trashed the landscape, killed animals for sport, and polluted the water with an elk's carcass.

The Bad. Sadly, nineteenth-century white America lacked compassionate leaders such as the fictional Dunbar who celebrated diversity, supported human rights, and championed environmental justice. Had there been more Dunbars, Indian peoples and their lands would not have been so brutalized. Also, there's something troubling about white people becoming Indians. In films, they often also act as saviors for Indians. I believe that such storylines are generated by the desire of white Americans to feel less guilty about the history of Indian-white relations. Scriptwriters and novelists like Blake pander to this need by constructing stories with compassionate characters such as Dunbar and Stands With a Fist in order to allow their audiences to divorce themselves from such brutality.

Wolves falls squarely in the genre of the Hollywood Western in which Indians are cast as troublemaking savages whose vicious nature justifies their murder by John Wayne and other silver-screen heroes. And yet, Blake's version of the West is supposed to be more sympathetic toward Indians because of its depiction of the virtuous Lakotas. However, the movie glosses over the devastation caused by the U.S. invasion of Plains Indians and glorifies Costner's role. One example of this is the scenes in which individual U.S. soldiers and individual Pawnees bear sole responsibility for the Lakotas' (mis)treatment. Such episodes, repeated in various places in the film, serve to deflect blame away from the criminality of federal Indian law and policies over Indian lands. Washington officials used the military as a means to ethnically cleanse Indian lands to make way for settlers. All Indians, not just Lakotas, suffered the debilitating effects of U.S colonization and genocide. In the end, Pawnees paid a tremendous price for possessing fertile lands that were generously "opened" to settlers by the federal government. During the Indian removal that ensued from such largesse, hundreds of Pawnees died, while the tribe as a whole lost its traditional lands.

Another problem with *Wolves* lies with Costner's character. No evidence is available to support the existence of a Lieutenant John Dunbar, or any other officer, living as a deserter among Lakotas or Comanches during the 1860s. However, a missionary with that name lived with the

Pawnees during the 1830s and 1840s. The real-life Dunbar (who incidentally converted very few, if any, Pawnees to Christianity) wrote a series of detailed letters describing the tribe's seasonal round of activities as well as troubled relations with white Americans and surrounding Indian nations. He also documented a particularly destructive 1843 Lakota attack on a Pawnee town on the Loup River in what is now Nebraska. Despite missionary Dunbar's racial bias regarding Indians, his correspondence provides a rich record of Pawnee history during the early nineteenth century and is worth investigating.

Yet, instead of drawing upon historical sources, screenwriter Blake most likely fashioned his gallant Dunbar in the image of James Fenimore Cooper's Natty Bumppo, the main character in *Leatherstocking Tales*, published as five novels from 1823 to 1841. Bumppo (also known as Hawkeye, the Deerslayer, and other names) is a Euro-American who "goes native," becoming a hero among his vanishing Indian friends. Bumppo and his noble Indian allies outwit and destroy their evil Indian opponents, as does Blake's Dunbar and his Lakota friends. Now it is true that Indian peoples have often opened their cultures for non-Indian participation. But Blake depicts Dunbar as becoming more Indian than the Lakotas in a remarkably short period of time. The scene in which Dunbar tells the Lakotas where a nearby herd of buffalo grazes is just plain nonsense. Equally inconceivable is the scene where Dunbar teaches a group of Lakotas, including women and young boys, how to use rifles against battle-hardened warriors in a blink of an eye. Is this nothing but a kinder, gentler version of the usual Hollywood hokum of the innate superiority of whites to Indians?

Then, there are the names of important Lakota characters. The real Ten Bears was a Comanche chief; Kicking Bird, a Kiowa leader. In the novel by the same name, the Lakotas were Comanches. Sadly, the filmmakers saw no need to use authentic Lakota names for Lakota characters. Equally disturbing is the scene in the beginning of the film in which the Lakotas appear to be living in a pristine, "natural" state untouched by U.S. expansionism. According to Blake, they had merely heard rumors about white Americans. In actuality, by the early 1800s, Plains Indian nations had experienced numerous contacts, friendly and otherwise, with citizens of the United States. Trade for firearms, cloth, beads, metal goods, and other items constituted an important element of those interactions. Lakotas had also entered into treaties with U.S. representatives and visited U.S. military posts and settlements.

Sioux interaction with white Americans began in earnest during the early 1800s and increased in frequency throughout the century. In 1823, Lakotas participated in a military operation that temporarily drove Arikaras, northern relatives of the Pawnees, from their homes on the Missouri River. The Oregon Trail, established in the early 1840s, was an especially contentious point of contact. Thousands of white settlers in rut-carving wagons with large herds of livestock traveled this route to reach the West Coast. They polluted the water, destroyed timber, spread disease, and slaughtered game along the way. The immigration of settlers had serious consequences for Lakotas and Pawnees alike, including epidemics and conflict, as well as famine. Additionally, the Oregon Trail brought the formidable U.S. military to Pawnee and Sioux country to protect the settlers from Indians.

During the early 1850s, Lakotas took up arms to defend their lands, resources, and culture from U.S. encroachments. In 1864, many of them fought valiantly alongside their Cheyenne and Arapaho allies against U.S. soldiers and settlers in response to the Sand Creek Massacre.

Their armed resistance resulted in important victories and continued into the 1870s when, as a consequence of attrition, they lost the ability to continue the struggle. In other words, their opposition to immigrants did not begin and end abruptly in 1864, as the movie suggests.

Another problem lies in Blake's failure to provide a historical context that is so desperately needed to comprehend the complex nature of Pawnee interactions with both white settlers and Lakotas. Before 1864, Pawnees had conducted frequent horse-raiding expeditions and military operations against their Sioux, Cheyenne, Arapaho, Comanche, Kiowa, Kaw, and Osage adversaries as well as white American and Mexican intruders. In fact, Pawnee land tenure pre-dated the arrival of *all* of these other groups, Indians and non-Indians alike. In simple terms, the Pawnees viewed them all as invaders of their homelands. In the end, American expansion disrupted Pawnee lives, left them weakened, vulnerable to colonial domination, and struggling to carry on their traditional lifeways. Facing these and other deplorable conditions, Pawnee leaders reluctantly ceded millions of acres of land to the United States in 1833, 1848, and 1857 in return for promises of assistance. In 1859, the Pawnees moved to a small reservation near the confluence of the Platte and Loup rivers in what is now central Nebraska. Federal policymakers expected them to remain there and adapt to their new circumstances.

By the early 1860s, the Pawnee reservation had become a beleaguered cultural enclave surrounded by growing numbers of hostile white settlers, including many who wanted the U.S. government to either remove or exterminate all nearby Indians. Compounding matters, recurring Lakota, Arapaho, and Cheyenne attacks on Pawnee reservation homes and on buffalo-hunting parties resulted in high mortality rates and the tribe's increasing poverty. Pawnee parties occasionally ventured into enemy territory for horses and revenge, but by then they were largely on the defensive and mostly fought to protect themselves from enemy encroachments. It's these kinds of conditions that forced the Pawnees into military alliances with the federal government. From 1864 to 1877, hundreds of Pawnee men served as scouts in five different enlistments. Ironically, helping the colonizer to subdue common enemies was a way to eliminate one of the conditions that often made life precarious for Pawnee people.

The Ugly. (My term for describing Blake and company's depiction of Pawnees as uncontrollable, bloodthirsty savages.) Though not elaborated in the film, the Pawnees' alleged proclivity for violence is very much a part of Blake's novel, where he depicts Pawnee warriors as crude, demented, methodical killers.

"They saw with unsophisticated but ruthlessly efficient eyes, eyes that, once fixed on an object, decided in a twinkling where it should live or die. And if it was determined that the object could cease to live, the Pawnee saw to its death with psychotic precision. When it came to dealing death, the Pawnee were automatic, and all of the Plains Indians feared them as they did no one else."[1] According to Blake's fiction, Pawnees were the functional equivalents of the *Saturday Night Live* "land shark," killing unoffending men, women, and children of all races without mercy, and devoid of the ability to distinguish right from wrong. In both the novel and movie, readers and viewers alike see Pawnee warriors as a marauding band of brutal murderers who scalp Timmons (a crude but likeable Indian-hating teamster who helps transport Dunbar and military supplies to his post at the fort). As one-dimensional serial killers, Blake's fictional Pawnees express themselves with violence. Wes Studi, an Oklahoma Cherokee and brilliant actor, recognized the shortcomings of his role as the "fierce" Pawnee. In a May 8, 1999, interview titled "Meeting Magua: A Wes Studi Interview,"[2] Studi expressed concern that *Dances with*

Wolves had failed to provide an understanding of Pawnee behavior. The Magua role (*The Last of the Mohicans*), he said, enabled him to give a voice to the tragedies that motivated Magua's ferocious acts. The same opportunity had not been afforded him in *Dances with Wolves.* "I think," said Studi, "Magua was a more developed Pawnee. Yeah . . . I think it was really a matter of demanding that same character with the ability to speak a lot of different languages as well . . . and have a similar story. Cause that's more or less the way I played the guy in *Dances with Wolves* . . . he probably had gone through the same kinds of tragedies as Magua had, but Magua had the ability to voice some of those things."

I must respond by saying that the fierce Pawnee war leader, who is violently killed near the Lakota encampment, in no way resembles a real person. A war leader, or *kahiki*, obtained his position and followers by having demonstrated wisdom, bravery, skill, and success in warfare. A successful war leader was one who accomplished his goals without losing party members. In the scene depicting the Pawnee warriors' discussion about whether they should attack Timmons's camp, an expedition member complains that the vicious one "will not quit until we are all dead." A leader who functioned so irresponsibly as to needlessly risk the lives of his people would have had no followers.

In closing, *Dances with Wolves* is a stereotypical work of popular culture. Although the presence of Indian actors playing Indian roles, and the use of Indian languages give the movie an appearance of authenticity, its storyline reeks of crass historical misrepresentations. The good and bad Indians in this literary and cinematic cesspool are romanticized and villainized props for a love story involving a white man and white woman who turn "native." Even worse, the novel's and the movie's depiction of Pawnees is nothing short of a bloody hatchet job delivered by a wrinkled scoundrel with "unsophisticated but ruthlessly efficient eyes" who should have stayed in the dishwashing profession. The most troubling prospect to me is that mainstream audiences may have swallowed whole Blake's perverted version of the Pawnees as merciless psychopaths who just kill saintly Lakotas.

I end this review with a postscript. I first began work on this project in mid-March 2010 while my wife Ida and I were visiting our daughter and son-in-law in Rapid City, South Dakota, not far from where several scenes in *Dances with Wolves* were filmed. We were awaiting the birth of our first grandchild, but our daughter's baby was overdue. A baby girl arrived several days later. She will be raised in a nurturing environment with multitudes of Pawnee, Oglala, and Santa Ana Pueblo relatives. Our grandchild will thus be a living expression of the multicultural realities of twenty-first-century Indian life. Although time, familiarity, and shared cultural experiences under colonial domination have done much to heal the animosities that once divided Indian nations, uninformed novelists and filmmakers have a penchant for reopening old wounds with sensationalized stories that lack any understanding of the cultural and historical realities of nineteenth-century Indian life. Time is long overdue for the movie industry to reconsider the consequences of its mythmaking about American Indians. Can they create films about us more responsibly? A good question.

NOTES

1. Michael Blake, *Dances with Wolves* (New York: Fawcett Gold Medal, 1988), 21.
2. See *http://www.mohicanpress.com/mo06018.html.*

CHAPTER 6

Indians with Fangs

Dear Diary:

I've recently thought I would profit from having a live-in medicine man, as I often feel that I'm possessed by evil spirits. Are these demons merely the product of my watercress and caviar diet, or are they actually the mission control of my every thought and deed?

Note to Self: Must consult my astrologer and aroma therapist on what steps to take.

Love yah, babe.

Hollywood

The Manitou

Harvey Markowitz

Until it ceased operation in 1986, the Sandhills Outdoor Theater in Valentine, Nebraska, was the major venue for residents of Cherry County and South Dakota's neighboring Lakota Sioux Rosebud Reservation to gather and enjoy B- to Z-list Hollywood fare. I'm unashamed to confess that while living on the Rosebud from the mid-1970s to mid-1980s, I was among the Sandhills's most loyal patrons, regularly indulging in its cinematic equivalents to the cheese fries that local teens dished out in the theater's cinder-block concession stand.

Dwarfed by many of today's outdoor megaplexes, the Sandhills boasted a single whitewashed screen whose many stains and pock marks lent a common complexion to every movie projected onto it. And yet, I cannot recall anyone ever complaining that these imperfections somehow compromised their viewing pleasure. In fact, the business of watching movies at the Sandhills seemed to run a distant second to the primary activity of chatting up one's fellow patrons. Whether seated on car hoods, the tailgates of pickups, or in folding chairs generally reserved for powwows, a sizeable percentage of the Sandhills's audience, at any given moment, was more likely to be engaged in socializing than in paying attention to what was transpiring on-screen. In fact, I think it is fair to say that, during its existence, the Sandhills did more to encourage the lively art of conversation than film appreciation.

However, during the summer of 1978, there occurred a remarkable, if short-lived, aberration from this norm, occasioned by the arrival of a movie whose trailer had succeeded in generating a considerable amount of reservation buzz. Word of mouth had it that this movie, entitled *The Manitou*, depicted a Lakota medicine man's struggle to keep an evil spirit from conquering the world—a contest evidently of sufficient gravity to lure throngs of Rosebudders to plunk down $5.00 a carload at the gate.

Alas, the Indian-centered feast that had enticed these Lakotas to the Sandhills, and kept most of them uncharacteristically glued to their seats, was a quite different kettle of fish than that which schlockmeister William Girdler, director of such deliriously entertaining cheapies as *Three on a Meathook* and *Asylum of Satan*, set before them. As a vehicle for fading stars Tony Curtis and Susan Strasburg, *The Manitou*'s heroes turned out, once again, to be white folk, with the Lakota medicine man, played by Syrian-American actor Michael Ansara (Cochise of television's *Broken Arrow*), tagging along as the heroes performed their courageous deeds.

Now, given its priorities, it's hardly surprising that most of *The Manitou*'s action unfolds in San Francisco, rather than in Indian Country. As the movie opens, two doctors are seen scrutinizing a rapidly growing tumor on the back of patient Karen Tandy's (Strasberg's) neck. Much to their astonishment, this lump is not a tumor at all, but a placental sack containing a willful fetus, which, in subsequent scenes, will turn scalpels and laser beams on doctors who attempt to abort it. As if this weren't enough, Karen has also taken to growling the strange incantation "Panna wichi salatu" while sleeping; but when awake, she acts and behaves like the *Exorcist*'s possessed Linda Blair on speed.

Troubled by Karen's worsening condition, her erstwhile lover Harry Erskine (Curtis), a fake psychic whom she berates for frittering away his true spiritual calling for a quick buck, sponsors a séance at which the culprit, an evil manitou or spirit, makes himself known. Wishing to learn more about this entity's identity and motives, Harry consults a professor of anthropology (Burgess Meredith) who quickly deduces that it is the manitou of a long-deceased medicine man that is using Karen's nape as the expendable (and, as it turns out, highly expandable) vessel for his rebirth. When Harry asks how he can save Karen's life, the professor advises him to make a beeline for South Dakota and find a good medicine man to "fight fire with fire." Harry's quest ultimately leads him to the doorstep of John Singing Rock, who, as we witness from the following dialogue, initially voices righteous indignation at the white stranger's pleas for help, but whose wife ultimately convinces him to accompany Harry back to Frisco.

HARRY: Why won't you help me?

JOHN: Mr. Erskine. You see this valley? From where we stand there's one-half million acres of land; some of the richest farmland in the world. Two hundred years ago my ancestors owned all this land. Now it's under title to the Missouri Holding Company. I don't want your pleas for help Mr. Whiteman! I don't need your money!

HARRY: Wait a minute, John . . . please!

JOHN: Would *you* help if you were me?

HARRY: No, I guess I wouldn't.

(*Mrs. Singing Rock suddenly appears and gives John a compassionate glance that immediately melts his heart.*)

JOHN: Mr. Erskine, normally I wait three risings of the sun before I take on a job. My fee will be one hundred thousand dollars to the Indian Education fund.

HARRY: And you?

JOHN: Well, I need some tobacco. I'm running a little low.

(*Both Harry and John grin at one another as the scene ends.*)

Smile while you can, boys, because the manitou you have chosen to challenge is none other than the spirit of the most powerful medicine man of all, Misquamacas. And indeed, as the movie plods on, none of John Singing Rock's ceremonies turns out to be potent enough to keep him inside the womb. (By the way, Misquamacas is reputedly played by two midgets, one of whom—Felix Sella—starred as Cousin Itt on the late and much lamented *Adams Family* TV show).

Before long, Misquamacas is breaking through the sacred circle John Singing Rock has created to contain him, and perpetrating your typical schlock-movie mayhem, including beheading a nurse, conjuring up a huge lizard, and turning one of the hospital's wings into a giant popsicle. But then, just as Misquamacas appears on the verge of winning the day, a desperate Harry heaves an IBM SELECTRIC typewriter at the sneering medicine man, causing him to beat a hasty retreat, much to Harry's astonishment. Unfazed by this turn of events, John Singing Rock patiently explains to his sidekick that Misquamacas was undoubtedly frightened by the typewriter's powerful manitou; after all, he continues, all things, even human-made objects, have spirits.

Now, contained within John Singing Rock's matter-of-fact observation is the metaphysical tenet that will figure prominently in Misquamacas's defeat. However, the privilege of converting this principle into a strategy of war is awarded to Harry, not to the Lakota medicine man, as is made clear in the following exchange:

HARRY: Didn't you say that a machine has its own manitou?

JOHN (*quizzically*): Yah.

HARRY: Suppose we took the manitous of all of the machinery in this hospital, turned it on all at once and directed it against [Misquamacas] . . .

JOHN: It might work . . . It just might work. There's just only one thing.

HARRY: What's that?

JOHN: The machines' manitous could turn against us.

HARRY: But John, we gotta take a chance. We've got nothing else . . .

JOHN: Harry, do you still have room for a South Dakota Indian with a bag of tricks?

HARRY: John Singing Rock, it's not your problem anymore.

JOHN: Yes it is. Come on.

As Harry puts his plan into action, and the climactic battle between good and evil is joined, the hospital is miraculously transformed into a portal to a celestial dimension, suspiciously reminiscent of the tacky star-spangled scrim often seen in the original *Star Trek* series. At first, it appears that even the combined power of the computers is no match for the sneering Misquamacas. However, just when all seems lost, Karen, clad in a loose-fitting examination gown, comes floating in on her hospital bed to save the world.

Now, it would be easy to dismiss *The Manitou* as pure trash. And while trash it most certainly is, I would take exception with claims to its purity on this count. For festering beneath its garbage-heap plot and poor production values lies a fascinating crypto-imperialist mediation of several counterpoised stereotypes, attitudes, and values associated with white-Indian relations.

The most obvious of these antitheses is, of course, that of "Indian as ally" versus that of "Indian as adversary," here represented by John Singing Rock and Misquamacas, respectively. While, as we have seen, John Singing Rock initially responds to Harry's plea for help with a litany of wrongs that whites have perpetrated against Indians, in virtually no time he has enlisted in the latter's fight against Misquamacas. Now, given Harry's desperate need of John's services, it would make perfect sense for the medicine man to be calling the shots in this alliance. And initially, this is the case. However, once Harry appropriates John's nugget of spiritual wisdom, the balance of power immediately tilts in his favor, achieving its ultimate asymmetry in the degrading scene in which John describes himself as a "South Dakota Indian with a bag of tricks," and then begs Harry to allow him to remain in the contest.

An equally interesting set of oppositions is found in the triangular relationship between Karen and the two men in her life (one quite literally): Misquamacas and Harry. On one level, this pair's contest over Karen can be viewed as a figurative, horror-movie variant of the libidinous narratives of savage captivity and rape that abound in American literature and films. However, in addition to her role as "the prize" in this struggle, Karen also serves as a mediatrix of life and death for both men. Thus, in Misquamacas's case, she is initially the medium of his birth, or rather rebirth, and then, in the film's finale, the agent of his demise, being the only human deemed immaculate enough to channel the computer's superior spiritual power against him. Karen's relationship with Harry reverses the sequence of life and death, with her illness serving as the catalyst for his selfless and sacred mission in which he first dies as a pseudo-psychic and is reborn as an authentic spiritualist.

Now, had the creators of *The Manitou* limited their ambitions to telling the story of Harry's spiritual redemption, framed within a tale of good's triumph over evil, one could dismiss it as a dopey, if ethnically insensitive entertainment. However, their grander aspiration is to draw upon yet another pair of opposites—that of savagery versus civilization—in order to present Harry's salvation as a miniature for the redemption of Western society. It is one of the movie's underlying theses that although the West has outstripped American Indian cultures in technological progress, its success has blinded it to the spiritual dimension of its own creations. American Indian societies, by contrast, are portrayed as technologically simple, yet spiritually in tune with that sacred power that permeates and enlivens everything in the cosmos, even human-made objects. The lesson for the West in all this is simple. It must listen to, learn from, and finally appropriate Indian spiritual wisdom in order both to understand and to save itself.

While this portrayal of the mentor-student relationship suggests a reversal of the model that has characterized the history and theory of Indian-white relations, a more considered interpretation reveals it to be a conservative rationalization for the West's subordination of American Indians. For, in the end, the movie not only glorifies Euro-America's techno-economic superiority to Indian peoples, but its spiritual supremacy to them as well, objectively calculated on the basis of the superior spiritual, as well as physical, horsepower of its machines.

Were this a master's thesis, it would be interesting to detail the differences between *The Manitou*'s conservative program for appropriating American Indian traditions, and New Age disciples of so-called medicine men who are willing to sell distorted versions of their tribes' religious traditions to the highest bidder. Not only does the antimaterialist ideology of these disciples turn *The Manitou*'s alliance between material and spiritual power on its head, but it also indicts materialism as the primary agent for the pathologies plaguing the contemporary world. Their appropriation of American Indian spiritual beliefs and practices is fueled by a countercultural attack on the status quo, not an attempt to prop it up.

Looking past these differences, many contemporary American Indians consider any form of appropriation, no matter what its philosophical bent or goals, to be a part of the continuing legacy of political and religious oppression. This common heritage, some of these critics have noted, is frequently manifested in the assumed right shared by many such appropriators to yank Indian beliefs and practices out of their spiritual and community settings. Commenting on this sense of entitlement, the late Vine Deloria Jr. once noted in *For This Land*, "The non-Indian appropriator [thus] conveys the message that Indians are indeed a conquered people, and there is nothing that Indians possess, absolutely nothing—pipes, dances, land, water, feathers, drums, even prayers—that non-Indians cannot take whenever and wherever they wish."

When viewed in this context, one is liable to view Misquamacas and his mission with a bit more charity. One might even go so far as to regard him as the red blood brother of Marlon Brando's motorcyclist antihero in *The Wild One*, who, when asked by a cop, "What are you protesting against?" responds, "What have you got?" Had this been an exchange between John Singing Rock and Misquamacas, Harry Erskine would never have stood a chance.

Dear Diary:

Indians, hippies, and werewolves, oh my! This was going to be our greatest Indian movie yet, but Albert was such a scene-stealer . . . Brits! . . . the werewolves weren't the only ones chewing up the scenery. I think it's time for a good ole Western again. Must think on that.

Note to Self: Write Johnny Depp a love letter. Dear J. What about Tonto? You would look good in leather tights with a bird on your head.

Goodnight sweet prince,

Hollywood

Wolfen

Carter Meland

Crazy things are going on in this movie *Wolfen*. I mean it's a werewolf movie, but it is set in the city—and not just any city, but New York City. Manhattan Island, to be even more specific. Didn't the director do any research before putting this thing together? Everyone knows werewolves haunt the countryside. There's nothing especially chilling if you hear a prolonged howl when you are crossing the George Washington Bridge—it might just be a siren in the distance—but if you are walking through the woods on your way home from grandma's house and hear that howl, your blood will turn to ice, guaranteed.

Then there's the Indians. Yes, you heard right: *Wolfen* is a werewolf story set in a teeming metropolis, and there's Indians as well. Sometimes Indians howl too, at least in this movie. But again, I have to ask, didn't the director do any research? Indians *sold* Manhattan, right? How could they live there? There's no deer to hunt, no bears to commune with, and the cops in New York are the only ones who get horses. I mean everyone knows that Indians, like werewolves, live in the woods, and if you are on the way home from grandma's house and see one, you are likely to let loose a howl that will chill the blood in poor old granny's varicose veins. Woods are scary, werewolves are scary, and, come to think of it, Indians are scary too. I have seen enough movies to know that these things are true. When you are out in the woods, you've got to watch out for flashing teeth and flaming arrows! Especially at night. Werewolves and Indians prefer to get around after dark.

So I was kind of surprised when *Wolfen* ended up being pretty scary, even without any woods. One thing that works is you don't really get to see the wolfen until the last third of the movie; that's a good-quality monster-movie trick. Show us the monster's mayhem—a few bite wounds, a couple of puddles of blood, maybe a dismemberment or two, but don't show us the monster. It's kind of like *Alien* that way, or *Jaws*. I think director Michael Wadleigh did a good job of research on this count. It's a good thing to fear the monster before you see it, and Wadleigh, whose only prior effort at film directing was the documentary *Woodstock* (you know the one: it's about hippies singing along to classic rock and wrestling in the mud), also pulls off a neat cinematic trick by showing us how the wolfen see things. Lots of the camera work takes place at the height of a four-footed wolf-like creature as it runs through the streets and slums around Manhattan. You really feel as though you are stalking humans with this trick. It feels as if you are hiding behind benches and sculptures, or in the doorways of about-to-be razed brownstones, moving stealthily when stealth is necessary, and speedily when speed is needed. What is even more cool is that the wolfen see with a kind of heat-vision, and the movie replicates this way of seeing with some kind of color-solarization process, and this way of seeing renders the well-known Manhattan cityscape simultaneously familiar and otherworldly. It kind of reminds me of that old silent vampire movie *Nosferatu*, where Thomas Hutter is going to the count's castle, and the forest outside the carriage's window is made from a negative print of the film so all the blacks are white and the whites black. Those are scary woods, and the negative print makes things eerie, makes familiar settings strange, and the wolfen's heat-vision achieves the same kind of disorienting orientation. When someone is being stalked, the wolfen see in cool blue colors, but when someone *realizes* they are being stalked, their skin flushes with warm reds. Cool as this effect is, I wish the wolfen would lay off the voyeurism. Seeing the male lead and female lead make love in heat vision could lead to performance issues for some folks. Especially when the male lead is Albert Finney. Some things are better left unshown, even if those things are shown in heat vision.

The story is complicated, and not all of it is really comprehensible. At first I blamed the director for making a mess of things, but then I heard that the studio cut the film from its original running time of three-plus hours down to the more audience-friendly two hours. The length may be friendlier, but the cuts didn't help clarify the story. Studios always want to suck up to the audience, but confusing the audience is not a good way for a studio to separate you from your money. Maybe that's why relatively few people talk about *Wolfen* these days, but they should. The movie has interesting things to say, even if I wish some things had remain unsaid.

So here's what I think is going on in the story: The movie, released in 1981, is set in times contemporary with its making, and the Manhattan of the early 1980s is portrayed as a city in tumult. Rich folks are tearing down blighted neighborhoods to put up expensive office buildings and condominiums, poor folks are squatting in the blighted neighborhoods, and a number of homegrown and international militant groups (à la the Weather Underground and the Red Brigade) are trying to save the poor folks in the blighted neighborhoods by blowing up the rich folks in their office buildings. The movie suggests that society is out of balance. The rich are getting richer and the poor are expendable. Like the militant groups' terrorism, the wolfen also sow terror in the heart of high society when they brutally slaughter the real estate developer

Christopher van der Veer (a Trump-like mogul, though less pompous and better coiffed), his wife, and bodyguard. As the story unfolds, we learn that the wolfen are sending a message with van der Veer's death: they don't want their blighted neighborhood developed into a sumptuous playground for the wealthy. They prefer the poor. The wolfen seem to be leftists that way, until you realize that they prefer to *eat* the poor, at which point they seem more like Reaganites.

I'd be lying if I said this portrayal of the wolfen didn't bother me. Everyone knows that anti-wolf propaganda like "Little Red Riding Hood" seduces American youth into wolf-hatred before they even have a chance to learn about the creature's true nobility. The wolfen get painted with this same broad brush of disgust early in the movie.

Anyway, back to the story: The van der Veers' social status makes their murders a high-profile case, and the NYPD bring in their sharpest detective, the intuitive Dewey Wilson (played by the almost always clothed Finney). Wilson's keen detecting skills quickly lead him to suspect that terrorists were involved in the van der Veers' deaths, and when wolf-like hairs are found at the scene, Wilson's nimble mind immediately leaps to NAM. Not VietNAM, mind you, but NAM, the Native American Movement (a stand-in for the American Indian Movement). Wilson's logic, in leaping to NAM, runs something like this: dead white people plus wolf hairs equals Indians. For Wilson, NAM doesn't mean just any Indian either; it means Eddie Holt, the organization's former leader. Wilson knows Eddie; his arrest of the young activist had resulted in Eddie's imprisonment. In explaining Eddie's character to a colleague, Wilson describes him as "the Crazy Horse of the '70s," like that might not be a compliment!

With the NAM angle, I thought, Oh yeah, this movie's getting good. Now I knew why the movie was set on Manhattan Island and not in the woods, and why there were Indians and super-powerful wolf-like beings living in the city. You see, the Indians didn't *sell* Manhattan, they were *conned* out of it, and I was thinking Eddie Holt and NAM were going to reclaim the island, liberate it from *the man*, and restore the Native homeland. Eddie, I believed, was a seeker after justice, a holy warrior leading a battle for the people's redemption, a Crazy Horse for the '70s!

Wilson goes looking for his suspect and tracks Eddie down high atop what I think might be the George Washington Bridge. In a nod to the Mohawk steelworkers who helped build New York City's skyscrapers, the movie puts an Indian crew, including Eddie, to work on the "high steel" doing critical bridge maintenance. Good research, I thought. Give the people recognition for their role in building the city.

Wilson meets Eddie up on top of the bridge, and the detective's overtures to the young man are met with sneers. "So you guys do have a head for heights," Wilson comments to Eddie from where they stand on a walkway hundreds of feet above the city, and Eddie jabs back, "Just like we're all born alcoholics, huh?"

Eddie hears a boneheaded stereotype about Indians in Wilson's comment and calls the detective on it, and a moment later, after Wilson has suggested (rather cruelly) that Eddie is in touch with Mother Nature, Eddie explains sarcastically that of course he is, because he can "swim like a fish" and "fuck like a bunny." Right on, I was thinking. Way to go, Eddie. Don't let this agent of the *status quo* stick you with the pin of racism. Prick him back with sarcasm and put him in his place. That's just the kind of thing I like to see my holy warriors doing.

The movie was shaping up quite well at this point. This Indian was nobody's Tonto; he was fighting to restore his land and resisting racist stereotypes: that sounded like a movie worth watching, especially if the Indians had created an alliance with the wolfen. Having a pack of werewolves on your side would surely be invaluable in any effort at liberation that I can imagine. They'd kind of be like the Hessian mercenaries the British hired to fight the American revolutionaries, only cooler. (How could they not be cooler? Wolves are infinitely tougher than a bunch of guys in red coats standing in straight lines.) I was beginning to forgive the movie for trying to sell me that typical line about wolf-hatred. That was a trick the director had been playing, not a truth he was selling. With Eddie's sarcastic deflation of Wilson's trite attempts to create a bond through stereotypes, I thought, Okay, this movie is *Indian.*

And it got even better when, after a dramatic pause, Eddie tells Wilson that in addition to swimming like a fish and effing like a bunny, he can also "shift with the best of them." "Shift?" Wilson asks, and Eddie responds, "Shape-shift. We do it for kicks . . . Turn ourselves into a different animal. One night a salmon, the next night a deer."

"Or a wolf?" Wilson wonders, to which Eddie replies, "Sure."

I couldn't believe my ears. If I was following things right, and I seemed to be, the movie was suggesting that the Indians didn't have an alliance with the wolfen; rather it seemed to be suggesting they *were* wolfen. This was a hot development! Not only did I have a holy warrior engaged in the task of Indian liberation, I now had a holy warrior who was a shape-shifting shaman. Now *that's* Indian. Who would ever want to see a story about an Indian man working a difficult job, perhaps sending money back to his community to help care for his elders, while also being involved in the struggle for Native rights, when they could see a movie about an Indian man who becomes a wolf in order to change the world? That first guy seems kind of ordinary, and everyone knows from every movie they've ever seen that Indians are never ordinary.

With such a great setup, I thought nothing could go wrong; but then, you guessed it, everything goes wrong. This Indian story becomes a story about what white men think Indians are like. It all goes amiss when Wilson spots Eddie coming out of a bar one full-moonlit night with a couple of other Indians, including a gray-haired elder who, with great Indian solemnity, puts something in Eddie's mouth and then leaves the young man alone. With Wilson shadowing him, Eddie runs down to the river's edge after ingesting this substance and proceeds to take off his clothes and run around acting like a wolf. I kept waiting for a painful, but revealing transformation scene where the man becomes wolfen, but all I get is the naked Eddie (played by the Latino actor Edward James Olmos) splashing in the water and howling at the moon. He's not a shaman, or a holy warrior, or even a shape-shifter (though he is easier on the eyes than the naked Albert Finney). It turns out he's just another stoner who got lost on the way to Woodstock and ended up in New York City.

This hippiness wrecked Eddie's character for me. I'm supposing the old man gave Eddie some peyote, and even though I've never seen a movie about it, I know that peyote is not used recreationally to get in touch with your inner wolf. It's absurd, and if I were a religious type, I would even be tempted to say blasphemous. The production's research team once again came up short. It's like when they made this movie they didn't bother asking Indians how the movie might handle these situations. When will Hollywood ever learn?

Eddie stops being a sacred warrior at this point and becomes Wilson's Tonto. No more radical promises pointing to indigenous liberation, because Eddie, it turns out, is a reformed revolutionary trying to get right with the Earth by swimming in the Hudson River (which seems kind of like getting right with your lungs by smoking). The Indians cease to exist as characters at this point in the movie and instead become mannequins with great hair, guiding Wilson towards an understanding of things that no white man could ever hope to fathom on his own. At this point fiction becomes fantasy, and I lost interest in these Indians. I had seen plenty like them before. Tonto's job has always been to guide the white man, rather than helping his people in their struggle for justice.

I got to wondering why the movie seemed to have changed its mind about Indians just when things were going so well. The answer was staring me in the face all along. Woodstock. The counterculture. The movie seemed to be sympathetic to Indians and their causes, but what the movie was really sympathetic to was *its* idea of what Indians are. And Indians, as far as the director of *Woodstock* was concerned, were hippies. A movie that might have been interested in the symbolic battle for Indian ownership of Manhattan was really more interested in a kind of anti-authoritarian Just let me do my own thing, brother, and maybe I'll help you out with this wolfen thing. Give me my space, man, and I'll help you understand.

And this is how the Indians play out in the movie. They help Wilson figure out the wolfen, what they are, and why they're doing what they're doing. Given that these Indians are really hippies, they help Wilson realize that what he's up against is the spirit of Nature, and there's really nothing you can do about that except recognize it for what it is.

But are they the spirit of Nature? If you think about it, the wolfen's killing of the ultra-rich van der Veers seems nicely anti-authoritarian and might seem to offer a message of Nature righting the balance of out-of-control capitalist development. The wolfen don't kill to right the balance of Nature, though. They kill the van der Veers in order to protect their *hunting grounds* from development. The wolfen want to preserve the slums and blighted neighborhoods where homeless people root through rubble for scraps they can use to fill their bellies, but the wolfen are not interested in recognizing the intrinsic humanity the destitute possess. They are interested in *eating* them. The wolfen are worried about their bellies, not about justice. The wolfen feed on those society has cast aside, they don't sympathize with them, and at the end of the movie, when Wilson achieves some kind of telepathic, trans-species communion with them, I suddenly understood why this movie was released in the year of Ronald Reagan's inauguration. The wolfen were the perfect symbol of a counterculture that forsook its anti-authoritarian ideals of social transformation (and empathy for the struggles of Indian peoples for social justice) and instead consented to a social order where self-indulgence was more important than justice. Starting out as hippies, the wolfen became yuppies and, if they were drivers, they would at this point trade in their rusty VW microbuses for shinier, speedier BMWs. What better cars could there be for laissez-faire capitalists, or for killing machines like the wolfen?

CHAPTER 7

Walk a Mile in My Moccasins

Dear Diary:

Wooeee! Did the Canadians do a number on poor old Thomas Wolfe, or what? Go home young Indian man, go home. Hummm, our marketing kids might not like the sound of that.

Note to Self: Make a film on the return of the Pilgrims to England? Who can we get to direct this with class? Must do lunch with Steven Spielberg.

Still Number 1,

Hollywood

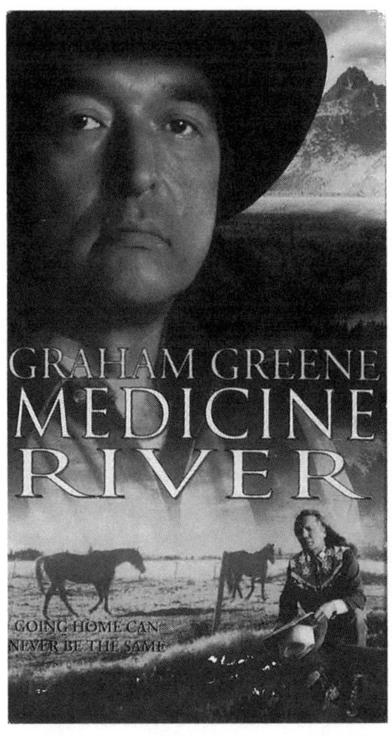

Medicine River

Jacki Rand

When Indians go home following a long absence, you can be sure that the road will likely be as bumpy as the roads in Medicine River, a fictional reserve town set in western Canada. No one knows what to make of long-lost returnees whose changed markings are fully observable to the home folks. Will, a long-lost Cree played by the ubiquitous Canadian actor Graham Greene, narrates his return to Medicine River to attend his mother's funeral. When he arrives, he finds that his mother's funeral has already taken place, and his brother James, who had left the phone message notifying Will of their mother's death, has skipped the reservation to satisfy his wanderlust. Will, by now a famous photographer based in Toronto, is left to engage with a community of people with whom he is no longer intimately linked.

Watching Will's awkward return leaves me feeling worried about the film's narrative on two levels. Already averse to Indians on the big screen, I instinctively think, "Oh, no. This one's gonna be bad." Will is a long-lost relative whose discomfort signals his broken ties with Medicine River. Greene's performance is awkward and at times overacted. He lurches through his return to Medicine River and reconnection with some of the local Indians. Harlan, his Indian guide and distant relation, plays on Will's unmistakable discomfort, overplayed by

Greene, with just about everything: the modest reserve town, rapid-fire introductions to local Indian people, teasing and humor, and Will's obvious memory loss of things familiar before he left for Toronto.

The soundtrack plays to the strained comic journey from Toronto to Medicine River. Where had I heard that before? And why did it seem so out of place? The director of the film is Stuart Margolis, best known for his role as "Angel" in the 1980s series *Rockford Files* starring James Garner from Norman, Oklahoma—where, coincidentally, I obtained my PhD in history. Rockford plays a private detective on the coast of California. Angel and Rockford are former cellmates who, against Rockford's private wishes, cannot get their lives disentangled. Angel turns up all too regularly at Rockford's door to beg for money or for help to get out of a jam. *Rockford Files* was one of my favorite shows in the '80s, and James Garner (also from Norman, Oklahoma, and "part Cherokee") has been a favorite actor of mine. I rarely missed an episode, and watched the show in syndicate throughout graduate school. All of this goes towards explaining the soundtrack of *Medicine River*. Check out the scene where Will wakes up in his mother's house the morning after a bumpy ride into town. Derivative "Rockford Files" soundtrack plays to the first meeting between Will and Harlan and turns up throughout the rest of the film.

Harlan must coax Will into taking photographs of the elders for a calendar. But nothing is ever that straightforward in Indian Country, where robbing Peter to pay Paul becomes an art form. Will learns that Harlan is not so subtly enlisting him in a ruse involving a grant application for a fictive project (wink, old Indian trick), "Photographic Study of Wildlife Migration Patterns in Southern Alberta." "It was the only grant available." Harlan and Big John Yellow Rabbit, director of the Friendship Center, want a van to take elders around to traditional social events like "hockey games and bingo." But the grantors have given them cameras instead of money. Harlan and Big John get a loan on the cameras and buy the van. And that's where the calendar comes in. They get the money for the calendar from the band council, "small business loan," and buy basketball uniforms—"to give the boys pride so they'll win the championship." Will's time away from the reserve leaves him lost to the logic of Indian projects. "So, there's a loan on the cameras that you got from the government but you bought the van. And you got a loan from the band for calendars, but you bought basketball uniforms." Harlan's pride in Will erupts, "Bingo!" And I'm rolling on the bed laughing at the Indian shell game. There's hope for the movie.

Harlan is far from being done with Will. Harlan is social glue in human form, and he has many uses for Will. There's Louise, the beautiful, pregnant Native accountant who has vowed to remain unmarried and to raise her child on her own. And the elders who watch the young people leave and hope for their return. Will, despite his resistance, is slowly being pulled into the Medicine River community. Bertha, the Friendship Center assistant, wears Will down with her aloof reception of, and pointed remarks to, this "world-famous photographer," "the one who didn't come home for his mother's funeral." Life in Medicine River makes the women independent. While Will's new assistant is photographing Bertha for an Internet dating site, she assesses her chances while she preens to the camera, "Pickin's around Medicine River would starve a vulture." Bertha and Harlan collaborate to throw Will and Louise together.

Does the matchmaker's strategy succeed in joining Will and Louise, and thus Will to Medicine River? That is the question around which this flimsy, yet charming movie revolves.

Dear Diary:

What's all the fuss about John Wayne's teeth? It was his bad breath that bothered me. Those Indie Indians... (Indie Indians, I kill me.) Not to worry; what we need is a good old-fashioned cowboys and Indians shoot-'em-up, but set on a sexy outer space planet. Think blue.

Note to Self: Call Kathryn Bigelow.

Still The One,

Hollywood

Smoke Signals

LeAnne Howe

Sometime in 1997, the Native listservs had really begun to cook. It was the heady early years of the Internet, and even Indians were drunk with the e-power. Everybody was posting stories on old AIM members, arguing over history, arguing over who had the most corrupt tribal chiefs and chairmen, and still debating about what really happened to Custer's ears after they were cut off. I remember getting into a tizzy with another Choctaw e-warrior about whether Pushmataha was a good leader or just some hang-around-the-feds-for-some-coin kind of a guy. All these early posts were fast and furious, and I was just as guilty as the next person for letting my fingers do the talking. Apologies all around; even after fourteen years it's never too late to say you're sorry.

So, back in the day, even Sherman Alexie (Spokane/Coeur d'Alene) used to post his thoughts along with all the rest of us Indians. Remember, it was fourteen years ago, and though Alexie was a big success even then, he would still engage us. In 1997 *Smoke Signals* was undoubtedly in postproduction, and Alexie was posting about his screenplay, the film, and some of the challenges of making the movie. This was also Native director Chris Eyre's (Cheyenne and Arapaho) first major project. Everyone was very excited and hopeful that *Smoke Signals* was going to change the landscape for Native films. And in some ways it did. Yet, as I recall, a terse e-discussion broke out on the listserv somewhere between the "Congratulations, Sherman," and "Oh no, not another Indian joke movie." What started it was a discussion of Adam Beach's shitty wig in the last third of the film. There were those who sided with Beach's decision NOT to cut his beautiful long hair and wear a wig, and then there were Indians on the listserv who thought he should have sucked it up, cut it onscreen for the sake of authenticity. After all, most of us grow our hair long; even if it looks bad we wear it long. And rarely do most Indians cut their hair unless a relative dies. Somewhere I have all these e-mails. I printed dozens and dozens of posts about this one discussion. At the time, I was a visiting writer at Carleton College and printed out the e-fights. Finally, in one of these e-mails, Alexie says to someone who shall remain nameless, at least until my memoir comes out, "You are starting to piss me off." He went on to staunchly defend Beach's right to keep his hair and play the scenes in a bad wig.

Okay, to the review. I finally went to see *Smoke Signals*, but "I didn't mean to." I'm using the line that Arnold Joseph (Gary Farmer, Cayuga Nation) counters when he is praised for saving the life of Thomas Builds-the-Fire (Evan Adams, Sliammon First Nation). I'm fessing up that I didn't intend to see the movie until it came out on DVD, because over the years, I've been so disappointed at Indian movies that I'm gun-shy (pun intended). But when the film opened, my friends tricked me into going to see it.

So, *Smoke Signals.* I liked it, and loved the brilliantly edited time shifts and poetic voice-overs, yet I also disliked the film. It's based on the short story "This Is What It Means to Say Phoenix, Arizona," from Alexie's short-story collection *The Lone Ranger and Tonto Fistfight in Heaven.* It's about two young Indian men, Thomas Builds-the-Fire and Victor Joseph. In some ways, it's a buddy film, a two-for-the-road kind of thing. The opening tease shows a house on fire, with a voice-over by Evan Adams explaining that Arnold Joseph saves the life of Thomas Builds-the-Fire. As a result, Arnold remains heroic to Thomas. But to son Victor, Arnold is a terrible father. Victor endures Arnold Joseph's alcoholism, and his verbal and physical abuse.

Thomas and Victor grow up together on the Coeur D'Alene Reservation. Often Victor beats up Thomas, but as in all codependent relationships, they remain friends. Sort of. When Arnold Joseph dies in a trailer park in Phoenix, Arizona, after deserting his wife Arlene Joseph (Tantoo Cardinal, Métis of Cree descent), the two young Indians go on the road to take care of Arnold's affairs and to bring him home. The scene as they're about to leave the reservation when Thomas and Victor meet up with Velma (Michelle St. John, Wampanoag and Carib heritage) and Lucy (Elaine Miles, Cayuse/Nez Perce), two Indian girls driving backwards on the highway in a Rez car, is one of my favorites. Director Eyre deftly lets the camera roll on the two women, showcasing the comedic timing of Adams, St. John, and Miles. For any Indian who's ever driven a true Rez car, this scene remains with us long after the movie ends. It's too funny. I once had a 1973 Ford Pinto. I used chicken wire to keep the driver's door shut and I would crawl through the driver's window to get in and drive. Yeah, when it rained, the seats were soaked.

Once in Phoenix, Victor learns about his father's life in Arizona through his father's friend, Suzie Song (Irene Bedard, Inupiat Inuit). It's through a series of flashbacks that we learn of the true origins of the fire that killed Thomas's parents. Arnold was drunk one night and accidentally shot off fireworks into the living room of his neighbor's house.

The last act of the film centers on the ride back home to the reservation. On the way back, Victor and Thomas get into a fight; there's a car crash with some drunken white people. There's a good-bad cop, and some heroics on Victor's part. Even though so many of the scenes favor

Victor's character, the film really belongs to Evan Adams. His performance captures the audience's imagination, and he wins many awards.

In the end, Victor and Thomas return Arnold's ashes to the reservation. Road trip over. Thomas goes home to Grandma Builds-the Fire (Monique Mojica, Kuna, Rappahannock). The last scene is beautiful, in which Victor Joseph mourns his father by returning Arnold's ashes to the river. In montage and poetic voice-over delivered skillfully by Adams, the ending of *Smoke Signals* stands in for all Indians—our ability to release our anger at the American government for its 250 years of abuse directed at tribal peoples. And maybe, like Victor, we can at last forgive.

What I didn't like about the film was that it relied on the tired stereotypes: drunk and absent fathers, abused mothers, rebellious Indian children, John Wayne's teeth, and the religion of frybread. Listen, all Natives didn't/do not live off frybread. Many southeastern tribes ate cornbread with little to no bear grease. In fact, frybread is a foreign import into Indian Country by a federal government that wanted us to die. Wheat flour, hog fat, salt, milk—"fried bread" is killing us. Check out the diabetes rate among America's Natives. It's an epidemic. One in four American Indians dies from diabetes, and films that celebrate frybread irk me.

Speaking further about stereotypes in *Smoke Signals*, I grew up with relatives who were barbers, soldiers, sheriff's deputies, bakers, cleaning ladies, farmers, bronco riders, teachers, local feed-mill workers, and Avon ladies. Two of my great aunts worked in an airplane factory in California during World War II. All these people were Indians. As a child I didn't know any alcoholics; I would have to seek them out on my own as a young Indian woman in Oklahoma City. My great-uncles and aunts went to stomp dance, and would also host family reunions. Relatives would come home each summer from California, Arizona, New Mexico, and even Texas. There were all-night sings with a great-aunt playing the piano, my grandfather playing the fiddle. Elders fed the spirits (and me) squirrel dumplings and corn. But with the success of *Smoke Signals* and films like it, mainstream America will only view Indians as victims.

However, despite my objections, *Smoke Signals* went on to win a bucket of awards in 1998 *and* 1999. Among them are American Indian Film Festival best film (1998); First Americans in the Arts: Outstanding Achievement in Writing, Sherman Alexie; Outstanding Performance by an Actor in a Film, Evan Adams; Outstanding Achievement in Directing, Chris Eyre (1998); Sundance Film Festival's Filmmaker's Trophy, Chris Eyre; and in 1999, Independent Spirit Award for Best Debut Performance, Evan Adams.

Even when I was living and teaching abroad, I showed *Smoke Signals* to a group of Jordanian graduate students in the English department at the University of Jordan. They read poems, short stories, and a novel by Sherman Alexie. At the end of the film, they all cried. (What can I say, I did, too.) And no one mentioned Adam Beach's awful wig. Go Indians.

Dear Diary:

I don't know why Indie folks bitch and moan about minuscule profits. What do they expect when they pick topics nobody wants to see.

Note to Indies everywhere: Film snobs are cheap bastards and never pay full price.

Love ya,

Hollywood

The Business of Fancydancing

Dean Rader

No one knew what to expect in the early days of the new millennium when word hit the street that Sherman Alexie was going to make a film called *The Business of Fancydancing*. After all, is there any film genre more beloved in America than the volume-of-poetry-to-screen adaptation? I remember my first viewing of the film version of John Ashbery's *Self-Portrait in a Convex Mirror*. Good times.

Imagine my surprise (and that of the other twelve people in the theater) when *Fancydancing* turned out not to be an adaptation of the collection of poems, but an actual narrative film with characters, scenes, dialogue, and editing. We were all a little shocked. But, leave it to Alexie to have fun with an audience.

And fun he has.

He goofs on Indians, Indian writers, readers of Indian writers, lovers of Indians, haters of Indians, haters of Indian writers, and journalists, who may or may not have any interest at all in Indians. He also plays with the genre of independent film with its montages, its self-important quirkiness, its juxtaposition of dramatic action and interlude, and its high devotion to transgression. At its core, *Fancydancing* is, above all else, experimental. Whether that experiment is a success or not may depend less on how you see Indians and more on how you see movies. In fact, the people I know who liked the movie are film people—either on the production or academic end of film—while most I know who didn't care for *Fancydancing* are scholars or students of American

Indian Studies or absolute devotees of *Smoke Signals.* Such anecdotal evidence might tell us much more about ourselves than it does about the film, but no pop-culture experience may be more subjective than viewing a movie in a darkened theater, where reactions, prejudices, and desires are shrouded by a heavy cloak of passivity and extrahuman inattentiveness. Furthermore, there may be no space in American culture more fraught with complex semiotics about Indians and Indian identity than the cinematic space. Alexie helped alleviate some of the anxiety tethered to viewing American Indian movies with the lovable *Smoke Signals*, so his follow-up project was ripe for drawing on that complex and contradictory space that had not only been filled with *Smoke Signals* but also *The Searchers*, *The Lone Ranger*, *The Dakota Incident*, and *The Battle at Elderbush Gulch.* In other words, working on the assumption that most of his audience will have seen and laughed lovingly with *Smoke Signals*, Alexie goofs with our expectations of what an Indian film might be and what a Sherman Alexie film about Indians might be.

These surprises come in both plot and style, though the butter on the film's popcorn is to be found in the latter. The plot of *Fancydancing* proceeds along a fairly conventional route; the truly interesting aspects of the film are directorial detours that take our expectations, not the narrative, in new directions. Seymour Polatkin, a gay Indian (Coeur d'Alene) poet who has achieved uncommon literary celebrity, functions as the film's protagonist. The first part of the movie explores his writing life (fulfilling) and his love life (perhaps less so) as it traces his experimentations with heterosexuality in college to his present life as an out gay man. Living in Seattle and partnered with a white man, Steven (Kevin Phillip), Seymour's life feels far away from the reservation in all possible ways. He no longer talks to his best friend from childhood and former college roommate Aristotle (Gene Tagaban), who seemed unable to exist in Seattle. Comfortable inhabiting reservation life only in his poetic imagination, Seymour refuses to go home, but the news of the death of his childhood friend Mouse (Swil Kanim) jerks him back into the realities of his former world and its many tentacles. He returns to the reservation for Mouse's wake, where he also faces many of the people who see him as both a turncoat and a favorite son. Based as loosely as is humanly possible on Alexie's collection of poems *The Business of Fancydancing*, the movie feels more like an adaptation of the text of Alexie's life as a writer turned celebrity city dweller. Shot in just about three weeks on a minimal budget and within a restricted time frame, the film's production qualities are less sophisticated than *Smoke Signals* (see the review in this chapter) or *Skins*, but the acting and the script are considerably better than that of *Naturally Native*, in part because Alexie resists the temptation to take on the cornucopia of Indian issues.

For me, the best feature of *Fancydancing* is its awareness of itself as a text. At no point during *Fancydancing* does the viewer ever suspect that he is viewing a documentary (unlike *Skins*, for example). Alexie keeps reminding the viewer that she is looking at a screen, not looking out a window. *Fancydancing* is not real life—though it is realistic; it is a construct, a simulation, a play on cinematic verisimilitude and the questionable history of ethnographic films. It locates authentic Indianness within its experimental, performative, anti-diegetic design—a design reflective of Seymour Polatkin himself. As the film suggests, "Seymour Polatkin" is a text, a self-invention made necessary by his fame. Additionally, the idea of Seymour Polatkin is also an external construct, concocted by those who want an image of "the Indian poet." So, most viewers don't know what to do with *Fancydancing* because they don't know what to do with Seymour; he bears no resemblance to any other iconic Indian (unlike Victor Polatkin and

Thomas Builds-the-Fire from *Smoke Signals*). It stands to reason, then, that a film reflecting Seymour's aesthetic sensibilities and his complicated identity, and also perpetually reminding the viewer of its own fictionality might be difficult to decode. Indeed, its textuality problematizes expectations of fictional Indians, forcing viewers to rethink not just their notions of Indians, but all inventions of the left-wing bookstore demographic, like "the sensitive poet," "the passionate Indian," "the Indian writer," and "the sage scribe."

Alexie loves to hack away at myths, and *Fancydancing* wastes no time pulling out the ax. In the second scene of the film, only a minute into the movie, Alexie substitutes mimetic scenes of reservation life and family interaction with a bizarre shot of someone who looks a lot like Thomas Builds-the-Fire sitting in a bookstore window, facing the street like a mannequin, and reading a poem called "How to Write the Great American Indian Novel." A close-up of the book tells us its author is Seymour Polatkin, and almost immediately, a black-and-white intertitle appears on the screen:

> "Seymour Polatkin's poetry is funny, angry, authentic, and ultimately redemptive." —*New York Literature Quarterly*, May 21, 2001.

At this point, the viewer has been prepared for an earnest portrayal of the Indian writer, chronicling the woes, magic, and dreams of his people. But, as soon as the audience settles into this easy reading, Alexie irrupts with yet another intertitle:

> "Seymour Polatkin is full of shit" —*Indianz.com*, May 22, 2001.

The second intertitle brings the entire scene into focus and tells the audience how to read the film. Seymour (Evan Adams), perched in a bookstore window, ceases to be a poet giving a reading and instead looks like he is in an exhibit at the zoo—a live Indian on display and safely tucked away behind glass. A passerby, a confused Anglo man, stops and looks quizzically at Seymour before entering the bookstore and ignoring him altogether. Then, almost as quickly, the film cuts to Seymour placing his hands on the cheeks of a famous statue of Chief Seattle in Pioneer Square, at which point Seymour gives the chief a long, passionate, open-mouthed kiss. While all this is going on, the audience listens to Seymour's voice-over, which is the text of the poem—an actual poem of Alexie's—that riffs on the readerly expectations of Indians, "Native Americans," stereotypes, and the stereotypes that some highly regarded Indian literature romanticizes. To be sure, it is an unusually rich scene. It's rare, for example, to see someone on film make out with a statue, and even more rare to see an Indian French-kiss a statue of another Indian, and it engenders an entirely new image of the sacred and the profane. In fact, the entire first five minutes of the film unnerve preceding and perceived assumptions of what to expect from a "small budget Native American film."

This three-minute section I describe above, beginning with Seymour reading the Alexie poem, through the intertitles and the statue kiss, and ending with the final lines of the poem, is one of the most revolutionary three minutes in Native film. In that span of time, the movie moves from modern to postmodern, from earnest to ironic, from predictable to performative like nothing before it. One of the great contributions of *Smoke Signals* is its ability to perform like a buddy movie or a Western, but ultimately to embody, better than any other text, a new genre we might call "the American Indian Independent Film." *Fancydancing* picks up where *Smoke Signals* left off. *Fancydancing* begins as yet another seemingly depressing but ultimately uplifting American Indian independent film that audiences have been prepared to view, but Alexie's deep play with cinematic grammar in these scenes deconstruct the very genre he helped construct. If a viewer cottons to such directorial flourishes, then that viewer will probably enjoy the experience of watching *Fancydancing.* But, for many viewers—and critics—Alexie's heavy-handedness both as a director and as a social commentator is distracting.

It is worth inquiring into Alexie's audience for *Fancydancing.* With *Smoke Signals*, he, Chris Eyre, and Miramax engaged in strategic efforts to market the movie as a comedy and to make it as widely accessible as possible. Even though *Dances with Wolves* was wildly popular, Miramax's market testing revealed that many Americans assumed that movies about Indians would be a downer, so they went out of their way to make *Smoke Signals* hip, funny, and mainstream. Alexie goes to no such effort for *Fancydancing.* In fact, in many ways he estranges the viewer, mixing Indian issues with gay issues, offering visual critiques of both Anglos and Indians, poking fun at successful writers (like himself) who write about how awful life on the reservation can be, and lastly, making it hard to like many of the characters we're spending time with. In one of the many inside jokes, Alexie himself makes a cameo appearance in the film as a kind of ambitionless slacker who won't leave the reservation. In what must have been the single most enjoyable scene to film, Alexie's character pokes fun at Seymour's new life as a fancy writer: "When was the last time Seymour talked to Mouse? Writin' all those poems, walkin' around here, thinking he's too good for us. He always did." Seymour's college girlfriend and closest friend on the reservation, Agnes Roth (Michelle St. John), defends Seymour, suggesting that perhaps Seymour communicated to Mouse through the poems, reminding everyone that Mouse read Seymour's work. Alexie's character retorts, "And, I don't even like those poems! Do you?" What a treat to get to make fun of your own poems in your own film. That's just about as fun and as postmodern as it gets, but for many viewers, that's just not very *Indian.* I mean, what does it have to do with the mascot issue? And, like, where are the dream-catchers?

Alexie's not much help stylistically either. There are confusing montage scenes, interscenes of Evan Adams and Michelle St. John fancydancing, and random clips of interviews Seymour does with a cranky journalist about being a writer and an Indian. It is as if the composition of the film mirrors the composition of Indian identity. Seymour patches and pastes and shifts and adjusts. He edits and reedits, as though his life (like his writing) is a series of takes and reshoots he can do until he gets it right.

In a world of inconsistency, one aspect that is consistent—at least within the film—is music. Even more than language, music seems to tie the characters together. The secret star of the film is Mouse, whose astonishingly good violin playing smoothes out the harsh edges of the movie and reservation life. He even draws in the lovely Cynthia Geary of *Smoke Signals* and *Northern Exposure* fame, whose character comes to the reservation to teach school, but who falls for the self-destructively compelling Mouse. Even though Mouse dies, his music lives on—more vibrant, it would appear, than the memory of him. Alexie might be suggesting that it's the work that endures, the work's effect on people, how it gets integrated into their daily lives. In other words, Mouse's Mouseness is best embodied in his music, just as Seymour's Seymourness resides most authentically and profoundly in his poems.

Alexie's Alexieness is all over *Fancydancing.* I like that. But, for those viewers who are turned off by self-referentiality and postmodern gestures of play, you might be better served watching *Skins* or sticking to the edited Alexie of *Smoke Signals.* Ultimately, as a film, I think *Fancydancing* succeeds despite itself. It helps us see Indians through surprising lenses, and if film can't do what it does best—bring the world in and out of focus—we might as well just stick to poems.

CHAPTER 8

NDNS: The Young and the Restless

Dear Diary:

Now I have my very own plastic Indian—and a pretty wooden cupboard to lock him in. If I'm lucky, Litefoot will rap in my dreams tonight!

Yours forever,

Hollywood

The Indian in the Cupboard

Pauline Turner Strong

As I sit at my computer, a three-inch plastic Indian stands beside the monitor. He has a scalp lock, and wears leggings, a breechcloth, a knife sheath, and a pouch, all of yellow. Next to him is the case for a videocassette of *The Indian in the Cupboard*, with the cover reversed, so that the case resembles a weathered wooden cabinet. Beside the cabinet is a plastic skeleton key, almost as large as the miniature Indian. Although it is possible to purchase the Indian figurine independently, as well as figurines of other characters that appear in *The Indian in the Cupboard*, mine was packaged with the video.

Equipped with the plastic Indian, the cabinet, and the key, I can imitate Omri, the nine-year-old American boy whose coming-of-age story is told in the film. Omri, like his English namesake in the popular children's novel by Lynne Reid Banks, is given an Indian figurine that comes to life when locked inside a magical cabinet. My figurine does not come to life, but I do have a CD-ROM version of *The Indian in the Cupboard* that allows me to animate an Indian figure. This computer-generated image reminds me of a miniature cigar-store Indian, or a ship's figurehead.

When I move the cursor in order to place the figurine in the cabinet and turn the key, the Indian begins to move and to talk to me. Like Omri's miniature friend in the film, this animated Indian is named Little Bear. He identifies himself as an Onondaga of the Wolf clan and introduces me to his Ungachis, his "friends" on the toy shelf. He gives me the name of Henuyeha, or "player."

Using the cursor, I accompany Little Bear to a promontory overlooking his palisaded village, where his people live in three longhouses.

Descending to the village, I meet the Ungachis, whom I will later bring to life as my guides. I recall the many Indians who have made their living as hunting guides or ethnographic consultants, as well as a YMCA organization to which my brother once belonged known as Indian Guides. Foremost among my new Onondaga "friends" is a clan mother, Gentle Breeze, who will introduce me to Onondaga words, stories, and symbols referring to the ancestors of the clans—Turtle, Bear, Wolf, Snipe, Beaver, Hawk, Deer, and Eel—as well as to the underwater Panther, the Keeper of the Winds and his Spirit Animals, the Peacemaker, and the Tree of Peace. Another Ungachi, a male "chief" named He Knows the Sky, will introduce me to Grandmother Moon, the Path of the Dead, the Bear, the Seven Children, and Star Girl, telling me their stories.

An Ungachi named Shares the Songs will teach me to play water drums, a flute, and a variety of rattles, challenging me to remember ever more complex rhythms. Swift Hunter will teach me to recognize and follow animal tracks, while Keeper of the Words will show me how to make a headdress in the style of each of the Six Nations of the League of the Iroquois. Two children will teach me their games: from Blooming Flower I will learn how to decorate carved templates with beads; from Runs with the Wind, how to play a challenging memory game with seeds of corn, squash, and several varieties of beans.

Succeeding in these various activities requires a certain degree of patience and attentiveness. Each time I succeed, I am rewarded with effusive praise and a symbol for my "wampum belt." Upon its completion, a ceremony is held to present me with the completed wampum belt and to name me an Ungachi, a "Friend of the Iroquois." I am feasted with a meal of corn, pumpkin, potatoes, squash, deer, roasted turkey, and cornbread.

This concludes a disconcerting episode of what the anthropologist Michael Taussig calls "mimetic excess," with a panoply of resonances: Camp Fire Girl "council fires" at which, proudly wearing my deerskin "ceremonial gown" and the beads I had "earned," I paid homage to Wohelo ("Work, Health, Love"); campfires under the stars at Camp Wilaha and Camp Katomi; school lessons and pageants about the first Thanksgiving; Louis Henry Morgan's activities in the fraternal organization he helped found, the Grand Order of the Iroquois; the assimilationist group of reformers known as the "Friends of the Indian"; and Vine Deloria's caustic dismissal of "anthropologists and other friends" in *Custer Died for Your Sins.*

Despite my initial discomfort with the power of bringing miniature Onondagas to life—and especially with the power to turn them back into mute "plastic"—I find myself intrigued and rather charmed by this simulated world. So is six-year-old Tina, whose favorite game is the Trading Game, in which we bring an English trader named Spaulding to life. In the process of bartering with Spaulding we learn a fair amount about Onondaga hunting, farming, and material culture. By the time Tina and I are presented with our wampum belts, we have been introduced to many aspects of Iroquois life in the early eighteenth century: the forest, the river, and the clearing; the powers of various animals; the Onondaga names and legends of the moon, Milky Way, and several constellations; the Three Sisters (corn, beans, and squash); the architecture and layout of the village; the manufacture of goods and the practice of reciprocity; the importance of clans and clan matrons. We have heard many Onondaga words and learned to recognize a few. With the exception of Spaulding and his trade goods, however, we have encountered little evidence of Iroquois relations with Europeans or with other indigenous peoples.

Little Bear's world is one of order, beauty, and tranquility, free of disruptions from warfare, disease, displacement, or Christian evangelism. It serves to arouse both powerful feelings of nostalgia and nostalgic feelings of power. This is a world under control; a world in which people treat each other with respect; a world pervaded by the soothing, rhythmic music of flutes and rattles. It is a world in which human relationships tend to be dyadic and free of conflict, a world in which, as both the textual and celluloid Omri teaches his friend Patrick, "You can't use people." That we enter this world through the conceit of controlling the lives of miniature Indians and "mastering" the knowledge they have to teach us; that we feel we can be "Friends of the Iroquois" without confronting the political and economic claims that a real friendship would make upon us: these are among the ironies that pervade *The Indian in the Cupboard* in all its incarnations.

Destabilizing stereotypes is a tricky business, as others easily rush in to fill the void. In Banks's original book series, the figure of Little Bear explicitly replaces the stereotypical Plains Indian with a more localized and complexly rendered representation. When Little Bear comes to life, he does not live up to Omri's expectations of an Indian: he lives in a longhouse rather than a tipi, walks rather than rides a horse, and is unaware of the custom of becoming "blood brothers." In other ways, however, Little Bear more than meets expectations: he is a fierce "Iroquois brave" who has taken some thirty scalps; he is volatile, demanding, and interested in "firewater"; he becomes "restive" while watching a Western on television; his English is broken and, early on, mixed with grunts and snarls; he initially thinks of Omri as the Great White Spirit, only to be disillusioned when the boy fails to live up to his notions of a deity. The most racist stereotypes, however, are voiced not by the narrator but by "Boohoo" Boone, a humorous cowboy who, when brought to life, denigrates "Injuns" and "redskins" as "ornery," "savage," and "dirty," only to be convinced otherwise by Omri and Little Bear. Although passages like these and cover illustrations reminiscent of nineteenth-century dime novels have attracted some criticism, the moral of the tale is clear: although Omri at first cherishes his power over Little Bear, calling him "my Indian," he comes to respect Little Bear as an autonomous human being with his own life, times, country, language, and desires (as Omri tells Patrick).

Lynne Reid Banks, an Englishwoman who spent the war years in Saskatchewan, set her series during the French and Indian War, and the friendship between Omri and Little Bear plays upon the alliance between the English and Iroquois. The historical context of the book series is almost completely absent in the film. Except for a brief dreamlike sequence in Little Bear's world, the film takes place completely in Omri's time and place. The film, for this reason, has far less cultural content than the CD-ROM, though what there is has been carefully rendered, following the advice of Onondaga consultants Oren Lyons and Jeanne Shenandoah. The film is equally nostalgic, however. When Little Bear, preparing to return to his own time, asks whether the Onondaga are always a great people, Omri sadly answers in the affirmative, then reluctantly reveals that "it isn't always so good" for them. While this is indisputable, the scene misses a valuable opportunity to show something of the resiliency and contemporary life of the Onondaga people. Portrayed in the past or in miniature, and without visible descendants, Little Bear is out of place, out of time, and an object of intense longing. The film does nothing to help viewers imagine Little Bear's descendants as persons who share a world with Omri even as they share a tradition with Little Bear.

Nevertheless, the film is more successful than the book or CD-ROM in presenting Little Bear as more than a stereotypical representation. As played by the Cherokee rap artist Litefoot, Little

Bear dominates the film, even at three inches tall. The film's Little Bear is not to be patronized, earns Omri's respect, and teaches him to appreciate the awesome responsibility that comes with power over other human beings. Given this, it is jarring to have power over Little Bear, voiced by Litefoot, in the CD-ROM version of *The Indian in the Cupboard.* The CD-ROM encourages the Henuyeha, in the spirit of playful learning, to mimic just what Omri learned not to do—but in the service of understanding Little Bear's world. It is doubly disconcerting to possess a plastic figurine of Little Bear. Omri's rejection of objectifying human beings was, predictably, lost on the marketing department—and is sure to be lost on many of its young consumers.

Dear Diary:

Although I often present a tough exterior, you know I'm as soft as a cashmere sweater inside. That's why I can only watch Ol' Yeller *backwards, so the dog doesn't really die at the end.*

Reminder to Self: Men's Drumming group meets this Sunday at 5:00 at the Hollywood Bowl.

See ya there, babe,

Hollywood

The Education of Little Tree

Daniel Heath Justice

I cry every time I watch *The Education of Little Tree.* It annoys the piss out of me, but I can't help it. Even though I know that the book upon which it's based, originally advertised as the homespun autobiographical reminiscences of the Cherokee storyteller Forrest Carter, is actually a complete scam-job written by Asa Carter, a violently defensive alcoholic and rabid KKK segregationist. Even though I know that there are nasty undercurrents of bigotry beneath the story's apparently antiracist surface. And even though both the movie and the book, in differing degrees, perpetuate tiresome stereotypes about Indians in general and Cherokees in particular, I still end up with sniffling nose and brimming eyes, caught up in the sentimental, Depression-era story of a wide-eyed mixed-blood Cherokee boy raised up by his loving, salt-of-the-earth, Tennessee hill-country grandparents.

It's pathetic. But it's also powerful.

My emotional response to the film makes me cautious about being entirely dismissive of the many thousands of nonacademic readers and viewers who've fallen in love with the story. And this is what worries me. It's still one of the University of New Mexico's top-selling books, even now, more than a decade after the full nastiness of Carter's true identity was exposed. What is it about this tale that captures so many peoples' imaginations, even those of us who know very well that it's far from the lovely, gentle autobiographical reminiscence it was originally said to be?

In my own case, I'd never been much into the Hollywood Indian at the heart of TV Westerns—he (invariably a "he") was generally a stallion-riding, long-haired, bare-breasted, war-painted Plains warrior who howled a lot and didn't offer much eloquence to a kid who loved narrative and story. I was raised in the mountains (the Rockies, not Appalachia) with a plaid-wearing, buzz-haired Cherokee father who's a hunter, outfitter, and wilderness wanderer who has occasionally skirted the letter of the law and who's old enough to be "Granpa," and a mountain-born and bred mother who's an amazing country cook and has always been the spiritual seeker of the household. *Little Tree* was the first book I read as a kid that made being Cherokee—not just generically Plains Indian and pseudo-Lakota—something to be proud of, something mysterious that belonged just to my family, something that distinguished us from all the other poor mining families in the district, so that all explains a bit of the appeal for me. (Sure, I had pugs instead of hunting hounds, but that disconnect didn't bother me too much.)

But it only explains a bit. It still doesn't offer a convincing rationale for the whole *Little Tree* phenomenon, both movie and book, especially for those who aren't Cherokee or even Indian at all. Why do *so* many viewers and readers without any related history or experience so enthusiastically want to love Little Tree and his moonshine-runnin', moccasin-wearin', church-goin' heathen grandparents and their mysterious friend Willow John, the sorrowful and Noble Savage hermit who, accordin' to Granpa in the movie, "has the magic"?

Indians are appealing to most Americans as an idea that can be claimed and appropriated; the reality of Native sovereignty, land claims, and political autonomy is much less palatable to the American (or Canadian) public because it doesn't offer the same transportability. So the Indians that people love to love are the Indians as wearable costumes, the Indians devoid of complexity or depth, the Indians as symbol, the Indians as ghosts. And, ultimately, that's what the *Little Tree* phenomenon is all about.

This is supposed to be a film review, but it's hard to talk about the film without referencing Forrest (Asa) Carter's 1976 novel, because the two texts exist in a strange relationship. In some ways, the film is a significant improvement on the novel; in others, it replicates or even exacerbates some of the problems of its source text.

"It begun," an adult Little Tree (Jeff Jeffcoat) tells us in soft, rhythmic mountain tones, "at the Jericho Mine, Jericho City, Tennessee, in the year nineteen and thirty-five, the day after Ma died." The camera pans through a ruinous mining town filled with crumbling brick buildings, mountains of waste rock, and weathered white folks, all washed over in dull tones of gray, brown, and black. It's a place custom-made for the Depression. Continuing in his ever-so-slightly flavored hillbilly drawl, Little Tree informs us that his Ma had "lasted only a year after Pa was kilt in the army. And that's how I come to live with Granma and Granpa when I was eight years old. One time Granma told me, that when you come on somethin' good, first thing to do is share it with whosoever you can find. That way, the good spreads out where no tellin' how far it will go. Which is right. So I'm tellin' the story of them days, and how Granma and Granpa got me away from Aunt Martha, and taken me to live in their mountains, where they'd raised my Pa before me, and which I know now was the secret heart of the world." Now, who could argue with that?

In the aftermath of her sister Sally's death, Aunt Martha (Leni Parker) is gathering up her sister's belongings, eight-year-old Little Tree (Joseph Ashton) among them, when Wales (James Cromwell), a white mountain man gone native, and his shy Cherokee wife Bonnie (Tantoo Cardinal) show up to take their young'un back to the mountains with them. Little Tree runs to grab onto Granpa's leg, and Martha, true to bad whitey form, starts a-screechin'. Her concern about the boy's welfare seems far less compelling than browbeating her chickenshit husband and railing against Wales's "backwoods white Injun" ways. Though white, Granpa has the stoic Indian thing down pat, and with a simple "Martha, leave him be," he leaves her sputtering in impotence, collects his wife and grandson, and heads out for the hills.

Though it's certainly a melodramatic start, it's also effective, because the principal actors—Cromwell, Cardinal, and especially Ashton—are incredibly engaging and charismatic. There's an undeniable chemistry among them that makes the grandparent/grandchild relationship convincing. Ashton's Little Tree is cute without being saccharine, wide-eyed and innocent without being cloying, and expressive in ways that seem almost effortless. Cromwell, for his part, fully inhabits the rumpled, world-weary Granpa, complete with scruffy half-beard and stringy hair over his balding pate, and he's as believable in his feisty antagonism toward yammering preachers and petty bureaucrats as he is in his tenderness to his wife and grandson. As usual, Cardinal takes what is an underwritten role and gives Granma a quiet strength and dignity, making her the wise, gentle heart of the family. The viewer *wants* Little Tree to go with Granma and Granpa; the old folks are a bit wizened and tattered, but they're fiercely protective of their orphaned grandson, and clearly far more loving and welcoming than his mean-assed Aunt Martha.

So, after a long journey by bus and shoe-leather express, Little Tree comes to the little cabin on the sunny south slope of a pine-wooded hill. This enchantingly bucolic locale is rendered complete by the presence of a half-dozen hunting hounds—including Blue Boy, who becomes Little Tree's fast friend—and the occasional unexpected appearances and disappearances of Willow John (Graham Green, in a rather underwhelming performance).

The first two-thirds or so of the movie chronicles Little Tree's rather accelerated mountain education, which we can summarize thusly:

1. Follow "the Way," an incredibly vague philosophy of cosmic disinterest, human passivity, and barely veiled social Darwinism that apparently makes anyone a little bit Cherokee. You get extra points if your grandparents can stand in a cornfield and add some vague lesson about fit raptors and slow prey birds, and offer a lame interpretation of why that illuminates the complexities of colonialism and sociopolitical oppression. The most points come if your white Granpa can hisself learn to "see the world through Cherokee eyes," as it makes your own efforts at being Cherokee just a matter of following "the Way"—it's easier and less messy than those trivial little matters of culture, history, kinship, worldview, or political relationship.
2. Learn a trade. If it's one that involves moonshining, and offers a young kid the opportunity to flee from federal revenuers and "big city criminals" and gives the authorities reason to doubt the suitability of said kid's grandparents as fit guardians, all the better.
3. Moccasins are good if Indians and white-men-gone-native wear them, as they help the wearer get all knowin' and sensual with the ground underfoot, but other white folks tend to get all put out and concerned about savagery if you offer them some mocs of their own (see lesson 7 below).
4. Slightly strange Cherokee hermits are mysteriously magical, like the Lucky Charms leprechaun, and there's nothing wrong with putting a loud frog in said hermit's pocket if it causes them

to make a scene of themselves in church, as that's really the only chance you'll have to get them to emote onscreen.

5. Don't trust Christians, because they'll cheat you out of your moonshining money and sell you a diseased calf that will die very shortly thereafter.
6. Don't trust politicians, because they're fat, racist, and wear too-small suits, and their wives are wasteful with their cigarettes.
7. Don't trust poor white sharecropper girls with scabby knees and dirty feet, because their racist and grammatically challenged "pa's" will call you names and spray tobacco spit at you, especially if you give them moccasins (see lesson 3 above).
8. Most mountain whites not married to Indians are goobers with bad dental hygiene and worse fashion sense, who don't talk, and dance *really* badly.
9. The main thing you need for preventing death or disability from a rattlesnake's bite is to kill a bird and press its bloody corpse on the wound. Not sure what it does, but if a wise old Cherokee woman does it, it must work.

It's a pretty full curriculum for a kid who has to learn these lessons in between memorizing dictionary words with unlikely applicability in his present milieu, running up and down the mountain trails (sometimes with a tow sack full o' whiskey), picking up woodchips for the owner of the local general store, looking for his own special "secret place" in the woods, and attending weekly services at a church where Indians and white Indians are clearly not welcome.

The last part of the film follows Little Tree's temporary departure from his mountain sanctuary. Aunt Martha—that nasty ol' woman!—has reported Wales and Bonnie to the authorities as unfit guardians, and because he's on the Eastern Cherokee rolls, they take him to the Notched Gap Indian School instead of back to her. (This act makes her doubly vile, as there's no benefit for her in taking this action apart from just plain polecat meanness.) So, Little Tree ends up back on the bus and heads off to the school, where his hair is cut, his name is changed to Joshua, he's forced to wear ugly denim uniforms and uncomfortable shoes, and he's thrown headlong into a world of strictly regimented schedules, educational propaganda, and social exclusion. A crippled fellow inmate, the bitter cynic-with-a-heart-of-gold Wilburn (Chris Fennell), offers him advice on how to survive defiantly in the school, but it's the lessons of Granma and Granpa that Little Tree relies on for survival when a casual observation about deer reproduction gets him beaten and sent to solitary confinement. (Though brutal, this punishment is far from the sadistic attack he experiences in the novel, which, surprisingly, is one of the more accurate scenes in the book, even though it takes place in an orphanage instead of an Indian school.) Little Tree talks to his grandparents via nightly vigils before the Dog Star, slowly drifting into a disconnected haze that he maintains even after he's released from solitary.

Finally, Granpa comes to rescue him, and Little Tree heads back to the mountains, taking care to remove "clobbers" because he "couldn't feel the trail." Granpa follows suit, they both toss their boots into the woods and dance like loons, and there's a big, happy reunion with Granma and the hounds back at the cabin.

Of course, since this is a movie with kind and loving Indians in it, most of them have to die, and that's what happens here. First, Granpa falls on the high trail, wastes away, and dies with his hat on, whispering weakly but sagely, "It's been good. Next time, it'll be better. Be seein' ye."

Not long after that, as the older Little Tree informs us in dulcet voice-over, Granma dies, telling Little Tree not to worry, that she and Granpa had an "understandin," that they'd be together always, "their spirits knowin.'" And if he'd ever need them, all he'd have to do is look to the Dog Star, and they'd be there.

Unlike the book, where Willow John dies naked in his lean-to after raving against the white man in fever-induced delirium, the movie offers a different ending. Little Tree is sitting on the front step of the cabin after Granma's funeral, surrounded by the dogs, staring at the ground, sad and alone. But he perks right up when Willow John appears at the edge of the cabin clearing to fetch him. So the boy rushes off with the hounds to join the hermit-turned-surrogate-grandfather and start the next stage in his education, to learn "all there was to know about being an Indian," having already learned a few more valuable lessons:

1. Unless they're white guys who marry Cherokee women and learn "the Way," most white people are backwards, bureaucratic, ignorant, greedy, racist, or slovenly, and some are all of the above.
2. Apparently, there are only four Cherokees anywhere in the hill country of Tennessee, even though the Notched Gap School is apparently full of Indian kids from the area.
3. All it takes is a big bowie knife and a little bit of elbow grease for your grandfather to rescue you from a government boarding school, and aside from some token bureaucratic pursuit, you'll pretty easily be able to avoid being taken back.
4. When your grandparents die, leaving you once again an orphan, the slightly strange and mysteriously magical hermit will come by to fetch you up to his isolated cabin in the hills, and there's nothing weird or creepy about that at all.

On balance, the film's ending is better than that of its source text. In the novel, Little Tree leaves the mountains with the hounds, having lost his grandparents and Willow John in fairly short order. As he travels westward to find Cherokees—"to the Nation, where there was no Nation" (a line that never ceases to piss me off)—the dogs die off one by one until, at the very end, the last dog, Blue Boy, dies, leaving Little Tree completely alone in the world, a proper adolescent last of the Cherohicans. At least the movie gives a sense that there's some sort of community in the east—if only Willow John, Little Tree, and the dogs—and Cherokees, Navajos, and other folks out west. At least the movie offers some hope for Indian continuity and survival (a hope that's moderated, however, by the fact that we learn in the closing narration that Willow John, too, has died).

There are many things to dislike about the film (fewer than the book, I should point out), but there are also some good things. Excellent acting by the principals is the high point, with the finest scenes being those that quietly observe the mundane, everyday kindnesses of a loving family. You've actually got Indians playing Indians in the movie, unlike the book, where the Indians are pretty much just symbolic stand-ins for Confederates in Asa Carter's twisted race-world of "guv'mint" hating. (In the novel, Granpa is half-Cherokee. The change from half-Cherokee to all-white might be a positive, in that they didn't want to replicate the Hollywood pattern of having white guys playing Indian, but a more skeptical analysis might be that all Indians need a white man to be a protagonist. In my more generous moments, I like to think it's the former.) Granma sings in Cherokee, and there are Cherokee baskets in the house, so there's at least some aural and visual presence of Cherokees in the film. The cinematography and locations are stunning (and particularly appealing to me, as it was filmed in Ontario, not so far from where I used to live), and the dulcimer-, violin-, and fiddle-dominated soundtrack by Mark Isham beautifully invokes the musical spirit of Appalachian mountaineers without succumbing to the flute music or eagle cries.

In the end, *The Education of Little Tree* isn't a terrible movie. Its strengths are impressive, and certainly far better than most Native-themed films out there. Given its subject matter, the film makes a pretty concerted effort to portray the experiences of Indians in the eastern United States with some small measure of accuracy. As part of the entire *Little Tree* phenomenon, however, it still reinforces the idea that Cherokees are just another ethnic group (albeit an incredibly wise and ecologically superior one) that all white people can become if they just learn "the way of the Cherokee," not a people with distinctive histories, worldviews, and political structures. Tribal nationhood, sovereignty, and self-determination are in no way represented in either movie or book, nor are the very real efforts of Cherokees—in Little Tree's time and our own—to maintain their ways and vigilantly affirm their values in spite of the assimilation efforts of the United States and its many colonial agents. The Cherokees in the movie offer a lot of down-home mountain goodness and the supposedly deeper wisdom of a simpler time, but they remain dim shadows of a greater, far more complicated reality, and the best of them are dead at the closing credits. In the end, they're nothing but fragments of a proud, living people; in the end, they end up ghosts.

And I still cry every time I watch *The Education of Little Tree.*

Dear Diary:

Why do all Indians say, "A?" Is it because it's the only letter in the alphabet they know? "A." Gotcha, "A."

Love ya,

Hollywood

The Doe Boy

Allison Adelle Hedge Coke

Tahlequah, Oklahoma. A feature film set in the Cherokee Nation's capital. Okay, I'm game. A coming-of-age story. There's deer hunting. Great. Complications within an interracial family, sure. Tahlequah, Oklahoma. *Hummm.* Here's a film I believe I'm ready to love. Finally. Yes, finally. Okay, click DVD. Note to readers: despite the fact that this film is touted as being Tahlequah-specific, shall we just forgive the pan-Indian overture while it's playing out? And, the deer running through the woods sporting an unexpected necklace. And the shaky cam POV. Intriguing.

I want to like it, really I do. And, hey, the three kids also running through the woods during the opening credits are pretty cute. The credit sequence gives the story a bit of family prelude. Nothing hokey about the kids, so okay, I'm in. One of the three boys eventually slows to pump a bit of his inhaler, thus falling behind the second runner still trying to catch the first. They race along, and the lead boy wins. All three gather on the hardtop road they reach just about the time a truly near-hokey voice-over is inserted into the scene. A Northern Cree accent narrates in Tahlequah?

> "Nobody cares how much blood runs through a deer, but everyone wants to know how much blood runs through an Indian."

I recognize that voice: Gordon Tootoosis as "Marvin." As a former director of the American Indian Registry of Performing Arts, I know his name is definitely on the A-list. Excellent record.

Maybe the film is going to be about intertribal families as well as interracial families. Okay, certainly this could be great, despite issues already named.

> "It's kinda hard to tell, unless you cut one of us open."
> Tahlequah, Oklahoma
> 1977
> "And watch all the stories pour out."

Nice opening lines.

The boy with asthma still attempts to calm his pain. The lead boy is an easy winner, so he suggests an agreed-upon bet for a Dr. Pepper has come due. He's then told to shut up by a declarative nickname "Band-Aid Boy" as the two other boys leave him in what should have been his glory. "Come on, Cheekie," the second runner says to the asthmatic boy.

A young Hunter (Andrew Ferchland) turns, tearing Band-Aids off his elbow. He leaves his victory depressed, or at the very least frustrated. Hemophilia. Point of provocative interest is clear. The hemophilia will complicate our protagonist's relationships worse than any childhood asthma might, and a deer runs through it, a deer wearing a necklace. The Northern Cree voice has instructed us to be aware of the story developing and pouring out through the blood, and yet while no one is worried about the deer's blood, moviemakers often think that everyone will accept a Northern Cree accent as definitively wise, thus a Northern Cree voice-over tells the story about a Southeastern tribe. You got to have your wise man. I'm a big fan of Gordon Tootoosis, but by now I am looking for admission that the Northern Cree character is part of the story.

> VOICE-OVER: "There was a boy who followed in the deer's footsteps instead of his father's."

Cut to Band-Aid Boy's home (interior, dinner-table scene). Indian mom, Maggie Kirk (Jeri Arredondo), and white dad, Hank Kirk (Kevin Anderson), both sit across the table from the boy who follows deer and evidently pours out stories through his blood.

The father (shooting for accent Southern) asks Hunter to work with him on his truck, tomorrow.

The mother (shooting for accent Southern) offers to cut his meat for him.

The dad complains about all the mothering, suggests that the boy is old enough to kill his own meat. Young Hunter agrees and adds that his grandfather kills his own meat. Good scene, believable. The conversation quickly changes to work and the day. Maggie is still wearing her nursing uniform and details the fact that Old Mrs. Deer-in-Water passed a kidney stone. She then pulls said stone from her pocket and places it on the dinner table after shaking it a bit in her hand. (Egad, isn't she worried about bringing someone else's sickness into the home and onto the dinner table? No taboo here, it doesn't seem!)

Complaints ensue from Dad and Hunter about the kidney stone. Mom argues that they should not be "such babies" as Band-Aid Boy begins to lazily and intentionally chew ice from his beverage. Maggie admonishes him to stop, suggesting he'll cut his tongue and have to get a shot. He spits the ice back into his drink as we cut to several bottles of antihemophilic medication vials and the visually implied knowledge that she can take care of Hunter's hemophilia because she's a nurse. Hunter then brushes his teeth carefully in another room. There is definitely potential for relational issues in this family. Okay, I'm hooked.

Next Dad, drinking in easy chair, laments an air-force pilot scene playing out on the TV underneath a trophy buck. Dad's disgruntled line: "Weakened their defense the day they lost me." Cut to the family's garage sometime afterwards, Dad underneath a truck asking for a crescent wrench. Hunter does not know one tool from another to help, so asks, while swinging his legs from the tailgate, obviously thinking of other things, including two buck trophies hung above, one stuffed, the other bone skeletal. Dad slides out from underneath on a creeper, asserts that he sometimes has a hard time believing Hunter "sprung from" his loins, clearly disappointed in Hunter and expressing it openly. The Oklahoma plates on the pickup are evident in the closing of this scene.

Another vehicle, possibly an earlier model Scout, complete with overhead spotlights and a longhorn trophy across the International grille, is coming down a road. The second runner, the boy from the opening scene, is the passenger next to a man in a cowboy hat, driving.

Voice-over returns. Telling the metaphoric story element prior to its occurrence, in case we cannot draw our own conclusions. The narrator notes facts about stronger bucks setting their territory and running away inferior bucks by attack.

Hunter and his dad Hank, wearing a military-green baseball cap, are outside a business having a snack as the vehicle arrives at what is probably a store parking lot. The second-place runner comes into the scene with what seems to be his cowboy-hatted dad, possibly a Southern Plains father. He insults Hunter's dad jokingly, and insults himself. A self-deprecating type, it seems. Hunter tells the second runner that he needn't pay up the (earlier) Dr. Pepper bet as his mom says they cause kidney stones.

Second Runner's dad mentions they've come for a hunting license. Hunter's dad speaks of the overpopulation of deer. Southern Plains man complains he hasn't killed a deer in three years, and then brags up his son's hunting ability. We cut to Hunter asking his father to take him hunting on their drive home. A beer can on the dash during the drive. Hunter's father agrees that he'd "better"—"Can't let those two jerks take all the glory"—then says he has to run it by his mom (for permission). Pan out to see them drive down the road alongside a sign declaring "Upper Shit Creek" and then cutting to Marvin playing flute with Hunter sitting next to him on a park bench in the town square. Another man passes by and places money in what looks to be a coffee can in front of the old man. This sets up a scene, inside a truck bed, where Marvin tells Hunter about his own father's flute playing—how he'd never play for money for a hamburger, only to get girls, and to expound upon his own playing for the courtship of Hunter's granny.

Sitting across from them is a man who appears to be from a Southeastern tribe. Marvin directs Hunter to look at him. He tells Hunter that the man, Tommy Deer-in-Water, is a real hunter (to which Tommy nods his head in acknowledgment), not a "weekend warrior like your Daddy." Insulting Hunter's father directly, Marvin explains that Tommy only hunts alone, only taking "one arrow." (Any American Indian hunter living in Oklahoma knows just how ridiculous this scene is.) He tells it that Tommy got so close to a deer once that he hung beads around his neck (hence the opening clips). Cut to cabin porch where Hunter sits on a bench across from his grandfather holding a pipe. He continues speaking of hunting and notes that real hunters don't need to "dress up like a tree" and wait for a deer to come along.

What did he say? This will be news to all the Native hunters around Tahlequah, Oklahoma. Oh sure, "real Indians don't need no stinking guns. Just give them one arrow and they'll make do." Phooey! Hundreds, perhaps thousands of Oklahoma Indians buy and wear camouflage when they go hunting. In fact, their wives or sisters or aunts buy "camo" for the males in their families for Christmas, birthdays, Halloween, and Valentine's Day! Male and female Native hunters sit in tree stands and wait for the deer to come into view. It's irksome that the Native filmmakers are trading in stereotypes for this scene.

Cut to a bedroom scene. Hunter's parents argue. Hank complains about Hunter's shortcomings (due to illness) and worries that Hunter will be like his mom. Maggie defends his right to be like her. Dad notes that Dr. Moore (Jim Metzler) warned her not to be overprotective. Maggie gives in. Says he can take him, but that he must pad him. Hunter's been in another room throughout this scene and raises his arms excitedly at overhearing the permission.

Cut to tomorrow. Hank and Hunter are sure enough dressed like trees walking through woods. Hunter has large shoulder pads underneath his shirt. Hunter complains about the camouflage clothing, as the woods fill with the sounds of rifle shots. Dad insists they sit and wait and let the shooters flush up the deer. Each selects a.tree to rest against. Hunter notices his dad snoring a bit later, and moves quickly around his tree when someone shoots at him, hitting the bark above his head. Cursing, Hunter then glimpses a buck and takes aim, releasing the safety to shoot. A doe walks past. He fires, and the kick of the rifle knocks him off his feet. Dad wakes up, realizes his son has shot his first deer. Hunter laughs joyfully. They stalk the bloody trail to the doe, still heaving. With, of course, more contemporary pan-Indian music playing in the background to ensure we know this is an Indian thing. Hunter states that it was a buck, and Dad says that "it ain't a buck no more."

The second runner's dad pulls up and teasingly asks why they've taken a doe. Dad explains, "Hunter had a little mishap," while the second runner in the first scene taunts Hunter for wearing his shoulder padding.

Cut to Marvin, obviously disappointed in Hunter's dad (and his grandson) for shooting "a woman" and losing out on an opportunity to have a "story to tell." Hunter's dad fires back that Marvin is filling Hunter's head up with stories about "magic beads" and "magic hunters" and says that there is no magic, just life here. All this buildup is to show how Hunter became known as the "Doe Boy."

The continuing music follows as we zoom out to an interior shot of Hunter's mom saying that it's not his fault and that she knew she should not have let him go, all while giving him an IV.

1984.

Cut to an older Hunter (James Duval) driving home, all the while through the music. He passes a caution sign on the road with a pictured of an injured deer painted on it. We then move into shaky camera, heartbeat, and breathing as we follow deer POV running through woods. Cut to a sign of Magik Burger, and Hunter leaning outside the joint with an *Oklahoma Game & Fish* magazine in his hands. A voice calls him "Doe Boy" and asks him to get to the customers on table five.

Night; an owl warns. Interior. Hunter watching Marvin shave wood, perhaps making a flute, next to a carved head. Voice-over of Marvin saying, "There was a boy who shot a woman while his father slept." Hunter is now driving in the dark. The voice-over continues, "A boy with bullets in his eyes and arrows in his chest." Next Hank, obviously drunk and drinking, slugs beer while watching military show on TV, says, "Yep, they offered me jets, offered me F16s. Fuck it." He continues complaining about what one might learn in a classroom, equating it with his working on planes instead of flying them. Maggie is next to him, drying her hair with a towel. Lauds Chuck Yeager while she lazily mocks his obviously often-repeated lines. Hunter returns to hear Dad yelling at Mom and questions the situation. Mom says nothing is wrong, and then Dad mocks Hunter's plaid pants, insinuating he might be gay. Mom defends him. Dad continues badgering his family about the money for his "wonder juice" (antihemophilic medicine). Isn't there an Indian Health Services hospital (IHS) at Tahlequah? Hey, note to filmmakers, it's located on Bliss Avenue in Tahlequah, Oklahoma. Inquiring minds want to know why Hunter, the son of a Cherokee mother, isn't able to go to IHS and receive free medical care for his condition.

In 1955, Indian Health Services was established by the Bureau of Indian Affairs to take over health care of American Indian and Alaska Natives. The provision of health services to members of the over five hundred federally recognized tribes grew out of the special government-to-government relationship between the federal government and Indian tribes. The relationship, established in 1787, is based on Article I, Section 8 of the U.S. Constitution. In short, the federal government agreed to provide for the health and education of American Indians in exchange for their lands. That the feds expected all Natives to be wiped out in the Indian wars (thus nullifying any contract provisions they'd made with Indian tribes) is another story. However, that still doesn't answer the plot problem set up in the film concerning Hunter's medical bills.

Back to the scene: Hunter eventually says that he's saving his money to move out. Hank says if he gets out of the house by the time he's thirty, he'll give him a thousand bucks (pun intended).

VOICE-OVER: "To a buck, every doe is unique . . ."

Hunter is spreading hair across his school desk, extending from the girl sitting ahead of him, without her knowledge. He kisses and smells her hair. His classmate looks at him like he is nuts, and Hunter's nose begins to bleed on the desk as the hair moves away with the girl's repositioning.

Clearly this is a lifelong issue, and Hunter is coming of age, with an interest in finding a buck to kill, and a woman to land, and that one is equal to two.

Hunter receives a flute from Marvin on his birthday (though he'd apparently vowed not to make anymore), and Maggie and Hank joke about the plaid pants (Dad admitting he doesn't hate them). The two other runners are also there (maybe part of the family). At a local pub, the girl of interest (Bird) has ended up with one of the earlier racers (Junior, earlier played by Kyle White, now Nathaniel Arcand), and the other racer (Cheekie, originally played by Kody Dayish, now as an adult, Robert A. Guthrie) also has a girlfriend with him. They tease him about being the worst hunter who ever lived and call him Doe Boy. He gets quarters to play pool. One couple begins to make out, and Hunter's obvious jealousy gets the best of him and he tries diligently to start a fight with the closest man to him (Oliver, Orvel Baldridge, the white man who Hunter just beat in pool and is at the bar buying Hunter a beer). When the fight is about to ensue, both racers rescue him.

Late at night, Hunter and his father visit (while Dad cleans gun, asks him why he reads hunting magazines). Dad insults him for reading and not doing. Both are drinking. Dad blames Hunter's illness for his leaving the military. Hunter insults his father and his dad slaps him.

Hunter leaves, bleeding. He doctors himself, then peels out, passing deer caution signs, and attempts to hunt drunk, lying in back of what appears to be an El Camino, spotlighting. A buck just out of sight. A full moon. He eventually passes out, and in the morning a buck comes up to smell him as he is dreaming of hunting with his face painted. He rises sometime afterward and fitfully breaks his father's gun.

Another voice-over intrudes. (It's beginning to bring a bit of didacticism to the viewer.)

Cut to Cheekie and Junior preparing for the Marines. Cut to Hunter moving out, meeting a Southwestern girl (Geri), and discovering he might have AIDS (Dr. Moore); he tells his dad he'd like the thousand bucks (yep, pun). I won't divulge the ending, no need to. It's completely set up, obvious. The story comes full circle with some poignant scenes and impressive acting from many of the actors. The film is heartbreakingly moving at times, a laudable storyline. Beautiful camera work. Often strikingly believable character portrayals by actors, though not always Cherokee. A thoughtful inclusion of '80s music in '80s scenes (including "Yeha Noha" and "Space Age Love Song"). The film is complicated by the intertribalism that should have been noted within the dialogue. As such, the complication of Northern accents sufficing for Southeastern Indians plays problematically. If you love the film (there is a lot to love; I love it, I do), you'll definitely want to mute the sound on the final narrations and the lovely and strange soundtrack of keenly recognizable Lakota (including Sundance) song lyrics sung in pan-Indian contemporized melodies during some of the ending scenes, and instead marvel at the great acting and story being told. Certainly others did: the film was winner of the Sundance NHK International Filmmakers Award, Best First Time Director's Award at Taos Talking Pictures Festival, AIFF American Indian Movie Award, and winner of the Best First Feature Film award at the Wine Country Film Festival.

In the end, a deer and a boy will always run through memory.

DEAR DIARY:

Just bought a butt-load of White Cloud toilet tissue. Do you think this is a product sponsorship for the movie Black Cloud*? Those clever Indians! What will they think of next?*

Love ya,

HOLLYWOOD

Black Cloud

MAUREEN TRUDELLE SCHWARZ

Black Cloud (2004) opens with violence: pounding flesh against muscle and bone in a practice boxing match between Black Cloud (Lakota, Eddie Spears) and his coach Bud (Lakota, Russell Means). Rick Schroder's screenplay is loosely based on the true story of Navajo boxer Carl Bahe of Chinle, Arizona. Bahe overcame alcoholism through boxing and established a successful boxing club for Navajo youth that to date has produced twenty-four national boxing champions. Schroder chose to tell his story within the familiar genre of the Western.

This film contains many of the predictable devices of the Western genre; however, it deviates from the genre as well. In particular, being Indian, Black Cloud is not a conventional Western hero. Moreover, the film's setting is marked by *two* signifying borders. The first divides a symbolic wilderness, in the form of an Indian reservation, from civilization. The second border divides the past, in the form of deceased ancestors, from the present, the living. Fists stand in for guns, the usual symbols that cowboys use to prove their masculinity in Westerns. As a result, instead of a memorable scene such as the shoot-out at the OK Corral, *Black Cloud* contains what might best be termed "the beat-down in the men's room scene." While there is no doubt that violence is part and parcel of the protagonist's redemption, it's arguably exactly that act of violence that provides Black Cloud's redemption. Or, maybe, regeneration. While a moral message is conveyed in the film, it deviates from a classic Western.

The film is filled with the usual suspects: Euro-American settlers (now townsfolk), cowboys, saloon girls (women in bars), a sheriff played by Tim McGraw, bartenders, store owners, and, of course, Indians and half-breeds, including Black Cloud, and a disturbing use of the Noble Savage, an anachronistic stereotype, wherein the only real Indians (read: traditional) are his grandfather, who dies during the film, and his deceased ancestors! The latter two categories are vital because Western mythology is inextricably linked with the often-contested relations among Euro-Americans and American Indians. Making an Indian the hero casts Anglos like Eddie Young and Sheriff Powers as enemies. Can anyone say binary? Black Cloud is a proper Western hero nevertheless; he abides by his word, *and* he is a skilled horseman. Eddie Spears is also a fine horseman, but never mind, the focus is on Black Cloud. Some of the best scenes in the film are when he supposedly breaks a wild horse and rides it with its companions to the home of Sammi (Julia Jones), where she and Black Cloud declare their love. The robust wild horses Black Cloud breaks look nothing like those commonly seen on the Rez, which are typically rail thin.

Driving the film's plot are Black Cloud's repeated crossings back and forth over the two signifying borders. He crosses the first border to go off-reservation in order to fight competitively, attend rodeos, beat up Eddie Young, visit bars or pool halls, and purchase alcohol, which is how he encounters the law. In multiple scenes, Black Cloud "crosses over into the spirit world" to commune with his dead ancestors. Bud is the first to realize that Black Cloud has begun to have spiritual experiences in the ring that empower him to overcome his opponents. Bud feels compelled to discuss these with his protégé:

BUD: You don't even know when it happens, do you?
B.C.: What? What happens in the ring? I don't know, I just fight.
BUD: Crossing over into the spirit world is a powerful thing.
B.C.: What do you mean?
BUD: Where you went. Our ancestors called for you, and you answered.
B.C.: There was this one voice that rose above the rest,
(*Smaltzy voice-over*) YOU ARE CHOSEN
BUD: Figure out why they are calling you.
B.C.: Great. I thought only medicine men had to deal with this. (*Sigh*)

While other errors in ethnographic detail are evident, these crossings are most egregious. Navajo people are *known* for their taboos surrounding contact with the dead. Typically, a Navajo family will not even mention the name of a deceased family member for at least four years after he or she has expired, and traditional burials involve as few people as possible to delimit contamination by the *ch'iidii* (the first two *i* vowels have high tone marks and are nasalized), "disembodied spirit capable of evil," released at the time of death. (Ironically, traditional Navajo burial customs are properly portrayed in the film when Black Cloud puts his grandfather to rest.) Given these beliefs, still held by a good percentage of Navajos today, the last thing most Navajos would ever want to do is cross over to the spirit world to commune with a deceased ancestor!

Violence is a typical masculine attribute in Westerns. In addition to the boxing scenes, the film is riddled with multiple forms of violence, such as bull-riding or the riding of unbroken horses at the rodeo or on the Rez, fistfights in rodeo staging areas or bar restrooms, domestic abuse, or the violence of language. This is most clearly evidenced in what Eddie Young says in reference to Sammi, the young woman with whom he fathered a child. While preparing to ride a bull at the rodeo, for example, he tells Black Cloud, "She's sweet meat, ain't she?" When

Black Cloud confronts him after the rodeo, Eddie Young says, "If you want that squaw, you can have her, I am done with her." A fight ensues. Black Cloud is about to leave Eddie to nurse his wounds, until the latter taunts him with "They are all whores, you know, including your mama," at which point Black Cloud replies, "You need to know when to shut up," and turns back to beat him some more.

The film also showcases the rape of a young Indian woman by three white men, which figuratively symbolizes the source of Black Cloud's inner turmoil—the treatment of Native Americans at the hands of Europeans and Euro-Americans since conquest. Black Cloud is filled with pent-up rage over his mother's death; his father's neglect, which is exacerbated by his alcoholism; and what Euro-Americans have done to Native Americans, as highlighted in his first encounter with Norm Olson, the Olympic scout. When Olson approaches Black Cloud, they have the following conversation:

OLSON: Excuse me guys, I don't want to disturb you; I am Norm Olson. Look, I saw raw talent today combined with clarity of purpose. I was just wondering, you know, you've got a gift, what are you planning to do with it?
B.C.: What's it to you?
OLSON: I am just a man who doesn't like to see talent wasted.
B.C.: Oh, I see, unless I play by your rules, I am a waste.
OLSON: Have you ever considered boxing in the Olympics?
BUD: The question's never been asked.
OLSON: Well he should; I mean he's incredibly talented. I mean, a man only gets so many highlights in his life, and I guarantee you box for your country in the Olympics and it will be one of them.
BUD: And your interest?
OLSON: I am an Olympic boxing scout.
B.C.: Forget it, I ain't interested.
JIMMY: Cloud, let's hear what he has to say, man.
B.C.: No, I ain't interested in what the man has to say.
OLSON: Why is that?
B.C.: Because it's lies. It always is.
OLSON: I'm sorry, I'm not following you.
B.C.: It's in their souls, they don't know any better. Why should I fight for your nation when all you've done is murdered and imprisoned my people, huh?
BUD: Black Cloud!
B.C.: I didn't invite you here. You're not welcome.
OLSON: Look, I've done nothing to your people. Look, there is an Olympic trial in Vegas; you should be there.
B.C.: I fight for the Navajo Nation.

The latter source of angst is complicated by Black Cloud's alleged torment over finding out that he is a mixed-blood. This plays off the stock half-breed character of the genre. The figure of the half-breed—long used to explore notions of race and assimilation, and as a means for Euro-Americans to ultimately claim ownership of the North American continent—fails in

Black Cloud. At no point is Black Cloud portrayed as naive, making this level of angst over mixed-blood heritage difficult to believe. Further undermining the tenability of this plot line is the fact that the mixed-blood status of Sammi's son, Tyler, is treated as a virtual nonissue by Black Cloud.

Here it is used as the catalyst for the protagonist's simmering inner conflict over the mistreatment of his people at the hands of whites, which comes to a head. His anger towards whites and his inner turmoil become almost more than he can bear. At this point in the story, he becomes self-destructive, consumed with shame and self-hatred. He falters, stumbles on his path, and believes his identity as a proud Navajo is undermined by this tainted heritage. After breaking up with Sammi, he launches into an almost obligatory town-drunk phase, nearly destroying his chances at a boxing career.

Black Cloud must conquer his inner demons in order to win in the boxing ring. (That plot device you could see coming a mile away.) One form of regeneration through violence occurs in the ring with Bud when Black Cloud breaks down and weeps over the loss of his mother, his father's drinking, and the knowledge of his white great-grandfather. Is it this violent act, the power of his own fists against Bud's gloves, that redeems him? I think not. Then, from where does it come? To answer this, we must consider how the all-important wilderness has been manipulated in this film.

In the classic Western, the wilderness is supposed to be a test of character, bringing out the best in the Anglo hero, and the worst in the villain. It is usually presented as a sacred Eden-like space of retreat for the protagonist. This is not the case in *Black Cloud*, where the Navajo reservation is cast as the wilderness, a colonized nation within a nation, the United States. Tension is created between what filmgoers see and what they hear. The beauty of the Navajo Nation makes cameo appearances on the screen when Black Cloud looks for solace, horses, or his grandfather. Yet, even when the natural beauty is shown, it's spoken of disparagingly by the Anglo characters in the film. For example, when Sheriff Powers drives out to Bud's home looking for Black Cloud, Bud greets him with "*Ya'at'teeh* (each vowel has a high tone) Sheriff. What brings you out here?" Sheriff Powers replies, "Well if I said it was the beautiful scenery, I would be lying, wouldn't I?" Later in the film, while standing in front of her parents' HUD home, Eddie Young says, "Look around you, Sammi; this is your future—pretty, ain't it?"

From the perspective of the Anglo characters in *Black Cloud*, the wilderness is a worn-out wasteland; it symbolizes the loss of their parents' or grandparents' frontier hopes. Such a reading echoes classics such as *Hud* (1962) or *The Last Picture Show* (1971). *Black Cloud* actually fits into the subgenre of the end-of-the-West Western, insofar as the West, the Nation's young region, is portrayed as no longer sustaining a viable way of life. The twist is that this is true for the Indian characters in the film as well as the whites.

Unlike typical Westerns that present indigenous peoples as one-dimensional stereotypes, this film at least attempts to portray multidimensional Native characters: Sammi's self-reflection, Bud's thoughtful mentoring, or Black Cloud's turmoil over identity. Pearl Means, Navajo, wife of Russell Means, said that in her opinion the film succeeds in showing that "we are human beings in the 21st century. We are portrayed with all the feelings, emotions, desires, failures, and successes as any other race."[1] Means continues, "If we are not shown as drunks, or in period pieces, or with the hero or savior being a white man, like in 'Dances with Wolves' and 'Windtalkers,' they are not interested in showing us as real human beings that can succeed."[2] One has to wonder if Pearl Means has actually seen the commercial version of the film, for indeed, contrary to her statement, many of the Native Americans in the film are portrayed as drunks.

While the portrayal of alcohol consumption is positive more often than negative in American films generally, alcohol use by Native Americans is almost always abuse. In *Black Cloud*, alcohol and its abuse prevails, in part, because alcohol is an important element of the Western genre. Classic Westerns are replete with scenes of saloons, whiskey bottles, alcoholic gunfighters, and town drunks. As an anti-Western, *Black Cloud* is nonetheless peppered with scenes of rundown contemporary bars, house parties, drunken cowboys and Indians, Navajo youths cruising in cars with liquor, and an alcoholic father who parties incessantly.

At another level, alcohol, and perhaps beer in particular, is used in *Black Cloud* to portray the devastation that colonialism has wrought. Navajo people on the reservation must deal with prejudice and issues such as unemployment, lack of opportunity, and problem drinking on a daily basis. In contrast to the snippets of beautiful landscape, many of the other on-reservation scenes depict rundown housing, drunken parties, or domestic violence. These images effectively convey dead-end lives, fractured culture, irreparable generational gaps, the clashes between modernity and tradition and youths and elders that collectively make up the American Indian end-of-the-frontier dream. For Black Cloud, boxing becomes a means to make all of this recede.

After his drunken binges, Black Cloud seeks out his grandfather for help with understanding what he has learned about his heritage. Upon seeing him, his grandfather says:

> GF: Things have changed, I can see it in your eyes.
> B.C.: I am a mixed-blood now.
> GF: The truth was always the truth, now it is known and it is good.... You have to lose yourself before you find yourself.
> B.C.: I can't find crap. It is all decided for me.
> GF: Are you done whining? Let's walk.

Grandfather takes him to a sweathouse and provides him with a special tea before telling him the story of White Wolf. As Grandfather sings, Black Cloud begins to have a vision that transports him to the spirit world. While his grandfather narrates the story, "In the last days, a girl named Nanibah took a pony to a special place where she would pick flowers for her wedding," Black Cloud spies her. He continues to watch as Nanibah is captured and raped after "Three white men came upon her. Nanibah was found, wandering, with her head full of demons, by a white hunter. He became White Wolf, your great-great-grandfather. He brought great honor to our people, we accepted him as our own." Afterwards, Grandfather tells him, "Rest, I will be waiting on the other side." In the morning, Black Cloud finds him dead outside the sweathouse. He buries him according to traditional Navajo custom.

By crossing the border to the place of the ancestors, Black Cloud learns that not all white men are evil; some are good. This squelches his anger against Euro-Americans. Thus, it is this violent act—the rape of his great-great-grandmother—that provides Black Cloud with redemption. When the violence of boxing surfaces a bit later, it offers him an opportunity to visit with his deceased mother during the last fight of the Olympic tryouts. She offers him guidance and then tells him to return to the world of the living in order to fulfill his destiny. After regaining consciousness, he wins the match.

Black Cloud's message puts a different slant on the Western genre. First, it is addressed to Native Americans rather than to Euro-Americans. Second, rather than demonstrating the ethical culpability of whites, or making an appeal for peaceful coexistence until American Indians can learn civilized ways, or claiming that Native American cultures are morally superior alternatives to modernity, as have previous forms of alternative Westerns, it calls for the indigenous peoples of North America to look at the past with open eyes, learn from it, and move on; that is, for American Indians to free themselves from the shackles of their colonial past that are causing them to live in what is held to be contemporary depravity, by acknowledging what was done to their ancestors by Europeans and Euro-Americans, but not allowing that knowledge to paralyze them. The message it promotes is, therefore, individualistic—live your own life and fulfill your own destiny—making this an anti-tribal, end-of-the-West Western.

NOTES

1. Brenda Norrell, "Denver Police Arrest 245 for Blocking Columbus Day Parade," *Indian Country Today*, October 14, 2004.
2. Ibid.

CHAPTER 9

Death Wish, Indian-Style

Dear Diary:

Today I watched the rough cut of N-Joe. Not bad, Burtie. Must schedule lunch and beg him to star in my newest property, Citizen Sitting Bull. *I weep just thinking about the sad ending that I've written (subtitled in Lakota): "Murdered by one of your own." Think of all the products we can market around C.S.B. I smell the money from here. Oh wait, that's my cologne.*

Love ya lots,

Hollywood

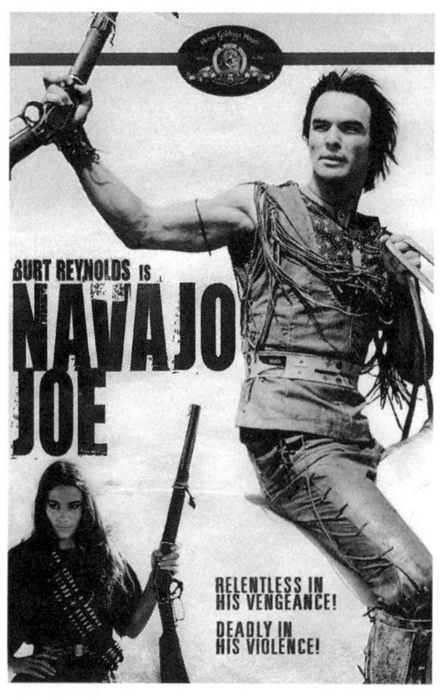

Navajo Joe

Theo. Van Alst

Somewhere in the wilds of northeast Connecticut, circa 2008:

student (proudly Irish-American, BTW): Well, just because John Ford used Navajos who spoke Navajo in *The Searchers* who were supposed to be Comanches, it's no big deal.

instructor: Why not?

student: Because nobody would know the difference.

instructor: The Comanches would know. The Navajos would know. Lots of Indians would know.

student: Yeah. But that's not that many people.

instructor: OK. I'm making a movie about the IRA and the UDF. I'm going to use people from Iceland speaking Björkian. Iceland is about as close to Ireland as Navajoland is to where the Comanches live. It all sounds the same, and besides, all you white people look alike to me.

student: But that's different. People would know.

instructor: But not that many. And we're showing it in America. Who would know? What's the difference?

student: B-b-but, but, but . . .

INSTRUCTOR: Young man, if I made a movie about the IRA and the UDF set in Belfast and used only people from Dublin as the actors and they saw it over there, the whole province would be pissed. Does that help you?
STUDENT: Uuuuh . . .

I believe that "seeing red" is mentioned somewhere in the title of this collection, and we will do that very thing, although we'll also see shades (or perhaps tints) of red as well. Specifically, I refer to the color "orangey" in this context. Remember this singular color when I tell you how my wife and children refer to our film, and taunt me with their doctored song lyrics sung loudly for days afterward, as you read about the totally fried and half-baked weirdness that is *Navajo Joe* (1968). So that you might understand the visual aspect of the man they all know as "Nacho Joe," my kids tell me that "Burt Reynolds looks like he fell in a giant bag of Doritos."

Navajo Joe (1966) was the first serious Italian attempt to portray a full-blooded Native character[1] since Sergio Leone's Dad, Vincenzo, and his Ma, Edvige, cranked out *La vampira indiana* back in 1913. The film opens with an "Indian" woman in the standard issue buckskins and headband. Carrying some animal skins and furs, she dreamily (yes, dreamily—and it's rather unsettling) makes her way to what looks like a small river or stream, where she is promptly met by a man on a horse. As she begins to pound one of the skins with a stone (I think she's doing the laundry), he dismounts. She smiles up at him, and he pulls out a revolver. She runs away, and he shoots her twice in the back. As other riders appear and begin shooting and riding through the encampment, the first man scalps the woman he has just shot; the accompanying Morricone soundtrack[2] abruptly announces the commencement of atrocities. We then see the scalp in bloody detail. It becomes readily apparent that this film will be quite unlike its German counterparts, which feature blood and gore only minimally. We also note that the theme song "Navajo Joe" sounds strikingly similar to the liturgical chorus of "Abolição,"[3] featured in Morricone's 1968 score of Gillo Pontecorvo's *Queimada* (Burn!), a film that also deals with interracial violence.

As the full company of horsemen ride off from their desecration, the credits roll, and the camera pauses on a scalp that is tied to a white horse. More scalps appear tied to other horses, and we confirm the profession of the riders. Corbucci has cut through to a Marxist critique of the American West; dead Indian bodies equal capital.[4]

Our introduction to the title character is through the first scalp hunter, the leader of the gang. As he spies a lone figure on a hilltop, he says: "Damned Indian. He's still on our trail." He sends two riders after who we assume is "Navajo Joe," and they are promptly killed. After hearing the gunshots that spell their doom, a blond-haired member of the bandits turns to the leader and says, "You should have let me do the job. . . . I'd be bringing you back his scalp by now." When the leader[5] (whose name we later find out from a "Wanted" poster is Mervyn "Vee" Duncan) tells him, "Maybe he would have had yours," the blond replies, "You're just too stupid. . . . You're real smart aren't you brother. Just like a true half-breed." Half-breed? This should be interesting; there would seem to be a conflict between mixed-blood and full-blood Native characters, though this is not clear from the scene. The leader says: "Be careful brother—I won't ever let anyone call me a bastard." Bastard? Half-breed to bastard is a pretty stretchy translation in any language, but it's Italy, so let's roll the dice and see what happens.

When they arrive in the town where they intend to sell the scalps, they find there is a price on their heads (*ooooh*, irony). The sheriff tells them he won't pay for scalps any more. The ones in the past he did pay for were those of "troublemakers." He tells the gang that now they're "attacking peaceful tribes, and that's murder." Mervyn replies, "Indians are all the same to me—they're red bastards." Hmmm. There's that word again.

A man who is an old friend of Mervyn tells them about a train arriving in the town of Esperanza (Hope! Double hope! A train to get us out of here!). He has this information because he's married to the banker's daughter. He is now a "respectable" doctor of medicine, but still a crook at heart. He tells the bandit leader to rob the train, and that he will provide the combination to the safe on board. We also find out what the murdered Native people were worth to their killers when the doctor compares the "half a million dollars" the safe contains with the "dollar a scalp"[6] that Mervyn and his gang would have received.

As we begin to wonder what happened to the last surviving member of the village who retained his scalp, we quickly receive an answer. Out in the gathering darkness, Joe strikes; he kills two men and leaves an unexplained double triangle symbol carved in a wooden post. Another question goes unanswered; audiences might wonder why there is no buildup to the train robbery, as we might expect in a "traditional" or American Western. The train robbery takes place shortly after we meet Joe, and the bandits make off with their prize, driving the train away to await the doctor's arrival with the combination so they can open the safe on board. American audiences surely experienced at least some disorientation at first view.

Joe returns in a low angle shot that frames him against the sky; we note that scenes with Navajo Joe usually begin or end with him so framed atop a hill, or against the sky, occasionally in silhouette. Joe takes on the bandits in the dark, and even gives one the old Shatterhand, knocking him out. He's extremely adept at dispatching his foes with the knife (a possible holdover from the German films and Karl May novels), as well as a feather-draped rifle. We also find out that he can drive a train when he takes it back from the bandits, and that he can communicate with his horse via whistles. I'm taking my dice back at this point on the Indian stereotype and half-breed thing, but I'll lay down my cards on the politics.

A great show is made of the ruling class of the town that is the train's final destination. Leftist Corbucci's smallish critique of the bourgeoisie is introduced in this scene. We are obsequiously introduced by a priest[7] to the mayor, the sheriff, and the banker and his daughter, who is married to the doctor who has set up the inside job of the train robbery. The piano player and the dancehall women[8] who escaped an earlier saloon massacre (these bandits always kill everyone they meet "so there are no witnesses") arrive in town needing medical aid; one of the women has been shot. This fact is explained in detail by a character named "Estella," who it appears may be meant to represent a Native woman. Her manner of dress is noticeably different from that of the other townspeople, and she looks in her clothing and physical appearance remarkably like the woman who was scalped in the opening scene. Since she speaks English with a marked accent retained in the English dub, and is told by the doctor's wife to "fetch his bag," we can assume she is at the very least an "other" or subaltern of some sort. The doctor who is to treat the injured woman is of course the evil ex-bandit. She will die later by his hand during "treatment."

Joe brings his captured train into town. He explains that it has "already cost many lives," and that he took it from Duncan to save the townspeople's lives. They all stare at him, and then express their true priorities, asking, "Where's the money?" When they find the money intact, the doctor's wife says: "Then we should take it to the bank as quickly as possible."

They soon find the telegraph wires are cut, and since the town of Esperanza is a "peaceful place, without a single gun," they are "doomed." They rather calmly ponder their fate, until Joe (after exchanging meaningful glances with Estella, confirming her "otherness") offers to kill the bandit leader "for a price." He is quickly told that the townspeople don't "make bargains with Indians." The doctor's wife wants at least to hear his offer. Joe's sense of justice asks for "a dollar a head, plus the reward for the Duncans, for every bandit" he kills. The evil doctor tells him: "Get moving, Indian." A steely-eyed (well at least they're brown) Burt Reynolds replies: "Why don't you try and move me?" He jumps on his horse, bareback of course, as Estella looks on longingly. He tells the townspeople that someone from their town helped Duncan rob the train and betrayed them all, and that this person could betray them again. He rides off. The doctor offers to ride off for help. The camera cuts to Joe framed (yet again) on a hilltop, his howling, haunting theme playing in the background.[9] He rides into an area filled with feathers, spears, skins, and skulls on sticks with long hair and feathered headbands still attached. This, the audience is meant to understand, is the ghost town that Joe's village has become.

Back in the town, one of the refugees from the saloon massacre tells the mayor that he has sent away the only man who can help them. The sheriff says, "That Indian was just a liar," but the priest says, "Maybe we can get that *boy* to come back here." The scene ends of course, with a cut to Estella.

Sure enough, up in the hills among the skulls and feathered sticks:

NAVAJO JOE: "What do you want?"

ESTELLA: "My mistress sent me . . ."

NAVAJO JOE: "Who's Indian? Your father or your mother?"

ESTELLA: "My mother. You're a Navajo, aren't you? What's your name?'

NAVAJO JOE: "Joe."

ESTELLA: "I've never known an Indian named Joe. And I've never seen a Navajo so far south before."

NAVAJO JOE: "And I never met an Indian girl that asks so many questions. Go back and tell your mistress I'll save her money for her. One more thing—I'll need some dynamite."

Yup. Dynamite!

Back in town, the bourgeoisie are nervous and say, "Damned Indian" and "Time was we'd pay a dollar for his scalp," even though the doctor's wife says, "The Indian will protect us." Joe returns to expose the doctor, who, according to a suddenly spiritual Joe, has "taken the wrong way." He then convinces them that he's the only man who can save them and sets out his demands. When he gets to "And one other thing . . . ," the sheriff says, "What do you want?" In an awkward moment, there is a pan to Estella, and the camera lingers for two or three heartbeats with Joe looking her way. Then it swings back to Joe pointing his rifle at the sheriff's star.

The tension builds as the first overtly political scene in the film continues. The mayor's wife asks Joe if he wants to be appointed sheriff, and he replies, "That's right."

The sheriff loudly protests: "An Indian sheriff? That can't be. The only ones elected in this country are *Americans.*"

Joe says: "My father was born here. In the mountains. And his father before him. And his father before him. And his father before him. Where was your father born?"

"What has that to do with it?"

Joe pokes him in the ribs with his feather-draped rifle and continues: "I said where was he born?"

The sheriff replies, "In Scotland."

Joe responds, "My father was born here, in America. And his father before him. And his father before him. And his father before him. Now which of us is American?" He takes the star and says, "That's mine. It belongs to me."

The bandits show up, pretending to have captured the doctor. Joe has told everyone to stay inside. After finding the bank empty, Mervyn loses patience and shoots the doctor. The sight of him dying causes his wife to run out from her hiding place and into the street after him. She is shot as well. They crawl toward each other, their greed binding them in their death throes. She tells him: "Darling. Chester. The Indian has it all. He hid it. It's my fault. I gave it to him." Mervyn interjects: "So. All the money's with the Indian." She dies, saying, "Forgive me darling." Mervyn (and the director) fills them full of bullets for good measure.

Joe lets the dynamite fly and the fight begins. Mervyn quickly finds Estella, and, like the caveman that he resembles, drags her out of the building by her hair, letting Joe know loudly: "Hey Indian. Come out. . . . Throw your gun down or I'm gonna kill this woman. . . . Can you see her? She's an Indian like you are. Get down here fast, redskin, if you don't want this squaw to die!"

Joe throws down his befeathered rifle, which the bandit leader picks up. The camera cuts to Joe being beaten while a man plays a harmonica and Mervyn sensuously strokes his horse. They're trying to make him talk, but Joe refuses. "Speak, you damned Indian! Where did you put all that money?" In a page taken from Karl May (German writer who wrote about the American West until his death in 1912), Mervyn breaks out the rawhide whip as his gang stands around grinning. The leader has them string Joe up by his feet, in an upside-down St. Peter–like position, leaving him to hang overnight.

Joe escapes with the help of the piano player. He comes back to attack the bandits, shooting a flaming arrow with a note attached into the side of the building. We don't see him do this, but Mervyn's brother lets us know: "It's a note from the Indian. It was attached to an *arrow*!" To save the townspeople, Joe tells them the money is in the train, but if he hears another shot he'll take off with both. Mervyn lets the townspeople know that if it's a trick, he'll burn down the church with all of them in it. We know he's serious; as we've seen, he insists on killing *everyone* at the scenes of his crimes. After the priest tries the "man of god" approach without success, he finally asks Mervyn what the problem is. We then discover the source of the "half-breed bastard" exchange from the beginning of the film. Mervyn tells the priest he was beaten as a boy, and even called "a bastard!" This "brought his hatred," he says, for "Indians, like my mother, and I kill white people, like my father. My father. A preacher like you, a minister. Bred by mercy. But I got a bad break when somebody killed him and beat me to the punch." He sends his brother out to check the train.

A shot of his brother at the train reveals the money in plain sight. He gives the prearranged signal that all is well and blasts the train whistle three times. The bandits prepare to leave. The priest says: "Thank you for sparing our lives," and of course Mervyn shoots him dead.

Just as we might have suspected, the train is a trap. Joe furiously attacks, employing his requested dynamite and many, *many* rounds of cartridges in a fight that shows no sign of the Magic Bullet theory. As I've worked it out so far, after a viewing of Ford's *Stagecoach* (1939), the

Magic Bullet theory states that white bullets invariably find their mark; and no matter what angle they are fired from, they are almost 100 percent fatal. It's as if the mere act of a white man firing at an Indian is enough to kill him. However, it takes many, many, *many* Indian shots to strike a white character, and if one does find its mark by some odd act of fate, it will usually hit him in the meat of the shoulder, or the lower leg, or better yet, graze his cheek, so as to give him that manly wounded-but-not-grotesque look that oddly enough often mirrors the "war-painted Indians" he's trying to kill. On other occasions, the "perfect" signifier will find its mark, and the character will take an arrow in the side, or some other place that he can easily access so as to perform the ultimate manly act of snapping off the head and pulling the shaft out of his own body.

Okay, back to the film.

As the bandits ride down the rails, Joe seems to appear along the tracks, riding on his horse just ahead of the engine. They shoot wildly, eventually bringing down the rider—who is actually Mervyn's brother, bound, gagged, and tied to the horse[10]—a ruse discovered when they all disembark, whooping and hollering, to confirm their kill of "the Indian." Joe shortly dispatches the remaining members of the bandits, and even carves the double triangles in a former torturer's forehead. This sets up the final showdown with Mervyn.

The sole survivor of Joe's revenge begins to yell. "You won't escape now, redskin!" Come on out, Indian! You're finished! You're through! I'll pin your scalp to my saddle, you filthy, stinkin' Indian! Damn you! . . . Face it Indian—I outsmarted you!" We see Joe sneak up behind him and quickly disarm the bandit leader, who pleads: "I know you're a bounty hunter. Let me live." Joe finds a double-triangle necklace hanging around Mervyn's neck—"This belonged to my woman! Do you remember her? You're gonna pay for her life!" Joe gives him a beating, but when he decides against using the rifle to finish him off and makes a move for the more personal "tomahawk," Mervyn pulls out a pistol and shoots him. Joe staggers around, but manages to throw the weapon into Mervyn's forehead before he collapses.

Joe's horse rides into town carrying the money. Someone asks, "Where's the Indian?" A townsperson replies, "Who cares? The money is all that counts." Estella tells his horse, "Go back to him." And it does. The film ends, along with, thankfully, no more attempts to represent "traditional" Native culture in a Spaghetti Western. Wait a minute, maybe Tarantino and Dario Argento will remake *La vampira indiana* . . .

NOTES

1. Burt Reynolds, whose Cherokee heritage is as well-known as it is apocryphal (though not deniable, at least according to the Department of Housing and Urban Development—see "Celebrities of Native American Heritage," *Public and Indian Housing-American Indian Heritage Month* at *http://www.hud.gov/offices/pih/ih/codetalk/onap/celebrities.cfm*, 30 May 2009, where they also list "Quinten Tarrantino [*sic*]—Cherokee Actor—Film producer") in the title role of Navajo Joe may be, like the casting of Lee Van Cleef in *Captain Apache* (1971), a stretch as well. However, it somehow makes more sense than Steve McQueen as a "half-breed" Nevada Smith (1966), though of course there are stories out there about his "part-Indian" heritage as well, which I can only ascribe to the power of the cinema. Other unconfirmed tales surrounding *Navajo Joe* have Burt Reynolds pronouncing it "the worst experience of my life," something we might attribute to the story that Reynolds only took the role because he believed the Sergio directing it was *Leone*, rather than Corbucci. And

though Corbucci didn't despise his actors as much as, say, Lucio Fulci, one story tells how Sergio Corbucci drove into the middle of the Almeria desert with Burt Reynolds and left him there to find his own way back to town on foot (*http://www.spaghetti-western.net/index.php/Navajo_Joe* [1 June 2009]).

2. Christopher Frayling describes a signature Morricone theme "as a simple electric guitar line . . . made more appropriate to the tone of the film, by the addition of yells . . . shrieks, gunshots, rifles being cocked, church bells, whipping sounds, trills, whines, rhythmic jew's-harp and other assorted electronic effects, to 'punctuate' the basically traditional Western score" (*Spaghetti Westerns: Cowboys and Europeans from Karl May to Sergio Leone* [London: I.B. Tauris, 2006]). *Navajo Joe* presents this cacophonous eruption (with the guitar line introduced afterward) as the murderer leans to his task.
3. A wonderful version can be found at *http://www.youtube.com/watch?v=yktc_P4FL_4*, filmed live in Warsaw, Poland (as part of the "TPSA Music & Film Festival"), performed by the Polish Radio Orchestra, the Mixed Choir of the Fryderyk Chopin Academy of Music, and the Warsaw Inter-University Choir.
4. Corbucci continued to work with political and social issues of the day. In addition to the Milián-as-Ché political tale *Vamos a matar, compañeros* (*Companeros*, 1970), he wrote and directed *Il grande silenzio* (*The Great Silence*, 1968). We can consider this film as notable for two things: one is the continuous presence of snow, the other is the presence of African American characters and the tensions and politics that surround them. A line from the governor in the film is most telling: "The Old West is finished. We must learn to live with people of all races and persuasions, and unite to make a New West." The main female character, Pauline (Vonetta McGee), is married to a man forced into a life of crime because no one would give him any work. Klaus Kinski is up to his usual evil ways; after he kills the man, he says, "What times we live in when a black is worth as much as a white man." Later in the film when the sheriff attacks Pauline, all the white women come out to help her (we must remark on signs of any feminist consciousness in a Spaghetti Western, as those moments are few and far between). In the end though, it is the man who is the hero: "He avenges our wrongs." "They call him 'Silence' because wherever he goes, the silence of death follows."
5. The actor who plays this character looks amazingly like late-night TV host Jimmy Kimmel, but with a beard.
6. Incidentally, the original Italian title of the film was *Un dollaro a testa* (A dollar a head).
7. A man in a Roman collar, at any rate.
8. Various reviews cast these women as "prostitutes," though that seems entirely unapparent to me. The site imdb.com lists them in the cast as "saloon girls." http://www.imdb.com/title/tt0061587/ (1 June 2009).
9. This image was apparently strong enough to resonate with Quentin Tarantino, who used Morricone's piece "A Silhouette of Doom" along with "Navajo Joe Main Title" to great effect in *Kill Bill Vol. 2*. We should also note that the bride's ax blow to the head of one of the Crazy 88s in *Vol. 1* is a direct echo of the climax of *Navajo Joe*.
10. This "astonishing" ruse is played to good effect in *V for Vendetta* (2005) and still seemed to shock those members of the audience around me who insisted on talking during a screening of *The Dark Knight* (2008).

DEAR DIARY:

Everyone knows that there are two sides to every story. The wrong side and the side those know-it-all critics write in Variety. *Hum? What if we give them a true story? Something true, like: "Manic-depressive Native American boy wants to get married, but first goes on a rampage, kills his would-be father-in-law, a Mormon, kidnaps his girlfriend, and inadvertently kills her desire to become a torch singer." Now that's a story!*

Note to Self: Call Robert Blake's agent! Maybe he can play a manic-depressive killer.

Happy trails,

HOLLYWOOD

Tell Them Willie Boy Is Here

CLIFFORD E. TRAFZER

Backstory. In 2006, the family of William Mike traveled in a caravan through the Morongo Indian Reservation on Field Road, winding their way up the foothills of the San Bernardino Mountains. Near the top of the hill, they passed the Catholic church and turned left into the old tribal cemetery. There they placed headstones on the graves of William Mike and his daughter, Carlotta Mike, both of whom died violently in 1909 from gunshot wounds. The family always knew the location of the two graves, but until recently lacked the resources to purchase respectable headstones for their relatives. They prayed and sang over the graves in a memorial service that included ancient Salt songs, performed to help the deceased make their way north, the direction of death. The family of William Mike remembers the events surrounding William and Carlotta's death as if they occurred yesterday. It was only with the publication of Harry Lawton's novel *Willie Boy* in 1960, and Universal Pictures's release of the movie *Tell Them Willie Boy Is Here* nine years later, that a portion of this story was made known to the wider public. The film stars Robert Redford as Sheriff Christopher (Coop) Cooper, Katherine Ross as Lola, Robert Blake as Willie Boy, and Susan Clark as Liz, the love interest for Coop, although it goes nowhere.

All are good actors, but the film feels like 1969, tainted by a decade of civil unrest. It's as if the filmmakers were banking on the audience to bring their disgust for the Vietnam War and their disdain for "the man" (read, the federal government) into the theater as they watched the film.

Tell Them Willie Boy Is Here never achieves the ambience of a 1909 California reservation. Even the costumes worn by the actors are off. It's also important to remember that in November 1969 a group of American Indians from the San Francisco Bay area began their occupation of Alcatraz Island. American Indians are fighting for their human rights, and tribal sovereignty over their reservation lands.

Plot: The filmmakers worked with a script based on Lawton's novel and historical documents; director Abraham Polonsky and Universal Studio's publicity department proclaimed that their movie was an accurate depiction of the tragic events surrounding William's and Carlotta's real deaths. Their claims notwithstanding, *Tell Them Willie Boy Is Here* is mostly a work of fiction—appealing and enjoyable at times, irritatingly bogus and contrived at others. For whatever reason, both Polonsky and his writers (for whom Lawton served as an advisor) chose to ignore what Indian people knew about Willie Boy's story, despite the fact that many of them worked on the film as actors and extras. This decision was especially reprehensible in the case of Katherine Siva Saubel, a respected Cahuilla Indian elder, noted historian, and accomplished writer, who was selected to play Carlotta's mother. Saubel and her family were close friends of Segundo Chino, one of Willie Boy's trackers, and had learned from him the finer points of the manhunt. Apparently Polonsky did not want this kind of indigenous knowledge to interfere with his simplistic adventure story, which is filled with clichés of good versus evil, and Indian savagery versus white civilization.

The Mike family and other Indians view the Willie Boy incident as a great tragedy that few white people get right. Chemehuevis and Southern Paiutes explain that the real story is one of love—not lust, liquor, and arrogance, as portrayed in Lawton's book and Polonsky's film. According to Chemehuevi elders, Willie Boy lived in Chemehuevis Valley on the California side of the Colorado River. He left the area as a young man and moved west, residing in such towns as Victorville and San Bernardino. Eventually Willie Boy moved in with his grandmother, Mrs. Teacup, at the Indian village at Twentynine Palms, which Chemehuevis shared with its original inhabitants, the Serrano Indians. William Mike also lived in Twentynine Palms, serving as a community and religious leader. Mike had a very large family of boys and girls, including the sixteen-year-old Carlotta, whom Lawton and Polonsky have renamed Lola in the film. Perhaps they thought "Carlotta" sounded too *Phantom of the Opera*-ish. Were they hoping it would make Katherine Ross's character seem, well, sexier? I dunno.

Back to the truer version of the story.

Chemehuevi people say that Willie Boy and Carlotta "made eyes at each other" (fell in love). However, when Willie asked her to marry him, she refused, waiting for her father's permission. And yet, the movie *Willie Boy* scarcely develops the romance between Willie and Carlotta, relegating it to a few of the opening scenes. Afterwards, the love affair is dropped, replaced by a narrative in which Carlotta is portrayed as little more than an object to be manipulated by Willie until he ultimately turns on her. Faring no better is Willie, who is reduced to a drunken Indian consumed with hatred for Mike. The fact that Chemehuevis insist that Willie did not drink and was a noted runner does not seem to have mattered at all to filmmakers Polonsky and Lawton's portrayal of events.

According to the novel and screen version of the story, Willie got drunk and made love to Carlotta in the bushes. (It is interesting to note that Polonsky juxtaposes Willie and Carlotta's—I mean Lola's—lovemaking in the wild with that of Sheriff Christopher Cooper [Robert Redford] with Indian Agent Arnold [Susan Clarke], who do their fornicating like civilized folk, in bed). When William discovers the couple, anger leads to accusations, etc.—and, so the story says, *Willie Boy* kills William Mike. In reality, no one knows what happened during that fateful encounter. However, Chemehuevis suggest that Willie went to see William to ask for Carlotta's hand in marriage, carrying a rifle with him because he feared William Mike, who was both physically and spiritually powerful. He did not intend to murder him. When Willie met William, however, the two men likely argued and fought, with Willie eventually killing William.

Following William's death, Willie and Carlotta fled into the Mojave Desert, going through a rocky pass known as The Pipes. A posse from the Riverside County Sheriff's Department chased the couple on horseback with the aid of volunteers and two Indian police officers, including Segundo Chino (Chemehuevi/Pass Cahuilla) and John Hyde (Kumeyaay/Diegueño). While passing through The Pipes, a bullet killed Carlotta. The film, however, fails to depict Carlotta's death at The Pipes, opting instead for the posse's account that Willie Boy viciously raped, tortured, and murdered her. Lawton based this version of Carlotta's death on posse members' testimony that she had left "signs" in the sand indicating Willie's abuse. In the film, Indian trackers also see these signs. Chemehuevis, however, dismiss this account, insisting that no such written language exists, and that the posse was using Willie Boy as a scapegoat. Scholars James Sandos and Larry Burgess side with the Chemehuevis here and propose that John Hyde most likely shot at a person in the rocks wearing or holding Willie's well-known leather coat. The lucky (or unlucky) shot hit and killed Carlotta, and the posse blamed Willie for her death. The posse took her body to the Morongo Reservation, where relatives buried her in the cemetery next to her father. The Chemehuevis sang Salt songs all night, just as Willie would have sung to direct Carlotta's spirit to the other world and to comfort himself.

According to Chemehuevi elders, after Carlotta's death, Willie traveled from The Pipes to Ruby Mountain, where he waited in ambush for the posse to return. When he spotted them, he killed their horses, wounding one of the trackers in the process. Indian oral tradition states that Willie could have killed and wounded many more, but he preferred to put his manhunters on their feet to see who among them could survive the Mojave Desert's brutal environment. In the film, Sheriff Cooper climbs a mountain to surprise Willie, who sits stoically wearing his Ghost Dance shirt. Of course, since Coop is played by Robert Redford, he gives Willie a chance to surrender peacefully. Willie, however, turns and fires and is killed by the sheriff. Only afterwards did Coop discover that Willie's rifle contained no bullets.

According to historical documents, the posse reported that Willie killed himself. (Lawton agreed, but Indian elders disagree.) They stated that as they pulled out from Ruby Mountain, they heard one last shot, and concluded that Willie had committed suicide. Rather than returning with his body, they claimed to have cremated it (which would have been difficult as the site contains little wood). On their last trip to Ruby Mountain, the posse had traveled with a professional so he could take pictures of Willie's corpse for the enjoyment of readers following the story. However, it's suspicious that rather than taking the usual close-up shots of dead outlaws, the photographer limited his photos to long-range shots of a body lying in the shadow of a big rock.

Indian elders again disagree with the movie and historical accounts. According to Katherine

Saubel, tracker Segundo Chino confided to her family that the posse never got Willie, dead or alive. Indians believe he left Ruby Mountain, traveling east to Twentynine Palms. Years later, Nellie Holms Mike told a columnist that Willie went to Twentynine Palms to get supplies and see his grandmother, Mrs. Teacup. She reported that Mrs. Teacup got so angry with her grandson for causing the deaths of Carlotta and Mr. Mike that she tossed his rifle into a pond located near the village. (It is of interest that years later, the owner of the pond drained it and found a rusty rifle). According to Nellie Morongo, Willie reacted by grabbing and violently shaking his grandmother, an outburst that some Indians claim led to her death. Chemehuevi elder Joe Benitez, the grandson of William Mike, reported that Willie fled from Twentynine Palms and traveled north, where he lived in a cave. When the posse ended its manhunt and concocted their story of Willie's suicide, Willie traveled northeast to the area around Pahrump. Indian historians Matthew Levias and Kenneth Anderson report that tribal elders claim that Willie lived among the Paiutes southeast of Las Vegas, Nevada, where he ultimately died of tuberculosis.

It is ironic that although Polonsky and Lawton claimed to be "friends of the Indians," the book and the movie versions of the Willie Boy story all but ignored Chemehuevi accounts. It appears that both the novelist and director cynically chose to cash in on public interest about the emerging Red Power movement of the later 1960s, yet created a crowd-pleasing action flick that was more in keeping with Hollywood clichés that had little respect either for historical accuracy or the feelings of the Mike family, the people it was based on.

William's and Carlotta's relatives have not forgotten the tragic events that befell them. They remember them at funerals and memorials, where they sing Salt songs and reestablish their relationship with the dead, just as the Mike family did when they met at the Morongo cemetery to place headstones on the graves of William and Carlotta. They have been laid to rest, but many believe Willie's soul is disquieted by false representations of his life, including those in the film *Tell Them Willie Boy Is Here.*

Dear Diary:

How can I lay my hands on some of that sweaty tourist money this summer? Politically speaking, the time has probably never been better for a big budget Billy Jack *remake. Yah, that's the ticket. Think of the cross-marketing possibilities: Wrangler, Tony Lama, Stetson, MoveOn.org. Does anyone know if Laughlin uses e-mail? He would be perfect to play the aging sheriff with a big belly.*

Love ya,

Hollywood

Billy Jack

Scott Richard Lyons

Three memories from my childhood come to mind as I consider the cultural tour de force that is the Billy Jack franchise. The first is my uncle Vern learning karate from a book sometime between the years 1973 and 1975. I remember watching him with great admiration and awe as he practiced his kicks in my grandparents' backyard, pausing only to take an occasional sip from his can of beer. The second is me at the age of nine or ten preparing for a schoolyard wrestling match with one of my chums by taking a good three minutes to dramatically remove my shoes and socks (and then learning a lesson about the pitfalls of brawling in bare feet); anyone familiar with *Billy Jack* will recognize the scene I was trying to replicate. My third memory is an entire generation of young Indian men my uncle's age—he was born in the 1950s—wearing variations of what is now considered to be the standard American Indian Movement (AIM) uniform, but which was originally Billy Jack's iconic outfit: denim jeans and jacket, cowboy boots, a black flat-brimmed hat with a beaded headband. These are just childhood memories, hence subject to all of the usual caveats. Yet they are also images of an era that should not be underestimated for its cultural and political importance to Indians: Red Power. Indeed, I would go so far as to suggest that in the early to mid-seventies, we were all, in one way or another, Billy Jack.

Tom Laughlin, a Minneapolis-born white man, directed (under the pseudonym T. C. Frank) all four Billy Jack films. He cowrote the final three with wife Delores Taylor (who plays Billy's love interest, Jean, in the films) under the pseudonyms Frank and Teresa Christina. He also starred in the lead role. Laughlin created a classic American hero in the character of Billy, a "half-breed" ex–Green Beret living in the dusty wilds of some unnamed Arizona reservation after his return from Vietnam, where among other things, as we learn, he refused to participate in the My Lai Massacre. Using a combination of martial arts, gunplay, and mystical Indian tricks, Billy protects children, Natives, horses, and hippies from local oligarchs, corrupt cops, and racist rednecks. Like his nineteenth-century cultural ancestor, Cooper's Natty Bumppo from the *Leatherstocking Tales*, Billy understands both the supposedly civilized world, which he thinks a sham, and the Indian world, which represents a vastly more compelling alternative. Unlike Cooper, Laughlin didn't situate his character between different groups of warring savages—a narrative maneuver that couldn't help but create a false distinction between good and bad Indians—but rather between two irreconcilable political worlds: on the one side, a white supremacist reign of terror waged by powerful elites who take whatever they want in order to forge a society in their own image; on the other, a diverse, radical, and democratic society privileging the young, the female, the poor, the marginalized, and of course the Indian. While occupying a liminal space himself, Billy Jack always defends that second world without apology, as did Laughlin.

Billy Jack was the second and by far the most successful film in Laughlin's quartet. The first was *The Born Losers* (1967), an extremely violent exploitation film introducing Billy through a confrontation with an obnoxious biker gang terrorizing a small coastal town and running a rape house. It is in the second film, *Billy Jack* (1971), that Laughlin truly begins to flesh out his melancholy character and develop the themes that run throughout the series: social justice, environmentalism, nonviolent resistance, and more. In this film, Billy Jack defends an alternative school and hippie commune, located on tribal land, from small-minded townspeople and local leaders with ulterior motives. Although the movie predates the real-life Wounded Knee standoff by two years, it remarkably concludes with an outgunned Billy Jack holed up in a small church trying to keep surrounding authorities at bay. As its title indicates, *The Trial of Billy Jack* (1974) is set in the aftermath of *Billy Jack*'s standoff and provides more background for Billy's character, while simultaneously airing countercultural grievances against the 1970s status quo. Once again eerily echoing the real world, this time in the form of nearly reproducing some of the actual arguments advanced during the federal trials of AIM leaders Russell Means and Dennis Banks that same year, *The Trial of Billy Jack* goes beyond issues of guilt and innocence to put the SYSTEM on trial! The final film in the series, and certainly the strangest, is *Billy Jack Goes to Washington* (1977), basically a transposition of Frank Capra's classic *Mr. Smith Goes to Washington* (1939) into our hero's world. Amazingly, Capra's son, Frank Capra Jr., produced this film. In this version, as any decent Capra fan could guess, Billy is sent to Congress by political cynics banking on the notion that he will simply sit there clueless while they garner youth support for themselves and their nefarious agendas. Alas for them, as in the original, Billy figures out their corrupt plans and rights their wrongs—yes, by filibustering like James Stewart, but also more characteristically by going berserk.

Let me set a few things straight at this point, especially in light of the fairly high rating I have bestowed on *Billy Jack* and by extension the entire series. From the perspective of what we might call "cinematic pleasure," these films are not exactly the sort of thing you enjoy with popcorn and a loved one on the couch. All four films were low-budget to the point of shoestring production; they reflected some of the worst (as well as the best, as I address below) cultural tendencies of their era; and their violence, especially in *The Born Losers*, is often gratuitous and hard to take. I'll admit that I find scenes in all four of the films positively excruciating to watch, and I don't necessarily mean the violent ones. Yet the Billy Jack franchise is historically important for a number of reasons, starting with a savvy marketing and distribution technique Laughlin invented and used after *Billy Jack*'s disappointing initial release in 1971, which has since been studied not only by big studios but by DIY indie filmmakers as well. Charging Warner Brothers with ignoring the film they had promised to promote, Laughlin raised funds to rent theaters and buy publicity in key markets in hopes of generating enough buzz to get the film re-released. This novel strategy, called "four-walling," worked beautifully, and the 1973 re-release earned over $40 million; adjusted for inflation, that places *Billy Jack* in the top one hundred most successful films of all time. The series is also notable for its practical invention of two filmic subgenres that became popular during the 1970s: the martial-arts film and the vigilante film. Martial-arts movies had long been produced in places like Hong Kong, but it wasn't until 1973's *Enter the Dragon*, starring Bruce Lee, that the big studios began producing them. To what extent did *The Born Losers* and *Billy Jack*, both featuring the use of hapkido as Billy's weapon of choice, inspire the martial-arts film craze? As for the series' invention of the vigilante film, it would be difficult to argue that Billy Jack didn't pave the generic way for *Dirty Harry* (1971), *Death Wish* (1974), and the scores of other vigilante movies produced in the seventies right up to our own bloodthirsty times. For those innovations alone, Laughlin deserves his kudos.

More than that, though, I like these films for the same reasons my college students do (I regularly teach *Billy Jack* in a course on the culture of Red Power): because the franchise stands for values that, despite their still vital importance to our world, rarely get defended by politicians, public figures, and least of all protagonists in big action films. I'm talking about principles like compassion, respect, community, ecology, economic justice, peace, and antiracism. Billy Jack upholds these principles by serving as their superhero; when they come under attack, as the film's slogan has it, "he is always there!" My students are usually willing to overlook the occasional narrative clunkiness, awkward seventies-style improvisation, atrocious music, and bad amateur acting, because they are simply amazed by the very idea of a tough, wisecracking action hero siding with progressive principles that they want to support, like caring for runaway children, protecting nature, upholding democracy, and even defending tribal sovereignty. In a society such as our own, where the growth of our problems seems matched only by our increase in pessimism, a liberal, idealistic hero like Billy carries no small amount of appeal. He fights for the things we believe in, at a time when most of us don't.

Many critics have charged Laughlin with inconsistency on this point—for example, Roger Ebert, who in his 1971 review of *Billy Jack* confessed to feeling "somewhat disturbed by the central theme of the movie. *Billy Jack* seems to be saying the same thing as *The Born Losers*, that a gun is better than a constitution in the enforcement of justice. Is democracy totally obsolete, then? Is our only hope that the good fascists defeat the bad fascists?" In similar fashion, Howard Thompson's bad review in the *New York Times* (1971) protested, "For a picture that preaches pacifism, *Billy Jack* seems fascinated by violence, of which it is full." I think *Billy Jack* resists these accusations of contradiction because the question of violence is placed at the very center of its narrative—this, remember, in a film released during a time of growing militancy on the left when such questions were constantly being debated. In *Billy Jack* the debate over violence takes the form of an ongoing discussion between Billy and Jean—for example, when Billy discovers that Jean has been raped, and prepares to exact his revenge. Jean, advocating the principles of nonviolence advanced by Gandhi and King, naturally tries to talk him out of it:

> JEAN: Billy, please. We haven't crossed over that thin line yet, but if you kill [the rapist] you'll be doing just what they want. Can't you see that? You just can't keep making your own laws. There's got to be one set of laws for everyone, including you.
>
> BILLY: That's fine. When that set of laws is fairly applied to everyone then I'll turn the other cheek too.

Even in this snippet we can see the basic positions taken by advocates of both violent and nonviolent resistance, and one would be hard-pressed to find similar discussions in other action films, then or now. This is not some sort of "ironic" discourse on violence, i.e., the usual unconvincing defense of gratuitously violent films made by directors like Quentin Tarantino. (Is that torture scene an appeal to our baser instincts, or a commentary on those instincts?) It is, rather, a relatively substantive discussion of the moral implications of violence as a political strategy during the civil rights era. Laughlin and Taylor used their characters to reproduce these kinds of debates, which, once again, were fairly ubiquitous among actual leftist groups at the time, so audiences could consider them for themselves. That's not the obsolescence of democracy so much as the enactment of it.

Later in the film, Billy and Jean revisit the themes of violence and retributive justice in order to address a popular misunderstanding about philosophical nonviolence being the product of a higher spiritual state or some naturally compassionate personality trait:

> BILLY: We're different, you and I. Your spirit is more calm and pacific in you than any person I have ever known. And mine has been in a violent rage from the day that I was born. And you know something? I didn't really want it that way.
>
> JEAN: Billy, that's a bunch of crap. I'm no different than you. Do you think when [the rapist] was on top of me grunting and slobbering, I didn't hate? I hated more than anybody else on this earth ever hated. And every time that picture pops into my mind . . . I . . . oh! I've never hated so much in my life. When I think of that, I dismember and I mangle and I castrate [him] over and over and over in my mind, at least a million times a day. The bad part is . . . I couldn't tell you. You couldn't get your hate out, so I had to keep mine in. I knew what you'd do. But I knew how important it was to the kids. And I knew that their lives and their needs were more important than any hate that I had . . . I don't know. I don't know anymore.

She knows, of course—what she knows is that violence always begets more violence, so it is crucial to stop the cycle—but the point of this scene, which comes at the end of the film, is not to conclude the discussion so much as keep the conversation going by presenting it to viewers as a difficult moral conundrum. It's a cinematic contribution to the public sphere, as is the claim she implicitly makes during that moment of uncertainty: that we do things not because we are destined to do them, even less because our "spirits" are inclined that way, but simply because we choose to do them. That's a significant idea to communicate in a political film, because it counters the old Hollywood habit of representing good and evil as essential characteristics rather than what they really are: decisions, actions, things that can be done differently or changed.

It is true that "good fascists" can be found in the vast majority of vigilante films, and, as I've been saying, Laughlin can take a little credit for them as well. The formula for most vigilante films, as Dennis Lim has observed, is "basically a biblical credo: an eye for an eye . . . a vigilante hero is wronged and because of the failures of the legal system must take matters into his—or, in some cases, her—own hands." Given this credo, it comes as little surprise that vigilante films tend to be strictly right-wing affairs, hostile to ideas like due process or sociological theories of crime, not to mention compassion and forgiveness. Billy plays the strong man for sure, but Jean is always there too, providing yin to his yang, or more appropriately a New Testament theology of kindness against his old-time religion of retribution. It's the combination of these characters in tension that takes this vigilante film out of conservative ideology and, however unlikely this may seem, places it in more progressive realms of thought. Billy, guided by Jean as his conscience, may be closer to Malcolm X than Martin Luther King, but surely that doesn't make him Bernard Goetz.

Besides, let's not forget that for many oppressed groups in America during those years, especially communities of color, the legal system *was* a failure. Indeed, that is largely why the civil rights movement came into existence. Laughlin's films cannot be divorced from the civil rights context without doing violence to them. I think the trajectory of the *Billy Jack* series might actually be read as a civil rights historical roadmap, moving as it does from defense of oppressed individuals (*The Born Losers*), to militant confrontation with "legitimate" power structures (*Billy Jack*), to engagement with the court system (*The Trial of Billy Jack*), and finally to an attempted seizing of power using national electoral politics (*Billy Jack Goes to Washington*). To the extent that the series mirrors at least the intended direction of the civil rights movement (actual results are always another matter), it seems unlikely that any progress at all would be possible without at least the suggestion of militancy, even if it is safely located in a low-budget film where the main protagonists are constantly debating the moral implications of violent revolution.

In the final analysis, *Billy Jack* and the rest of Laughlin's quartet reflect the best and the worst of the '60s and '70s civil rights period (and in so doing completely resemble Native American movements like AIM). For every painfully awkward hippie sing-along at the Freedom School, there is a refreshing and remarkable character like Jean. For every corny speech about becoming "brother to the snake" (spoiler alert: it involves being bitten by a rattler), there are moments of clarity regarding the real psychic devastations caused by racism and sexism. For every missed opportunity Laughlin had, but sadly ignored, to edit some of the film's more cringe-worthy moments, there are nonetheless other episodes where his idealism met with his considerable talents as a storyteller to produce a film that was, and remains, both politically ambitious and, yes, even cinematically pleasurable.

"Everyone wanted to be Billy Jack in those days," my uncle Vern tells me. It wasn't only because of his groovy clothes, or the way he handed it back to those racist, recognizable border-town bullies. It wasn't because sympathetic Native portrayals in cinema were still all too rare, or the fact that Laughlin compensated for his own "redface" by casting noted Native celebrities like Sacheen Littlefeather and Rolling Thunder (and perhaps here we can give a shout-out to Howard Hesseman, who appears in a supporting role as a hippie at the Freedom School—although he's not Native either, just a cool guy). And it really had nothing to do with a taste for vigilantism; if it did, one supposes kids like me would have played Dirty Harry just as quickly as Billy Jack, but kids like me didn't do that. Everyone wanted to be Billy Jack, I'm guessing, because he represented a visionary new world, one in which the old Indian world would have a significant and dignified part, as opposed to representing a marginalized, maligned embarrassment of history at the cusp of the civil rights era. Despite his flaws, Billy Jack gave us a sense of pride and possibility. The same can be said, incidentally, for the Red Power movement as a whole.

Laughlin never matched the huge success of *Billy Jack. The Trial of Billy Jack* was both a critical and commercial flop, and *Billy Jack Goes to Washington* wasn't released as a feature film (it did, however, appear on television and eventually on DVD). Still married (since 1954) to Delores Taylor, Laughlin has run for president three times (in 1992, 2004, and 2008). While he has done occasional work as an actor and producer over the years, none of it particularly noteworthy, he never gave up his dream to produce one last Billy Jack film. He attempted to make *The Return of Billy Jack* in 1986, but suffered physical injuries during filming in New York that permanently halted production. While in New York, Laughlin made headlines by breaking up a big street fight on the Upper West Side, reportedly telling the brawlers, "If it's killing you want, come and get it." He also threatened to rip a man's arm off. For years, Laughlin has been soliciting funding on his website for a film that has gone through various working titles, including *Billy Jack for President, Billy Jack and Jean, Billy Jack's Moral Revolution*, and, most unwieldy, *Billy Jack's Crusade to End the War in Iraq and Restore America to Its Moral Purpose.* I will admit that I have never been tempted to invest—perhaps donate is the better word—but I did happily buy one of the Billy Jack T-shirts offered for sale to fans both old and new.

REFERENCES

Ebert, Roger. Review of *Billy Jack, Chicago Sun-Times*, 2 August 1971. Accessed 15 June 2010 at h*ttp://rogerebert.suntimes.com/apps/pbcs.dll/article?AID=/19710802/REVIEWS/%20 101010302/1023.*

Lim, Dennis. "Vigilante Films, An American Tradition," *Los Angeles Times*, 19 October 2009. Accessed 15 June 2010 at *http://articles.latimes.com/2009/oct/19/entertainment/et-vigilante19.*

Thompson, Howard. "A Misguided *Billy Jack*," *New York Times*, 29 July 1971, accessed 15 June 2010 at *http://movies.nytimes.com/movie/review?_r=1&res=9900E1DA1238EF34BC4151DFB1668 38A669EDE&partner=Rotten%20Tomatoes.*

CHAPTER 10

Love, Indigenous-Style

Dear Diary:

I love the beaches, the waterfalls, hula skirts, and even the stuffed pig. Lose the poi, though, it tastes spoiled.

Note to Self: From now on all cowboys and Indians pictures must be shot in Hawaii. Call Carlos and Ricardo Montalbán and see if they'll consider starring in Hula in a Headdress. *(I just made up that title. Boy, can I pick 'em.)*

Nite-nite,

Hollywood

Waikiki Wedding

Jodi A. Byrd

Ah, Hawai'i. Land of pineapple, processed sugar, hula, and aloha. Well, for some I suppose, if you're into that whole touristic exploitation of someone else's land for your own pleasure, as most Americans tend to be. But for me? Not so much. I never in a million years thought I'd ever have anything in common with Shirley Ross, a 1930s Hollywood starlet who, it turns out, was born in Omaha, Nebraska, in 1913, and who ends up playing a reluctant Pineapple Princess on the silver screen in pursuit of the aloha dreams that the beaches of Hawai'i are supposed to promise. Yet watching Bing Crosby's 1937 *Waikiki Wedding*, the film in which Ross is cast as the aforementioned beauty-pageant princess, I found myself, at least initially, confronted with the possibility that I might indeed have to face the disturbing thought that this Chickasaw, born in Nebraska, had inadvertently stumbled into a horribly scripted Depression-era escapist fantasy and I didn't even know it. More importantly, I didn't even want it. Now, I'm not talking about the initial lesbian subtext between the Pineapple Princess and her sidekick, Myrtle (played in the film by Martha Raye), or the fact that said Princess was from Iowa. And let's be brutally honest, I could never be mistaken for a starlet or princess of any sort, so I'm not trying to make any self-deluded claims in *that* direction.

It's more that, like *Waikiki Wedding*'s Pineapple Princess Georgia Smith, I didn't instantly fall in love with Hawai'i the moment I landed to start my first tenure-track job there. How do you learn to love aloha as constructed by Hollywood when such love necessarily depends upon the ongoing colonization, subjugation, and appropriation of Native Hawaiian language, culture, and sovereignty? You don't. You do, however, learn to stop worrying and appreciate the absurd when the continental desires for wedded bliss collide with the whims of the American tourism industrial complex. It's a whole new heterotourism gone viral in the desires for the sanctity of marriage upheld by only the purest of flowers. Or something like that.

All right, all right. Fine. Back to *Waikiki Wedding.* Tinseltown's idea of Hawai'i as an exotic island locale had already been well established in U.S. continental and *haole* (a word that roughly translates as foreign and is used to describe white people) imaginations long before Bing Crosby started making films through the work of Jack London, Mark Twain, Robert Louis Stevenson, and the propaganda that emerged from the U.S.-backed overthrow of the Hawaiian Kingdom in 1893. By the 1930s, it was Bing Crosby with his silky voice who helped solidify U.S. longings for a romantic Hawai'i in the years that stretched out of the glittering tourism of the 1920s through the Depression, and culminated in the bombing of Pearl Harbor and World War II. All these events secure Hawai'i's place in Hollywood's imaginings. Crosby's 1937 *Waikiki Wedding*, including its songs "Blue Hawaii," "In a Lovely Hula Heaven," and "Sweet Leilani" (the 1937 Academy Award–winning song from the film) had a huge impact in shaping the *tiki* lounge fads that still accompany the stereotypical U.S. cultural productions about Hawai'i, "Polynesia," and the South Pacific. I can unequivocally assert that there is a genealogical pop-culture link that runs from *Waikiki Wedding* to *The Brady Bunch* (1969–1974) to *Joe vs. the Volcano* (1990) to *Forgetting Sarah Marshall* (2008).

Given its iconic status, the film does not disappoint. *Waikiki Wedding* tracks the hijinks of four main characters as they play hooky from their various responsibilities. Bing Crosby is cast as Tony, the employee of a local pineapple-plantation owner who'd rather sleep and fish on his boat all day than deal with the business he's been hired to promote. His best friend and sidekick, Shad Buggle, is played by Bob Burns and characterized primarily as a white local obsessed with his pig. As I mentioned above, Shirley Ross plays Georgia Smith, an Iowan who wins a beauty pageant contest and has been brought to Hawai'i by Tony's boss in a desperate gambit to promote pineapples and Hawai'i to Iowans who are growing uninterested in tropical fruit and destinations. Her best friend Myrtle (Martha Raye) chaperones her as comic relief in the form of a not-so-attractive woman looking to land a man during the trip. Myrtle's got eyes for Shaddie-pie, but she can't quite compete with his pig. This hour-and-a-half-long movie, directed by Frank Tuttle, follows Tony as he tries to convince the skeptical and hostile Georgia that Hawai'i really is magical and entertaining, by deploying all the Native Hawaiians he knows to create intrigue that will capture her imagination—complete with a giant fake (and cursed) black pearl and a fake erupting volcano. Though Georgia is engaged to a boring Iowa dentist at the beginning of the film, she falls in love with bad boy Tony during the course of her stay in Hawai'i. All hell breaks loose when said fiancé, played here by Leif Erikson, gets wind of her escapades and arrives in Hawai'i to petulantly demand she return to her real life in Iowa.

The film is bookended with weddings in Waikiki. The first actual, the second inferred. And for this Indian, watching the film for the first time not ten minutes from Waikiki on the island of O'ahu, and displaced from my own indigenous mainland, the first wedding scene was disorienting. Or rather, "orienting" in a strange cacophony where the Hawaiian music scored by Ralph Rainger, Leo Robin, and Harry Owens sounds like some forgotten love child that resulted from a ménage à trois involving a drumming Hollywood Plains Indian and the singing Siamese Cats from Disney's *Lady and the Tramp* (1955). And not nearly as self-aware as Jackie Chan's East meets Western *Shanghai Noon* (2000), in which he greets the Hollywood Indian with "Hau." It didn't please.

In the opening sequence of *WW*, which is supposed to represent a Native Hawaiian wedding, there is nothing Hawaiian in the "We are Siamese, if you please" musical structure, or in the "hey-ya, hey-yas" and "dum, dum, dum, dums" that punctuate the occasional "aloha oe." Native Hawaiians, it seems, are caught between stereotypes of Asians and American Indians, and the film draws upon the already established tropes of feminization on the one hand and savagery on the other to shorthand the threatening indigenous Pacific Islander within an emerging filmic lexicon.

The final and perhaps unintentional irony that accompanies the opening sequence is when baby-faced Bing Crosby appears for the first time onscreen. His character, Tony Marvin, is a local, and what's more, he's Hawai'i's epitome of the hapa haole, ballad-singing cowboy, complete with his insider knowledge of all things native and his total disregard for the rules of "civilized" business behavior. His first words onscreen serve to translate the "traditional" Hawaiian wedding ceremony for Shad, his pig-loving best friend from Arkansas, and to demonstrate to the audience the fact that he has "gone native," with his knowledge of hula and desire to avoid work at all costs. The scene continues with professions of love flowing like rivers to seas, and enduring like tides crashing into beaches, and then the Hawaiian bride and groom are asked how they would like to complete the "ceremony of the bowl" in the culmination of their Hawaiian, feminine receptivity. The groom, laughing slightly, points to Crosby and says, "I choose my friend. The friend of all my friends. I choose the haole," and the crowd of "Natives" goes wild, crying "the haole" as they run to cheerfully greet Crosby and bring him to the center of the ceremony. In what has to be one of the best examples of the Columbus complex—or better, in the Pacific context, the Captain Cook complex—the film presents Crosby as a god-like figure who is known to one and all in the Native community as "The Haole," a naming that assuredly does not carry such an honorific intent. Think the scene from 1925's *Vanishing American* where a stereotypical Southwestern Indian "chief" greets the Spanish conquistadors by first kneeling to recognize the superiority of their guns and horses, and then lifting the Spanish soldier's foot and placing it on top of his head while he grovels to represent the debased relationship Indians should naturally have to the newly arrived European masters, and you come close to the absurdity of the moment in this film.

Throughout *Waikiki Wedding*, Crosby's role as white patriarchal "god" is never challenged as he struggles to teach the Pineapple Princess the true meaning of the aloha spirit, as if he as a white man has any authority to determine what aloha might mean. Tony is an advertising mad man, a con artist, whose ability to think outside the box and manipulate women and Natives to sell product is unrivalled. He's the embodiment of the easy kind of self-serving capitalist machinations that underscored the pineapple-plantation owners' overthrow of Queen Lili'uokalani. His ability to control, manipulate, and script the events of the film demonstrate the kind of supposed white superiority that positions Hawai'i as a playground for vacationing imperialists. The film's plot follows one of Tony's ideas—which admittedly come to him while he's napping or fishing or generally lazing around, and are occasionally harebrained even if he is a fountainhead among men—and we learn that his Pineapple Princess marketing ploy is backfiring. The idea is this: Imperial Pineapple (yes, that is its name), in order to sell more pineapples and to get folks on the "mainland" to invest in the islands and the image that Hawai'i is a romantic, intoxicating wonderland, holds a beauty contest on the continent. The winner gets an all-expenses-paid trip to the islands, where she is to be swept off her feet by the allure of the night, the moon, and blue Hawai'i. Her job, aside from enjoying the fruits of the island and sitting under koa trees, is to have her photo taken in a calendar-girl pose next to a cardboard pineapple, and to write dispatches back home telling of her adventures. The problem is that Georgia Smith—from Birch Falls, Iowa—is not having it, or any fun for that matter, and is in the process of writing stories that report that Hawai'i is just like Iowa, only with palm trees. This will not do! Tony must be found, and must put a stop to her silliness before the business is destroyed.

The plan, with a couple of hiccups that include avoiding the overtures of the overamorous, pig-like Myrtle, has Tony orchestrating a Hawaiian adventure for Georgia and occasionally seducing her with songs about the moon and ocean breeze. While his bosses—the landed plantation owners—enjoy the spoils of their dominion over the islands, Tony is on the outs for his playing Hawaiian and refusal to take anything seriously. But it is his "gone Hawaiian" playboy ways that ultimately allow him to save the day by using his connections with his Native Hawaiian friends—remember, he's the "friend of my friends," "The Haole"—to administer a fictional stolen black pearl beloved by the gods, an erupting volcano, and romantic boat-ride escape from "hostile" Natives threatening to hold them all captive until the gods are appeased as remedy for the humdrums that have Miss Georgia Smith not liking Hawai'i. In the process, Tony and Georgia fall in love.

The catch in all this for Tony Marvin, however, is that everything he does is a fraud, and his artifice reaches volcanic heights when he gets his Hawaiian friend Kimo to help him (and yes, that is a reference to the Lone Ranger and Tonto). Kimo is played by a young Anthony Quinn, who will eventually go on from this role to be cast as Crazy Horse in *They Died with Boots On* (1941) and Inuk the Eskimo in *The Savage Innocents* (1960; see the review in this chapter). Kimo's role in *WW*, though, is to throw more logs onto the bonfire that's serving as the massive eruption of the staged volcano to underscore how angry Georgia has made the gods when she tried to smuggle the fake black pearl off the island. Tony scripts the entire adventure, from the moment Georgia is handed the fake pearl artifact to the fistfight between himself and Kimo, to give Georgia the excitement of a harrowing escape via white-knight chivalry. Through the entire course of the movie, Tony's easy-going paternalism and self-assured misogyny guarantees that he always has complete authority and the trust of his cast of fools. And Georgia is treated to an amusement park ride of Hawaiian romantic stereotypes.

Tony is eventually found out, though. While Georgia is distracted, Imperial Pineapple sends the dispatches that Tony wrote for her to the press to play up the fabulous locales and to lure more visitors to the isles. Her fiancé and Uncle Herman back in Iowa are horrified when they realize that they can't find her, and fear that they might lose her to one of the locals, or worse. They decide to intervene and miraculously arrive in plenty of time to confront Georgia with the truth of Tony's deception. Challenged by the continental version of his own colonialist masculinity, Tony's desire to marry Georgia is thwarted briefly, and Georgia, deceived and wounded, decides to return to Iowa and back into the arms of her stolid, if slightly violent, betrothed. In one last gamble to secure the woman he loves, Tony scripts two more deceptions: he sneaks aboard the ship as a stowaway, and when that doesn't work, he steals her luggage, and then sends his mother onto the boat to ask Georgia if she loves her fiancé. The movie ends with Georgia racing off the departing boat, and then laughing good-naturedly as Tony's latest deception is revealed and his "mother" turns out to be the "Mother Foster's Homemade Cookies" woman. Tony's last words before the curtain closes on the kiss are, "Well, she's somebody's mother! I think." *Oh Tony, indeed.*

While it may be easy to laugh at the ridiculous antics of Tony's self-assured white mastery over Natives and women alike, his "going Hawaiian" serves an important cultural and political function at a historical moment when continental Americans were uneasy with the racially threatening Hawai'i as a site for romance and escape. Tony Marvin's role in the film reassures American audiences that whatever threat the "Natives" might pose to a young woman traveling essentially on her own remains subverted and passive. He is, in a sense, a romantic safety valve for her Hawaiian adventures, at the same time that, whatever sexualized threat he might embody, his own masculine machinations to win the girl are themselves unthreatening in their colonial rube innocence, and if not that, then ultimately sanctioned because he is of the white ruling class. He intends to make an honest woman of her.

Despite all the songs, adventure, and humor that come at Myrtle's, Shad's, and the Hawaiians' expense, the film never quite recovers from its symptomatic need to protect white women from non-white Natives and locals roaming the streets of Honolulu. In the shadow of the Massie Affair and the Jim Crow miscegenation fears that dominated the minds of moviegoers in the 1930s, the film falters as it struggles to reassure moviegoers that Hawai'i remains an idyllic destination for beach blankets, Mai Tais, and sunset rendezvous. Bing Crosby's paper facade Hawai'i does its best to render a vanilla-safe romance by alchemically restoring Native Hawaiians to their Native aloha innocence in service to white patrimonial bliss. But *aloha*, as anyone who pays attention to indigenous politics and cultures knows, has more than one meaning. While Hollywood renders Native Hawaiians as romantic savages in search of a white fraud to rule them all, a hidden subtext exists between knowing how to greet and treat strangers with the proper protocols, and knowing when it's time to leave.

Dear Diary:

Things used to be so simple. When you wanted a cheeseburger, you went to McDonalds, and when you wanted an Indian, you went to Anthony Quinn. But whose brilliant idea was it to change "Indians" into Alaska Natives? What's the diff? Come to think of it, whatever happened to the word Eskimo? Inuit sounds too much like "I knew it." If you ask me, someone is making lots of moolah coining all these new words. Must call our copyright head. Follow the money, that's what I always say.

Note to Self: Cancel Alaska cruise.

Siesta time,

Hollywood

The Savage Innocents

Theo. Van Alst

E.S. (establishing shot):

Conversation in Chicago's Wooden Nickel on Wilson Ave., ca. 1961. A couple of guys from the neighborhood are debating going to the movies. They'll take the El up north and go to the Lakeshore or the 400, or maybe even the Devon or the Adelphi. But first, they've got some talkin' to do.

They sit in the heat and humidity that only the Windy City can unleash in the depths of summer. On the carved and pitted bar, centered in a ring of cigarette burns, a lone bead of water makes its way down a bottle of Schlitz, reflecting early morning slap-happy faces in a haze of smoke. Just as it obscures the "L" in the label, our first speaker takes a big swig and offers:

"You said it's a Western, right?"

"Mmmmm."

"And it's got a talking Indian in it?"

"Yup."

". . . Is it . . . Ricardo Montalbán?"

"Nope."
"Jeff Chandler?"
"Na."
"Couldn't be Anthony Quinn, could it?"
"Bingo."
"Dang. At least it ain't Sal Mineo."
"Ya, but it coulda been Paul Newman."
"Or Elvis."
"Elvis ain't an Indian."
"Is too. So is Wayne Newton."
"Now you're just makin' up stuff."
"Am not. They're Cherokees."
"Nuh uh."
"Uh huh."

And so it goes.

Well, *Les Dents du Diable* (1960) (or *Los Dientes del Diablo*, the only way you could find this title in the States until very recently) is not a real Western, but it is. Kinda. Maybe.

Not sure? Let's find out.

Does it star Anthony Quinn? Check.

Is he playing a Native dude? Check.

Does he kill someone? Check.

Vengeance is achieved!? Check.

It's a Western.

But it's not your typical Western. It's . . . well, let's go with that for a moment, as we head into the igloo of ignominy known as *The Savage Innocents.*

I must confess that my first viewing of this film came when I was a kid in Chicago. I only remembered it in bits and pieces, much like segments of other movies viewed on Channel 9, sometimes introduced by Frazier Thomas under the guise of "Family Classics" (*Captains Courageous, Boys Town, Miracle on 34th Street*, etc.), and sometimes just appearing during rainouts of wretched Cubs games. (I have long since shaken that sickness; I'm a White Sox fan). I remember thinking it was weird; weirder still was my second viewing. I watched a Spanish dub, which one supposes makes sense, given that the star is Anthony Quinn, *muy macho* Irish-Mexican (*Indio*—that's right) hero of stage and screen, a man who knocked out roles as Quasimodo, Osceola, Chang Tai, and Zapata, so why not an "Eskimo" in the appropriately oddly titled *Los Dientes del Diablo* (look it up).

Like an orphaned novel left in the seat back on a budget airline, this film is seen by some and remembered by few, yet it's still a thing in the world that affects those who encounter it. We should also consider that this film might be the possible vector for the insertion of indigenous concerns into the work of Franco Solinas (*The Battle of Algiers, A Bullet for the General, The Big Gundown, Z, Queimada*), whose later screenplays underscore and reverberate throughout the milieu of the Zapatista Spaghetti Western cycle of the late 1960s.

So, as the first two viewings were . . . fuzzyish, let's take a clear-eyed look together at *The Savage Innocents.*

Hey—it's an Italian-French-British coproduction. This should be exciting. It has very weird opening music, and it even sounds like a Western from the '50s. We are treated to some creepy jazz accompaniment of a polar bear's double harpooning; it looks quite realistic, so I'm hoping the pain dealt the bear in making this film was worth it.

On the weird music: Angelo Francesco Lavagnino put together many a score for an array of *peplums* and Spaghetti Westerns. He was also the composer on 1952's *Othello*, and *Chimes at Midnight* (1965), the film Orson Welles thought would get him into heaven, even more so than *Citizen Kane*, AEW.[1] And just so you know, it's true. Bob Dylan did, in fact, write "Quinn the Eskimo (Mighty Quinn)" after being inspired by *The Savage Innocents*. Figure that one out!

For a bit of official-type background, the sweet Turner Classic Movie brief synopsis tells us:

> When an Eskimo kills a priest for refusing his wife (an Eskimo custom), he becomes a fugitive and is caught by the Canadian Mounties, who then set him free in realization and respect for a different "nation's" set of laws.

How do you like that? It says, "nation," but it's in quotation marks, so don't get carried away. Should they have prefaced it with "domestic dependent," or would that make the already awkward style mostly unapproachable? Then again, the standard shouldn't be held too high; after all, these are the folks whose full synopsis misidentifies an airplane as a helicopter. Details, details.

Let us return to the task at hand. I have to mention the V.O. (voice-over)—if you can imagine Claude Akins on Demerol, sitting at your kitchen table drinking codeine syrup and Coke, projecting just the right hint of smugness as he's telling you the story, then you're halfway home.

Claude the V.O. tells us about "Laughter and love . . . when a third of the year is night." I figure out that "laughter" is a euphemism for sex, and between Claude and the unsettling use of the word "laughter" I realize now (as an adult) that I'm in for quite the ride.

Eighteen minutes and twenty seconds in, it occurs to me that, thus far, the movie has mostly been about Anthony Quinn trying to get laid, and people trying to get Anthony Quinn laid, while all the time he alternately laughs and scowls in an altogether unsettling performance. (I have questions for myself. I ask: Should he be "laughing?" What does that mean? Should he be mixing the two? What does *that* mean? Should *I* be laughing? How did I get sucked into this?).

So the plot: A buddy offers up his wife to Quinn, but he refuses and bashes the man's head against the wall of an igloo. That's more than a little rude. What does that mean? All these deep thoughts necessitate an onscreen break from reflection starring some action.

This film about "Life So Primitive It Will Make You Gasp! (imdb.com)" doesn't disappoint. Now Inuk-Quinn is out kayaking on the big water with a buddy of his (Anarvik, the first guy who offered up his wife for a little laughter and got his head bashed through the side of his own igloo). This seems invigorating enough, so of course we quickly return to some theoretical action.

> "Inuk. Listen to me. Everyone knows. One woman is as good as another."
> "But a woman is not a seal, or even a walrus . . ."

Whoa.

Quinn is having a hard time deciding which woman he'd like to have.

Here's some more from our ice-bound philosopher, Anarvik:

"More important than a woman is a man who makes up his mind."

Yeah.

Wait.

Shit. They've harpooned a walrus. I hope this is like the whale kill in *A Thousand Roads* (2005), and just coincidental to the shooting schedule for the film. Or just some stock footage. Then again, the seal he just killed offscreen certainly appears onscreen a couple of minutes later in a very, very dead fashion.

At any rate, he seems to settle on his woman choice—Imina. However, when he returns to Kiddok's house, he finds out from her mom that she's already taken off with someone else:

"Kiddok has given me a bowl and a lamp, so the marriage is made."

Quinn tries to bargain with a walrus head, a bearskin, and a "stone" knife, to no avail. They laugh and laugh at him (not *that* kind of laughing) and he decides to head off after Kiddok with some serious evil in his heart and on his mind; his grimaces and his facial expressions tell the whole story.

Though Quinn is working hard to win Imina, there is another woman in the story, and her name is Asiak. Have I mentioned that throughout this scene, Asiak is wearing some 1960s-era booty shorts, Arctic-style? She's got on leggings, sure, but over those she's wearing these snow-white go-go pants. Very Surreal.

And then . . . *whoa.*

Nudity.

Asiak just whipped off her top like it "ain't no thang."

Ah. This is 1960. Of course, we can see them naked/topless. They're just . . . Eskimos/Injuns. Whatever.

Quinn's immune to this display, though. He's still after Imina. And after puttin' the threats to Kiddok (and a spear to his throat), she's free to join the Mighty One. They seal the deal with much giggling and nose rubbing, and then head out into the sunlight. A minute later, Quinn changes his mind again (apparently he wasn't listening to his boating buddy and part-time philosophizing pal back in the kayak). He's decided he wants another go at those fur-trimmed booty shorts. More giggles, a bum rush on Kiddok, and everybody's sled gets a reload. Quinn's even takes Asiak's mom along for the ride.

Another bear scene: This time, though, no one has a pair of harpoons to drive into his lungs. Quinn decides to booby-trap some food. He puts together bait for the hungry bear that contains whalebone. When the whalebone springs open, the "bear will get stomachache," he tells us in fine Tonto-speak. The bear eats, obligingly bellows, and then goes for a little slide down a hill like the star of a Christmas-time Coca-Cola commercial.

Dang. I lied. Quinn *does* have a harpoon. Now where do you suppose he had that hidden? Anyway, we follow along for a bit, the bear's slow, agonizing death imminent now. This is one unhappy bear. It probably doesn't help that Quinn calls him "Nanook" (which, even though it's his name, still has uncomfortable associations for us in the audience), unfairly taunts him, and throws himself on Asiak, even as that whalebone causes the bear to roar in pain. Quinn is a real tyrant. Then, as he launches into another round of jokes at Nanook's expense, the bear can take no more and charges the humans. But wait . . . a shot rings out. What is this? Quinn covers his ears and rolls in the snow, ostensibly overcome by the sound. There's a cut, and then we see a very real, and very dead, polar bear on the ground. Shot in the head, blood everywhere. And this is how he meets up with a new buddy, Ittimargnek, who tells him how to trade with the white man.

What do you know? It's all about the guns. This is a Western, after all. After some childish shooting in the igloo, Quinn decides to "follow the way of the fox" (who happen to be *red* foxes in this Anglo-Franco-Italo Arctic; never mind that their ruddy appearance on the gleaming white snow is like a Michael McDonald backing vocal in a Metallica song). And though he pursues these foxes rather than "feed his family and make provision for the coming winter," he's the Mighty Quinn, and you'll just have to deal with it.

Inside the trading post ("one full winter and one full summer" away), a red-headed trader watching Quinn laugh his way in and out of a barroom brawl (no, not *that* kind) says: "Up 'til ten years ago, nearly all the Eskimos were like those three. Magnificent."

Quinn's wife looks at the nostalgia-filled trader and says: "This stupid woman expected him to be as white as snow, but he's a red man! Hahahahahah! Hahahahahahaha!"

Quinn gets his gun and tells one of the Native store employees to let the "white man" know that he is very happy. So happy, in fact, that Quinn offers up his wife for laughter with the white man. He is told "the white man does not allow laughter in his house." When Quinn tells his wife about this foolishness, she replies, "He must be very sad, this white red man." Indeed, sister. Indeed. We all smile knowingly at the double-entendre and await the next bit of Tonto-speak.

Funny, though, the next bit of Tonto-speak comes from a white man, offering a can of who knows what to Quinn. "Try some of this. It doesn't taste good, but it makes you feel warm and lively." Yup. Break out the whiskey. Quinn and the mother-in-law chug the better part of a bottle. That should do it.

A split second later and they're both completely crocked, laughing uncontrollably and clapping to the beat like white folks in a nursing home watching *Soul Train.* After a bit, Mrs. Quinn decides that the white man must be crazy from his lack of laughter. The family makes tracks for the great outdoors.

All is not destined to be laughter and light, however. Jesus and a priest from the trading post follow the little family back to their igloo. There the good reverend talks to them about "The Lord." He says that if they believe in his words, the Lord will be with them everywhere they go. Mrs. Quinn is like, no way, we don't need another mouth to feed, but Quinn turns briefly contemplative and wonders if "maybe He good hunter." He continues, "We will be pleased if your friend come with us." The missus? "He must bring his own sled." "Will this Lord bring everything he needs?" The rev replies, "He'll bring you faith."

When the priest turns down the couple's offer of a bowl full of maggots, Mrs. Quinn suggests, "Maybe he is used to different food?" The reverend, with a quick face-saver, says, "Men don't live by bread alone." This puts a smile on Quinn's face, and moves the missus to opine, "Maybe he want to laugh with a woman." Quinn quietly says, "Make yourself beautiful." (That means a big slather of blubber on the face, to me and you.)

The priest hysterically bows out, "No!" "No!" It's a sin! It's evil! Etc.! Etc.!

"You are rude! You have no manners!"

Uh-oh. You know what happens next:

"Maybe you bumped too hard," says the wife.

"Maybe his head was too soft," says Quinn.

Cut to the next scene:

Claude returns to give us some unsettling information about "useless mothers," elders wandering off to die on the ice, and the abandoning of baby girls. There is a scene back in the igloo where Asiak has given birth alone, and where, well, let's have Turner Classic Movies describe it. I just can't. "When Inuk returns, he is thrilled, until he notices that the baby boy has no teeth. The two adults blame each other for their bad luck, but eventually realize that he will grow teeth later." At any rate, Quinn interrogates Asiak, demanding to know why the boy has no teeth, accusing her of eating seal out of season, eating land animals with sea animals, etc., and wondering about "the ghost of the white man" (the one they killed earlier).

And then . . . a plane! Wha . . . ? What century is this again, in case you forgot the title? At any rate, after causing some people below on the ice to bail from their sled, the plane lands on the ice, and out come some official types with guns. "Are you Inuk?!" The man now putting his life back together yells, "No," and the two dudes in the sassy brown fur-lined winter tunics say, "We're looking for an Eskimo named Inuk! He's traveling this way with his woman and her mother. You seen him?" The people offer to make them some tea, but the well-dressed sergeants decide they must be going.

There's a quick cut to Quinn and the son with a bow and arrow and a herd of caribou.

The Mounties get the drop on Quinn.

Quinn protests: "But my father's laws have not been broken." (Quinn is a nationalist.) It's Peter O'Toole in his film debut, AEW!

A storm comes—Quinn asks them to allow him to drive the sled, but they refuse, and shortly thereafter Mountie #1 and the sled plunge into the icy seawater. Quinn knows he's a dead man, but #2 tries to save him, first pulling him out of the water and then cutting him out of his flash-frozen clothes. We watch #1 freeze to death. Quinn is, like, "later days, brother," but O'Toole hangs onto the Mighty One. They tussle for a bit, and Quinn points out that his hands are frozen. Quinn saves his hands and his life by cutting open a sled dog and sticking his hands in it (see this final full offering from Nicholas Ray in film school, did we Mr. Lucas?),[2] but the Mountie still insists that he'll be arresting Quinn when they get back to civilization. Quinn can't believe it, and starts to leave him to die on the ice. But because this film is what it is, he, of course, goes back and carries the "white man" across his shoulders and saves him.

The missus is *pissed.* Asiak says—"When you come to a strange land, you should bring your wives and not your laws." She should have told him to bring his voice too, because O'Toole's dub is weird (termed Spaghetti Western American according to the commentary) and that pissed O'Toole off. Pissed me off, too. It *is* weird.

O'Toole lets him go, but Quinn doesn't get it. Frankly, neither do we in this oddly underdeveloped part of the story, but Quinn heads off into the sunset. Like I said, this is a Western, kinda. As this washes over us, we can only be reminded of Quinn's mighty words of wisdom in response to his wife's questioning lamentation, "White men . . ." He says, "They're too difficult to understand." Roll credits (which turn out to be the principal cast only). Fade to black.

Perfect.

NOTES

1. AEW (I'm advancing this as a new appendage to "facts") stands for Apocrypha, Ephemera, Wikipedia—e.g., Burt Reynolds is half Cherokee, AEW.
2. *Star Wars Episode V: The Empire Strikes Back* (1980). A similar scene occurs in *Episode V* when Hans Solo cuts open a "beast of burden" and puts Luke inside to keep him from freezing to death.

DEAR DIARY:

Finally, an old fashioned bromance: boy meets boy, boy loses boy, boy finds Indian boy. How I wish Johnny Ford (that old softy) had been around to direct this tender love story with his faithful companions: John Wayne, cast as its star, and Jeffrey Hunter, costar. Of course, Ford would have insisted that the whole thing be shot in Monument Valley and titled Searchers 2.

Note to Self: Call studio to discuss 3-D possibilities.

Love ya,

HOLLYWOOD

Big Eden

P. JANE HAFEN

Big Eden (2000) is acclaimed as part of a second generation of gay cinema. The film is more romantic comedy than coming-out drama or confronting AIDS and its consequences. While those early gay films are certainly significant, the writer/director, Thomas Bezucha, presents gay relationships as normal parts of the community. His desire for that normalization is most clearly portrayed in his more mainstream film *The Family Stone* (2005), in which a family argument at Christmas Eve dinner unfolds over whether or not being gay is "normal." In that film, the Sarah Jessica Parker character is confronted with her own homophobia, and is put in her place by Diane Keaton, the protective mother of a gay son.

In *Big Eden*, homosexuality *is* the norm, and the community of ranchers, storeowners, teachers, and trades workers conspire to bring a gay couple together. The main character, Henry Hart, played by Arye Gross, is an artist in New York City. He is comfortable with his life, living among accepting friends. He returns to his hometown, Big Eden, Montana, to care for his ailing grandfather, played by veteran actor George Coe. Henry assumes that no one in his small hometown knows he is gay. He is afraid of disappointing his grandfather, and also assumes someone of his grandfather's generation would be less tolerant than his hip New York friends. His high school crush, Dean, played by Tim DeKay, has also recently come back, but is deeply closeted, married, and has children.

A meddling widow (Nan Martin) acts on her assumptions of heteronormativity and offers to set up Henry with a number of eligible single women. However, as soon as she realizes he is gay, she then moves seamlessly to have him meet other men. Eventually she and the townspeople would prefer to see Henry with Pike, the lone and generic Indian played by Eric Schweig. Pike is an imposing figure and stands out as the only person of color in the cast. As if we didn't know his ethnic heritage, he has a leitmotif of Indian flute music to emphasize his exotic character.

In Pike's first appearance, he is nearly speechless and classically stoic, a Noble Savage with emphasis on the noble. The background music is "Together Again" by Buck Owens. Later, when the film is crosscutting between Henry's ogling Dean and Pike's gourmet cooking, the song again emphasizes that Henry and Pike should be together.

Pike's character is double-edged. On one hand, having a contemporary Indian who functions in the mainstream and is cared for by the townspeople is idealistic. This modern character, who plays against historic Noble Savage stereotypes, is portrayed by the actor Eric Schweig (Inuit). Schweig is best known for his lead role as Rudy Yellow Dog in Chris Eyre's *Skins* (2002), and other iconic roles such as Uncas in *the Last of the Mohicans* (see the review in chapter 4), and as the title character in *Squanto: A Warrior's Tale* (1994). He observes the contrast to those earlier roles: "[I was] happy to get up in the morning and put on a pair of pants instead of leggings and moccasins."

On the other hand, as far as Indian characters go, Pike is generic—without tribe or community—and exists in a cultural vacuum. The director comments: "Very late in the writing of the script [I] figured out that he was Native American."[1] To underscore Pike's ethnicity, music was added to his characterization—as Bezucha remarked, "The music was indigenous that would pull out the Pike character, so we talked about the flute and the Native American drumming." Since the film is set in Montana, filmed around Glacier Lake on the edge of the Blackfeet Nation, having an Indian character in the plot is reasonable. However, the Blackfeet Nation is invisible to the white community in the film. The film denies the reservation border-town issues of resentment, racism, and colonialism. Pike is the lone Indian, the last relic of nature in the spectacular setting.

Additionally, the situation in the film is condescending. The writer's comments show a superficial understanding of Native issues. A person or a character does not simply become or turn into an Indian, especially not later in life, and especially NOT by listening to "Indian" music; I do not have an indigenous soundtrack to my life to remind me and others that I am Indian. Even de-tribalized Indians, those who are reared without family or cultural support, know the Indian core of their being. Considering the flute music, stoic silences, and conversations with nature that the author uses to make Pike an Indian, Bezucha's ideas about what constitutes Indianness reveal objectification that underlies conforming or institutional racism. By that I mean, Bezucha probably does not start out saying or believing he is a bigot, and he probably is not. Few people announce their own bigotry, especially in the context of trying to overcome bigotry against homosexuality. However, because he misrepresents Pike as a Native character, he reemploys stereotypes, regardless of how sympathetic they may be. This type of soft misrepresentation can be just as damaging as hateful misrepresentations, because it deprives the Native character of his own voice, and his right to his own identity formation.

For example, Pike is not monosyllabic, but he has very little to say through most of the film. He is the silent, stoic Indian, better quiet than revealing any emotions beyond his attraction to Henry. The one exception is when he and Henry sit down to visit, and Pike retells a story about the stars. The details of this scene reveal the deep problems with just inventing a generic Indian character for the script. Bezucha says, "There is this whole Native American tradition of storytelling as a gift." Admittedly, storytellers are held in high regard in many Native societies; however, the story Pike tells is from the wrong tribe, in the wrong place, at the wrong time. The myth is an indigenous rendering of the origin of the Pleiades, but it is identified as an Onondagan story. So, either Pike is a transplanted Haudenosaunee (Iroquois) from New York, or the myth is placed to serve the story, not the character. Indeed, the Pleiades story itself becomes Henry's symbol for his return to Montana and the community of Big Eden. He is inspired by the story and paints a representation that he later gives to Pike. The painting signifies Henry's coming home and his recognition of Pike as a potential love interest, yet allows Henry to appropriate Pike's story for himself.

The film also shows that all Indians must be alike—great storytellers, willing to serve and learning to cook, content to wait patiently and silently outside the church at the grandfather's funeral, and at the fireworks when Henry is still trying to hook up with Dean. Eric Schweig as Pike makes the most of the part and adds a wry humor in his interactions with other characters, including the dog.

The story ends with Pike and Henry dancing together at a community festival. Also dancing are a lesbian couple and other heterosexual couples from the town.

Big Eden is Henry's story, though—how he comes home, how he is welcomed as a gay man, and how he finds community and a partner. The question for me is: why is his true love an Indian? The film shows no sense of what being Two-Spirit means in Native cultures, and misses a prime opportunity to illustrate indigenous constructions of gender. Pike becomes part of the romance of the setting—the Montana mountains, the beautiful lake, and the rest of the invisible and silent Indians.

In many ways, I think this is a charming movie as a romantic comedy. The community of characters is rich with subtle details. The reconciliation that Henry feels as he finds love and a place in the community is satisfying. I like seeing a film in which the main character is developed and defined by a variety of his relationships and his occupation, not solely his sexual orientation. The only place, though, where I would use this film in class would be in an examination of gay cinema, a course I never teach. Even there, I would have to point out that noble Pike is deprived of his tribal identity, and that his Indianness functions more as a prop. Look at *Johnny Greyeyes* (2000) for a film about Native gay characters closer to the metaphorical tepee.

NOTE

1. "Director's Comments," *Big Eden*, directed by Thomas Bezucha (San Francisco, CA: Chaiken Films, 2000), DVD.

CHAPTER 11

Workin' for the Great White Father

Dear Diary:

It's so tiresome making movies about Indians in the swamps. All the blonds sweating like pigs, and what happened to Coop? He looks like an aging queen in that buckskin getup. This film barks.

Note to Self: Put Raoul on notice: If the back lot is good enough for Tarzan and the chimp, it's good enough for the cowboys and the Injuns!

Gosh, Diary, I'm in a black mood today. Profits are down. Must consult the stars. Is Saturn on our mid-heaven?

More tomorrow, sigh,

Hollywood

Distant Drums

Denise K. Cummings

About three quarters of the way through Raoul Walsh's 1951 Technicolor drama *Distant Drums*, the U.S. Army's Captain Quincy Wyatt (Gary Cooper) returns with his brigade in tow to the island he inhabits. In a point-of-view shot, the camera pans the charred remains of his isle's *chickees* (Seminole houses). We get a reaction shot of Wyatt, his face registering utter dismay, and then the camera follows him as he crosses a lagoon, slowly enters one of the blackened cypress log frames, and picks up two items off of the dwelling's sandy floor: a singed toy dugout canoe, and a small beaded shell necklace. The audience—along with Wyatt—instantly recognizes the objects as those belonging to Wyatt's young son, a mixed Anglo and Creek boy of six. Max Steiner's bathetic score summons our sorrow for Wyatt and his apparent loss.

On the surface, this scene suggests a sensitive rendering of a guy who believes he's just lost his son, and the last living connection to his beloved but dead wife. Yet placed in the broader context of what *Distant Drums* drums up for 1951 audiences, the scene, at least for this viewer, becomes one of irony.

At this moment in the movie, I just can't help but consider the larger-than-life Cooper—the handsome white man who typically plays big characters with big values and big ideals—but in this film, he's just another Hollywood dupe. But before I get ahead of myself, let's return to that key scene and consider the film's setup.

The story is a simple one of an armed conflict between the U.S. Army and Seminoles who are harassing white settlers—those attempting to establish their presence in a frontier region in keeping with the doctrine of Manifest Destiny in Florida, or Seminole land (at least for the film's purposes). The setting is Florida, 1840s. In most other ways, however, the movie's conventions suggest a classic Western, offering audiences, for example, an image of the American cowboy in Quincy Wyatt. He's capable, independent, and honorable. He's a rugged individualist, a hero who retains cultural ties to the community (though lives apart from civilization) and possesses knowledge of nature and the wilderness. Cooper's Wyatt wears buckskin and subsists off the land.

Those buckskin clothes, we learn, hold a deeper connection. What would a classic Western be without images of Indians? We get them here, first in the movie's establishing close-up shots of Indians drumming, followed by the credit sequence shot of a large drum being pounded (yet we can't see by whom). We are then, in turn, introduced to the "friendly" Creeks, some of whom share the island with Wyatt and from whom we assume he gets his attire, and later, the undeterred "savage" Seminoles. We also come to find out that Wyatt was even married to a Native woman—"a beautiful Creek Princess" who bore him a son.

The backdrop for the story is loosely drawn from a significant chapter in Florida's history in the early 1800s when the southeastern peninsula was a possession of the once great imperial power of Spain. At that time, various Native tribes inhabited the northern Panhandle area, including the descendants of Muskogee Creeks who, after 1750, had been driven out of such southeastern areas as Alabama, Georgia, and Mississippi by white encroachment. By the 1760s they were becoming known as the Seminoles. These groups managed to maintain significant autonomy under weakening Spanish rule. The United States, however, had a fervent interest in claiming the Spanish territory and, using the Seminole practice of harboring runaway slaves as an excuse, sent troops led by Andrew Jackson into Florida in 1817. Jackson attacked Seminole settlements, pushing some bands down the peninsula, and then attacked a Spanish outpost and illegally claimed western Florida for the United States. These events became known as the First Seminole War, and led to Spain ceding the Florida territory to the United States in 1821.

Under U.S. rule, Seminoles shifted southward and for several years lived in central and southern parts of the peninsula in relative peace. Following his election to the presidency and the passage of the Indian Removal Act in the 1830s, Andrew Jackson ordered all Native American groups in the southeast to relocate west of the Mississippi River to Indian Country (present day Oklahoma). The Seminoles, led by Osceola, resisted, beginning in 1835, and this opposition led to the seven-year Second Seminole War. Using their knowledge of the swampy terrain to their advantage, the Seminoles carried out a highly successful guerrilla campaign that eventually wore down the U.S. Army. Although during the course of the war several thousand Seminoles were indeed captured and moved west, a few hundred steadfastly remained. They weren't exterminated. They couldn't be conquered. In effect, by 1842 these peoples had won by resisting the Indian

Removal policy. In 1855, a series of limited engagements between the Seminoles and military, known as the Third Seminole War, was fought in southern Florida. By 1858, more Seminoles were moved west, again leaving only a few hundred in Florida. These Florida Seminoles are the only American Indian tribe never to have signed a formal peace treaty with the United States. Today, their descendants have sovereignty over tribal lands.

An early 1950s poster for *Distant Drums* announced: "The rescue—the throbbing jungle drums—the man-devouring marsh-wilderness aflame with unseen menace!" clearly indicating that the movie's plot didn't aim to adhere to all of this formative history. Instead, it focuses on Cooper as he leads a small band of U.S. soldiers to destroy a stronghold of gunrunners who are supplying arms to Native Americans during the Second Seminole War. They succeed in their mission of crossing Lake Okeechobee, storming a fort, and rescuing a group of civilian prisoners—among them a blond beauty and love interest for Wyatt (Judy Beckett, played by Mari Aldon)—but when their escape route is compromised, they are forced to flee into the Everglades with Seminole warriors not far behind them.

The Everglades, it turns out, offered an appropriately forbidding wilderness setting for Warner Bros. to maintain the invented traditions of the Western. With U.S. soldiers in the film referring to the area as "the mighty swamp" and "the rotting jungle," *Distant Drums* often brilliantly succeeds in perpetuating the centuries-old ignorance of the great ecological and environmental importance of the region. These concerns are naturally wholly disregarded, with the focus on the movie's characters as they wrestle alligators, dodge cottonmouths, and trudge through sawgrass and cypress (all the while donning anachronistic wardrobes and armaments). In one action-packed swamp scene after another, prefiguring the Indiana Jones character, Cooper's Wyatt valiantly navigates the Everglades, which ultimately allows him—and, by extension, the U.S. Army—to symbolically win the war against the Seminoles. At the climax, Wyatt kills the Seminole chief "Oscala" (a fictionalized Osceola) and the Seminoles retreat—but only after considerable bloodshed and death. On his inland island, Cooper reunites with his son (played by a non-Native actor in an uncredited role), reclaims his homestead, and captures the heart of Judy, a self-described white "cracker" who ultimately chooses to share Wyatt's maverick way of life over the comforts of "civilization." We are led to believe it is Judy who will help Wyatt raise his son. Is it just me, or is this film a metaphor for paternalism and federal Indian policy? What's more, it's Wyatt who gets to claim sovereignty.

And yet, there's another weird twist in the plot. Late in the film, we discover that U.S. soldiers actually killed Wyatt's Creek wife. Wyatt tells Judy, however, that he forgave the soldiers for being young and liquored up, and because "to them, all the Indians looked alike." For 1950s audiences, like the 1840s soldiers Wyatt pardons, the true menace is a misguided sense of white privilege.

Distant Drums is a perfect example of the classic Western that typically was uncritically accepted by audiences and, as we know, celebrated. Beyond its tacit support for ethnic cleansing and its blatant denial of the importance of the land, the movie's transgressions also include its stances on race and gender, established most saliently in the film's dialogue, its close-up reaction shots of characters' faces, and its characters' roles. In one scene, for example, Wyatt's naval associate and the movie's sometimes narrator, Lt. Richard Tufts (Richard Webb), refers to Wyatt's Creek wife as "the squaw." In a later sequence, Wyatt and Tufts repeatedly call the Seminoles "red devils." At various moments when the Seminoles close in on the soldiers, with the soundtrack endlessly repeating drum beats, the camera focuses on faces—the soldiers' intent, fearful; the

Seminoles' wild, bloodthirsty. Finally, women in the film are relegated to the silenced and the stereotypical: the expendable immigrant, the dark-skinned servant girl, and the Native princess, the object in which the white male hero plants his seed.

The representation of Natives in the film relates directly to Cooper's character. Wyatt draws a curious distinction between those he understands as the friendly Creeks from Georgia and those he perceives as the savage Seminoles, a willful misreading of the historical connections of these peoples (without drawing this distinction, the plot of *Distant Drums* could go nowhere). Moreover, we are beseeched to identify with the Creeks as human beings *only* because of Wyatt's connection with them—his own blood relatives. Otherwise, the Creeks, like the Seminoles in the film, are virtually undeveloped. All this brings us back to my crucial scene: audiences are most manipulated when we are led to believe it was the Seminoles who attacked the Creek-inhabited domestic site, and we believe Wyatt's son is dead.

If there is silver in *Drum*'s lining, it is its cinematography and Sidney Hickox's atmospheric camera work. The movie often offers beautiful panoramas of the real Florida. The last title card tells us, "This picture was photographed in the heart of the Florida Everglades, at Silver Springs and at Castillo de San Marcos in the southeastern National Monuments through the courtesy of the United States Department of the Interior, National Park Service." Due to this on-location shooting, we get important glimpses of mid-century Florida settings—a swollen Lake Okeechobee not beset by drought, untouched flora, bountiful riverways, and plentiful wildlife. Though on some crucial level, these sights also tend to all the more remind us of our plunder.

Dear Diary:

Donna Reed is such a babe. They don't make 'em like her anymore. Man, does she look good in a black wig and braids. Makes me sweat all over just thinking about her. Maybe we shoudda named this yawner How Lewis and Clark Won the Cold War. *Oh, but wait, then it wouldn't have been about Indians, but the Ruskies! Gag, it's so-o-o-o hard to dress "Communists." No feathers and boring . . .*

Time for my afternoon snooze.

Love ya, Donna. I'll see you in my dreams,

Hollywood

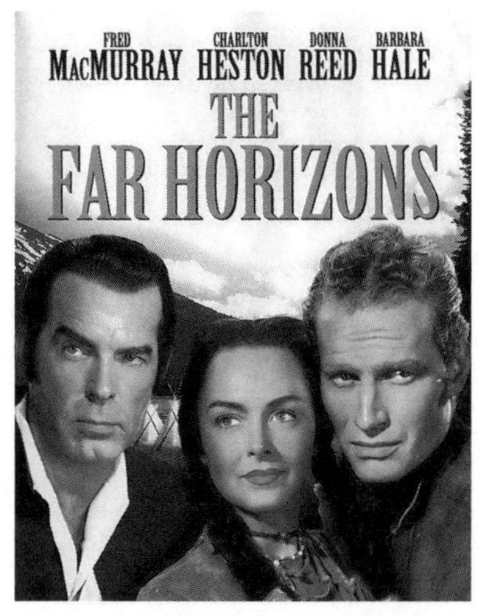

The Far Horizons

Frederick Hoxie

The historical errors in *The Far Horizons* (1955), Hollywood's contribution to the 150th anniversary of the Lewis and Clark expedition, come at you so fast, it is hard to keep up with them. The film opens with Meriwether Lewis in satin pants, and ends with the camera on Sekakawea (Donna Reed in pancake makeup) riding away from Thomas Jefferson's White House in a liveried carriage. Really, the fun never stops. The entire expedition takes place in gorgeous weather, seemingly over one long summer break. The crew travels by boat and is able to turn out in spiffy dress uniforms at the drop of the commander's Napoleon-style hat. Clark's manservant/slave York? AWOL. Where is the African American who went on this journey with Clark? If you're thinking that movie audiences might not want to see Charlton Heston with a black manservant, we might want to take that question one step further and ask, why not?

For their part, all the Indians wear beaded headbands like the ones we made in Cub Scouts back in the 1950s, and anyone who is *anyone* has great abs and an eagle-feather headdress. And having traveled the Upper Missouri several times myself, I was captivated by the movie's version of North Dakota's scenery: shining, snow-capped mountains, alpine meadows, pine forests! Who knew?

But wait. If, in the world of film, the errors are as thick as the Indians constantly lying in ambush, if good guys become bad guys and the Oregon coast is suddenly devoid of Native people, maybe this movie isn't really about Lewis and Clark at all! Maybe the screenwriters and producers had something else in mind. Could this miserable adventure have been intended as a forerunner to "Kabuki Macbeth" or "Hamlet in Drag?" Perhaps there is a core drama here that is more important than the costumes or historical moment. Perhaps that "1803" projected onto the screen in the first scene is a joke. Let's look for a deeper meaning. After all, the "errors" aren't really so bad. I mean, relax: a little scenery added here, a little makeup for the leading lady there, a war-whoop, a snappy red, white, and blue uniform in the background: why not? As a Hollywood executive said to me recently, "Don't get so excited; it's a story. We are selling drama, not accuracy." So how serious are those errors?

The Corps of Discovery—as the American expedition dispatched by President Jefferson was officially called—left Wood River, Illinois, in the spring of 1804 and returned to nearby St. Louis in the fall of 1806. Note the dates here. During the summer and fall of 1804, the commanders and their men traveled up the Missouri River as far as the Mandan villages in modern North Dakota. They made camp near the Mandans and Hidatsas from November 1804 until April 1805, when they continued upstream with two new recruits, Toussaint Charbonneau and his pregnant companion, Sekakawea, also known as Sacagawea. In August of that year, the group encountered Sekakawea's kinsmen, the Shoshones, in modern Idaho. They traveled on to the Bitterroot Valley and then, with winter fast approaching, they took advantage of new horses provided by Salish hunters and directions from a Shoshone guide to find their way along the ancient Lolo Trail to the Clearwater River. There, friendly Nez Perces helped the Americans descend the Columbia River to the sea. After a winter near the Oregon coast, during which time they dealt frequently with Chinook traders, the corps returned eastward, assisted by the same groups who had helped them on their outward journey.

Even the most celebratory accounts of Lewis and Clark's journey credit the commanders' Indian hosts and guides with providing crucial assistance to the expedition. Indians provided the food that kept the Americans alive during their winters in North Dakota and Oregon. Indian allies guided them across the Rockies and facilitated their travel down the Columbia. And Indians were the source of canoes, advice, and encouragement. None of this help diminishes the courage or achievement of corps members. In fact, the Americans' ability to make friends and elicit aid from Native people—all of whom were well-aware of the possible danger the Americans posed—should only enhance their reputations.

So it is not being picky to say that *The Far Horizons* incorrectly presents the Hidatsa chief Le Borgne (a well-documented figure with a long history of involvement in the international fur trade) as a duplicitous, slave-owning schemer. In the film, instead of welcoming the Americans to the Upper Missouri, the movie-Hidatsa leader plans to ambush them and rub them out. And rather than signing on with the corps as he did in real life, the movie-Charbonneau is a secret agent—an undercover spy who only pretends to help. The Frenchman promises to help the wily chief only because Le Borgne offered to make the Shoshone slave "his woman." The fantasy unfolds in true Hollywood fashion: the movie-Sekakawea gets wind of the plot against the Americans, escapes from the Hidatsa village on a stolen pony, and—after riding all night—reaches the Americans just in time to enable them to repel the—you guessed it!—flaming-arrow assault by Le Borgne's men.

Equally bizarre, the movie Nez Perces—who feasted the Americans on smoked salmon, boarded their horses for the winter, and accompanied the corps downriver to insure their safety—appear in *Far Horizons* in the prone position. "The woods are crawling with Indians," Sergeant Gass declares as they approach Nez Perce country, and soon afterwards the inevitable ambush occurs. Instead of helping the expedition downriver, the movie–Nez Perce hoist World War II–style submarine netting across the Clearwater, bringing the Americans' canoes to a sudden halt. (The movie-canoes are all flimsy birch-barks. Probably a good choice; if the filmmakers had put the Americans in historically accurate dugouts, the heavy boats would likely have sliced through the Nez Perces' nets with little difficulty.) The movie-soldiers are suddenly sitting ducks for the Indians' (surprisingly numerous) rifles and nefarious (but primitive) tricks: tribesmen aim logs downriver to sweep the corps towards shore. The attack spurs Meriwether Lewis into action. A knife firmly gripped between his teeth, the commander dives headfirst into the river and cuts through the Nez Perce netting. His men float behind him towards safety.

You get the picture. Indians are sneaky, violent, and dangerous. The only exceptions to this movie rule are Sekakawea/Donna Reed and her brother, Cameahwait, the Shoshone chief. In *Far Horizons* these two "get it." They understand that the Americans are a force for good. Their arrival signals a moment of progress. Sekakawea focuses on the corn seeds she wants to take to her people so "they won't starve," and Cameahwait agrees ("We will not grow hungry when the snow falls." So tell me again how the Shoshones survived in this region for 10,000 years?). After visiting Washington with the commanders, the movie-Sekakawea decides to return home. "There is much we can both do for our people," she writes to Clark as she rides away, "many things we . . . can teach to them: kindness and the wisdom to know the truth."

Sekakawea's departure resolves a complicated subplot in the film: the screenwriters have the Shoshone girl and Clark fall in love on the westward journey, despite Lewis's disapproval. Their romance suggests the possibility of a true-love-conquers-all ending, a Pocahontas story for the nineteenth century. (We are held in Hollywood suspense as, in its closing minutes, the film cuts from the characters' professions of love on the Pacific to Jefferson's White House. The screenwriters discreetly skipped the months of consensual sex during the return journey). But it is not to be: the Indian girl declares, "I have seen your country, but it is not my country and these are not my people. I do not want to be someone else." She appreciates the Americans, but she won't press them to alter their "country" to accommodate her. The perfect Indian: peaceful, grateful, patient. She accepts her fate; she is destined to be "different," an outsider.

The Far Horizons is more than inaccurate. The fundamental themes of the Corps of Discovery story—Indian diplomacy, cross-cultural interaction, mutual assistance—are completely absent. In their place we find not only stereotypes—tipis, feathers, flaming arrows—but a story that bears no resemblance to the original. Hollywood's epic of a few dozen white men in Daniel Boone getups fighting their way to the Pacific so that Lewis can declare, "I claim all the land we have traveled for the United States," is ultimately not about the age of Jefferson at all. The plot fits more closely with the age of Stalin and Truman: earnest Americans opposed by a treacherous enemy that will lie, break agreements, dispatch secret agents, and resort to the most nefarious tactics to thwart America's dreams. A few marginal members of the enemy's people will recognize the Americans' goodness, but their efforts count for little beside the firepower and unscrupulousness of the true enemy. (Imagine Sekakawea as a Hungarian freedom fighter, doomed to fall before the red menace.) The world is not a complex arena of competing cultures and crosscutting loyalties; it is a place where America's enemies hide from sight and await their chance. It is a place where Americans need to be vigilant and strong and, above all, to remember the differences between "my people" and "your people." This is the "truth" of *The Far Horizons.* I wish it had been a movie about Indians.

Dear Diary:

The British are coming. Those Brits seem hell bent on using more local Indian talent and expertise than I'm comfortable with, and they are mining stories that should belong to us. Come to think of it, whose side are those Indians on anyway? And the way those Brits skimp on their productions—not enough special effects for my taste, and too much good dialogue.

Bloody hell,

Hollywood

Thunderheart

Paul M. Robertson

"It's a five hundred year resistance." That's how Indian activist Jimmy Looks Twice, played by real life Indian activist and poet John Trudell, puts the events of the 1970s on Pine Ridge Indian Reservation in South Dakota into historical perspective. The activists and the Lakota people they support are a threat, he argues, because they "choose to be who they are." That choice puts them at odds with their corrupt tribal government, and with the revenge-bent FBI agent Frank Coutelle (Sam Shepard), for whom Jimmy is "an enemy of the United States."

British director Michael Apted's *Thunderheart* is a tale of exploitation, oppression, and violence that marks the recent history of Pine Ridge Indian Reservation, home of the Oglala Sioux (Lakota). It's a depiction of heroic resistance and steadfast refusal to cave in to pressures to abandon identity and culture. The movie unabashedly sides with ARM (Aboriginal Rights Movement) and the local people they support, against the feds and corrupt tribal president Jack Milton (Fred Ward) and his goons. Local ARM supporters, the "traditionals," have been marginalized by the corrupt Milton, who is ripping off funds meant for programs and schools, and getting kickbacks from land leases.

Parallels with actual persons, places, and groups are thinly disguised and are clearly intentional—the credits note that the movie is based on events that occurred on several reservations in the 1970s. The breathtaking badlands scenery is recognizably Pine Ridge Indian Reservation, as is the community scene from the village of Wanblee. The landscape is beautifully and accurately captured, even down to the dusty dirt roads, some of which are still regular arteries on the Rez, but many of which were paved over by the time the movie was completed in 1992. A remarkable sequence of Wanblee, near the northern reservation boundary, shot on a bright summer's day, simultaneously captures the promise and the desolation of a place that at the time ranked as the poorest in the United States. As Agent Frank Coutelle drives through that housing area, his young assistant, Agent Ray Levoi (Val Kilmer), who has been detailed to the reservation because of his Sioux heritage and is getting his first glimpse of the Rez, is shocked by the poverty. Frank offers that it is the "third world slap dab in the middle of America." The label sums up the grinding poverty but obscures the pulsing life of the place—children playing, elders sitting on porches—that signals a community. Touches like that make *Thunderheart* a rewarding treat that you can watch over and over again.

The character of President Jack Milton is modeled directly after Oglala Sioux tribal president Richard "Dick" Wilson, who served (more would say ruled) from 1972 to 1976. Wilson's reputation as a corrupt and brutal leader who functioned as a virtual dictator, and who was not above using violence to subdue his critics and consolidate his power, is supported by a not insubstantial body of evidence. But he had/has his supporters as well, who point to his strength and who benefited from the favors he distributed to selected constituents. *Thunderheart*'s Milton is more of a cardboard character than the late president; the undersized actor Fred Ward is not equal to the task of conveying the fleshier, more menacing presence that was Dick Wilson. See for yourself by watching *Incident at Oglala* (1992), Apted's outstanding documentary, the research for which clearly bleeds over into *Thunderheart.*

The goons in *Thunderheart* man roadblocks, careen around in pickup trucks, fire into homes, and brutalize local people. The depiction is spot-on, as far as it goes. And the casting decisions further strengthen the movie. Duane Brewer—a well-known, self-acknowledged goon-squad leader himself—along with some of his contemporaries play themselves in the movie. But why are their roles so narrow? They have families and lives, too—what's driving them to side with Milton? Why are they so opposed to the "traditionals?" What are their dreams and aspirations?

Milton's opponents fare better. By the time we enter the story, ARM has been decimated. Maggie Eagle Hawk (Sheila Tousey) and the redoubtable Jimmy Looks Twice are the only leaders left. Maggie teaches school, uses her Dartmouth education to help her people, and has clear pride in her culture, illustrating the ability of contemporary Native persons to negotiate "two worlds." ARM supports the "traditionals" on the reservation, and draws on the wisdom of elders and spiritual leaders for guidance. Chief Ted Thin Elk, in the role of the *wicasa wakan* (holy man) Samuel "Sam" Reaches, brings a quiet dignity, delightful humor, and familiarity with his beloved Lakota culture to a role he clearly relishes. Lakota elder Sarah Brave, Maggie's grandmother, conveys strength and resolution in her spare dialogue with Agent Levoi, as she tells him she hears gunfire every night—commonplace in those years. Her gift to him of a porcupine-quill medicine wheel is one of the ways *Thunderheart* achieves its authenticity.

The film captures the asymmetrical conflict between the opposing sides in spectacular fashion. The feds have a chopper, military assault rifles, and hi-tech communications. The goons in their pickup trucks are so heavily armed—and were, we now know, supplied with weaponry by federal authorities—that they are reminiscent of the "technicals" Somali warlords used against U.S.

forces in Mogadishu. Milton's use of their sardonic self-reference "GOONS," meaning "Guardians of the Oglala Nation," is a nice touch.

Thunderheart could easily be faulted for its "us and them" depiction of two sides—ARM and traditionals vs. Milton and his goons. After all, many people were not actively aligned with either side. Some felt forced, with good reason, to side with one group or another. Some were caught in the middle. Others made pragmatic choices. Granted, reality is messier, but the formula works in *Thunderheart* precisely because it captures a powerful dialectic that so starkly characterized the reservation in those conflict-ridden years.

Colonialism is a divide-and-conquer endeavor. It's an old story. Outsiders side with insiders who put their personal ambitions ahead of the welfare of their own people. The feds support the corrupt Milton because his personal goal of self-enrichment aligns with the planned exploitation of the remote Red Deer Table for large-scale uranium drilling, a goal favored by the United States. When tribal official Leo Fast Elk finds out about the deal, his murder is arranged by the FBI. ARM supporter Richard Yellow Hawk, in prison on criminal charges, agrees to do the assassination, snitch on his fellow ARM members, and act as an agent provocateur, in exchange for a dramatically reduced sentence. From there it's a simple matter to pin the murder on ARM activist Jimmy, and eliminate the last best hope of the movement.

Skeptics may scoff at the insistence that the FBI was an amoral colonial police force in that place and time. But *Thunderheart*'s union of a fine cast with a judicious sampling of the evidentiary foundation that underpins *Incident at Oglala* gives it credibility. The matter-of-fact way that Sam Shepard, who turns in a nuanced and compelling portrait of the corrupt Agent Coutelle, delivers a nearly verbatim quotation of real-life Special Agent Norman Zigrossi, who was in charge of FBI operations on the reservation during that period of the '70s on Pine Ridge that is often dubbed the "reign of terror," is chillingly convincing. "They are a proud people, but they are also a conquered people, and that means that their future is dictated by the nation that conquered them. Now rightly or wrongly, that's the way it works down through history." Tribal police officer Walter Crow Horse, engagingly and humorously rendered by Graham Greene, describes the FBI as "the second coming of the same old cavalry," an apt analogy for the antics and attitudes the movie highlights.

Thunderheart forwards the colonial situation into our era. Brutality visited on the people by self-identified conquerors; the consequences for identity, subsequent resistance, and revitalization—the elements are here and now. Colonizers, acting out of fear, hatred, and sometimes calculated attempts to humiliate, intentionally target the culture of the other. Postcolonialism? Not yet—not on Pine Ridge, anyway.

When an FBI agent grabs Sam Reaches's four-hundred-year-old rattle, passed down through the generations, conks him on the head with it, drops it in the dirt, and grinds it under his boot heel, you know Jimmy is right. *Thunderheart* explores psychological dynamics of racism and oppression, too. Walter Crow Horse recalls that, as a child, when they played cowboys and Indians he was always Gary Cooper. But resistance can rekindle the flame. Echoing recollections and interpretations frequently made by Lakota people, he credits the rise of pride in culture, elders, and language, variously evidenced in the movie by powwows, ceremonies, and respect for the power of dreams and visions, to the coming of ARM warriors.

In a parallel to the broader self-discovery that was going on during those years, Val Kilmer, as the cocky young FBI agent Ray Levoi, experiences his own transformation. Levoi is initially in denial of his Lakota Sioux heritage, and dogged by self-loathing and denial. As a person of principle, he is open to leads Walter provides about the murder, and is consequently troubled as the real intent of the FBI comes into focus. More importantly, the power of the place is stalking him. In a first exchange with Maggie, who tells him about Jimmy's ability to shape-shift, he dismisses her and the possibility with "Is that a hereditary thing or can one take classes?" But as he turns to go, he has a brief vision of dancers in buckskin up against the badlands wall. Sam Reaches gets under his skin too, nudging him to put his past into perspective as he shares his own visions about Ray's coming.

Once Ray has a vision of running headlong with other Lakota men, women, and children, who are being chased down by cavalry, and is shot in the back, he is a changed man. Sam explains that Ray is descended from a holy man named Thunderheart, who was killed there. "It is his blood, the same blood spilled in the grass and snow at Wounded Knee runs through your heart like a buffalo. Thunderheart has come, sent here to a troubled place to help his people."

Humor leavens the troubles in art as it does on the Rez. Locals on Pine Ridge who have seen *Thunderheart* laud it for its cultural knowledge and humor. Walter Crow Horse's reaction to Ray's story of running from the cavalry at Wounded Knee is a fine example of wry Lakota wit: "Man waits a long time to have a vision. Might go his whole lifetime and never have one. Along comes some instant Indian with a fucking Rolex and a brand new pair of shoes. Goddamn FBI to top it all off and has his self a vision." But what about that? That's how it works, Lakota people say. You might not want a vision and it comes. You might want one and never have it. It's a mystery.

When Jimmy cajoles Agent Coutelle, intent on searching Jimmy's home, into reaching into a hole under his house to get his key, rather than breaking down his door, and Coutelle gets a nasty bite by the resident badger instead, you can't help but cheer. And when Jimmy takes advantage of his coup, eluding the trigger-happy feds and goons, who lay down a withering barrage of bullets, by shape-shifting into a deer and bounding over a fence once the shooting dies down, there is real satisfaction in watching a modern Lakota trickster getting the better of an adversary that commands overwhelming force.

Thunderheart's sensitive representations of Lakota culture, spirituality, and sacred space give it power. Apted has the artistry to capture the dignity in Thin Elk's portrayal of Sam Reaches, and the enchanting beauty of the Lakota *inipi* (purification lodge) with songs sung by the renowned cultural practitioner, the late Severt Young Bear Sr., and to lift them magically right out of the Rez and onto the screen. There is a close attention to authentic detail—sage hanging on a wall, flag offerings tied to trees, a spirit dish Sam maintains, the Lakota *inipi*, the drum, the songs, the clothes they wear, the dust rising up after cars pass. It's all there, the grinding poverty, the violent history, the unbreakable spirit, the haunting beauty, and the power of the Lakota homeland, in a two-hour movie.

Thunderheart is a delicious exposé that, according to many of the Oglala Lakota (Sioux) students on Pine Ridge Reservation that I've taught over the years at Oglala Lakota College, gets it right. Not bad for a British director. How did he do it? First of all, he enlisted a cast of helpers and advisors and then listened to them. He tapped local people and listened to them. He sought out knowledgeable advisors, including WKLDOC (Wounded Knee Legal Defense Offense Committee) attorney Bruce Ellison, and listened to them too. He cast traditional people like Ted Thin Elk and Sara Brave in significant roles. And he had a heck of a story to work with. It is, for those close to it in particular, difficult to watch, evocative of tears. Why? Because it is so true.

Dear Diary:

I don't like mutton!

Signed,

Hollywood

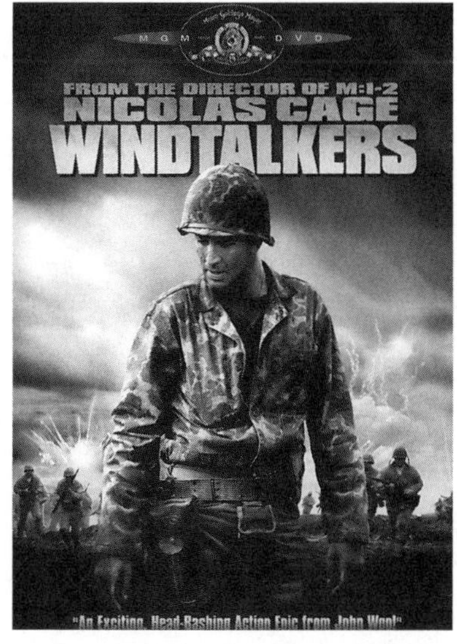

Windtalkers

Deborah Miranda

"UGH!" Unbelievable, Ghastly, Horrific.

That was my one-word indigenous review after first seeing *Windtalkers.* However, as it's been several years since I stumbled out of the movie theater spewing that primal utterance into the air, I now find it possible to be more restrained in my analysis of *Windtalkers.* What were my specific issues with this film? *Windtalkers*, as a title, seems to mean that the film will be about, well, wind talking (Hollywoodese for the Navajo Code Talkers who worked in the Pacific during World War II). But what the heck is a "wind talker" anyway? Someone who speaks into the wind? Why change the intense, intellectual job of coding and decoding into talking with wind? I know I'm not the only Indian insulted by what could be translated as "talks with farts." Hot air, indeed.

But what the film really ends up portraying isn't Code Talkers at all—it is Post Traumatic Stress Syndrome (PTSD) in a white man. I'm not saying war isn't hell; remember, we Indians have been at war and dealing with PTSD for hundreds of years. Joe Enders (Nicholas Cage's tortured character) is the sole survivor of a doomed platoon of Marines. With the help of a sympathetic nurse, Enders fakes his way to wellness in order to get back into action and avenge his buddies. Meanwhile, of course, the guy is a seething morass of guilt, anger and other manifestations of PTSD. So why wasn't the movie called *PTSD Talker*? Or *White Angst Talker*?

I'm so tired of seeing a White Man being serviced by people of color. Come on, you know what I mean: that old Hollywood plot where anyone who is NOT white in the film is simply there to save the White Man's life, save his woman's life, or bring about some significant character development in the lead (white) actor.

Here, Joe Enders achieves wholeness as a human being as he lies dying in the arms of Ben Yahzee (native actor Adam Beach.) And what's up with that spelling? It's Yazzie—but maybe that wasn't "indigenous" enough? After being a shell-shocked, angry, self-hating man for most of the movie, after refusing to relate to the Navajo soldiers as anything but walking code machines, after killing Yahzee's buddy and fellow code talker Charlie Whitehorse (Roger Willie) to prevent "the code" from being cracked by the enemy, Enders gasps that he's sorry he killed Whitehorse, is forgiven by Yahzee, and completes his quest to achieve redemption.

Once again, the White Man is served by a Faithful Darkie, and Faithful Darkie is just there to help White Man become a better person. *Geesh.* To top it all, the film ends with Yahzee, his wife, and his child on a high ridge somewhere in Navajo Country, performing a ceremony over Enders's dog tags. "He was a good man, a fierce warrior," Yahzee tells his young son. "If you ever tell a story about him, George, say he was my friend."

By this scene in the film, I wanted to scream. Can't we even have a decent indigenous ceremony without the white man taking center stage?!

Nobody told me this was a mystery movie. What mystery, you ask? How John Woo managed to make a movie not even remotely related to the actual event his film purports to portray. The "real" story goes like this: U.S. government sends Navajo kids to boarding schools where their Native language is beaten out of them, thus removing a major barrier standing in the way of Navajo Americanization. Some of the kids retain their language, in secret anyway, and at great personal cost. U.S. government becomes involved in war, needs a way for troops to communicate without the enemy understanding. They need a new code. All those American-educated Japanese soldiers can break English-based codes almost as soon as the Americans invent them. But wait! That's it! Languages are codes.

So maybe what the United States needs is a new language that is actually a very old language. One very few people speak. Even better, one whose speakers are totally within the control (not to mention actual borders) of the U.S. government. Hey, you know that Indian language we tried to stamp out . . . ?

So, the same kids who were beaten for hanging onto their language go off to war, successfully transmit crucial information back and forth, and basically save the world. Not only are these Navajo men heroes, but they wait decades to tell their story (and they do wait, every single one of them, quite faithfully obeying their last command despite the fact that they returned to homes without electricity or running water, poverty, and their own war-shocked psyches) just in case the United States needs to use that particular ace in the hole again anytime soon. Many Code Talkers died without one second of recognition. What a great story! What a powerful testament to the depth of indigenous devotion to, and protection of, their homeland!

Too bad John Woo didn't think so.

You can take the cowboy out of the movie, but . . . you're still gonna need a dead Indian. One of the weirdest plotlines here is also the movie's main tweak: the code must not fall into the enemy's hands. The only way the enemy could get the code would be to capture a Navajo and torture the code out of him. Therefore, the white soldiers assigned to guard the Code Talkers are ordered to kill the Indians if capture looks imminent (Joe Enders does, indeed, kill Charlie Whitehorse and his Japanese captors with a grenade).

Is this standard operating procedure for code signalers in the U.S. military? If so, it's the first time I've heard of it. In all the war movies I've seen (and I grew up watching a lot of them, all in black-and-white on our little TV on long rainy afternoons), never once has the guy receiving and decoding the incoming messages been assigned a "bodyguard" whose real job is to kill him if the enemy threatens. In a documentary for the History Channel, surviving Code Talkers disagreed about whether this plan was a reality or fantasy. The Marines simply deny the story flat-out. Some Code Talkers didn't even have a guard. Others suggest that guards were only necessary to protect Code Talkers from U.S. soldiers who might mistake them for Japanese (this actually happened). Hmmm. I hate to say it, but there's something about the idea of white U.S. soldiers killing Indians that appeals to an American audience. Holding it out like a carrot throughout the movie, Woo falls back on an old Western standard.

The sad thing is, this movie gave Woo the chance to reverse decades of cowboy and Indian movies in which the cavalry chases Indians into the ground. Rowdy savages full of rape and pillage, honest soldiers just protecting the good old homestead and homefolks. Now here's a radical thought: what if John Wayne and the Indians were on the same side? (Well, I guess we just answered that: then the cowboys would still have to kill the Indians because that's the way it's done. Just when it looked like we could get some brotherhood going here.)

"Stay on my ass," my ass. At one point Enders yells at Yahzee to stay down and stay behind him. I think it was about here that I realized there was a steady stream of whimpering throughout the entire scene—hell, the whole movie: it was Enders knifing, Enders shooting, Enders throwing a grenade, Enders charging a pit full of Japanese soldiers . . . and in between each of those scenes, we see Yahzee staring in horror, Yahzee wincing, Yahzee looking away, Yahzee crouching behind a barrier. Sure, eventually Yahzee starts killing the Japanese, but he continues to be portrayed as hesitant and, well, unmanly. While other Marines also respond to chaos and death with fear, their performance isn't noticeably impaired. What's going on here? Are Navajo men just wimps? Incapable of dealing with death and destruction? Unable to defend themselves or their buddies? I suspect what the writers and director might be trying to insert here is a teeny-weeny bit of Navajo culture. Dread of being near dead bodies, which is taboo and very difficult to circumvent for anyone raised according to traditional Navajo lifeways. The problem with this theory is that nothing about such a taboo is ever mentioned in the film, so all the audience sees is a really *wussy* Navajo man letting his platoon take bullets for him. In World War II, all Native men were young men in life-or-death situations who in reality adapted quickly to the needs of their military units, and staying alive.

Keith Little, a former Code Talker, readily agrees that his religion makes touching the dead or being in a place where a person has died a taboo because "there are evil spirits roaming around." But, he also adds: "You had to survive in combat. If you had to crawl behind a dead person for cover, that was it." In other words, Navajo soldiers, whether Code Talkers or not, didn't spend a lot of time staring, wincing, looking away, or hiding. They adapted, and perhaps the cleansing ceremonies performed for them when they returned home helped them deal with some of the horrors they endured. In *Windtalkers*, however, the stereotype of Indians as passive, lazy freeloaders gets perpetuated again, even if it is unintentional. And if someone edited out an explanatory scene about Navajo religious beliefs, what does that say about intention, anyway?

Another reason to hate *Windtalkers*: anti-Catholic bonding. In what is meant to be the obligatory macho-bonding moment of the film, Enders and Yahzee meet in a small village and enter a house where a woman and child cower in one corner. Enders then tells Yahzee that he was confirmed in the Church, where "They told me I was a soldier of Christ. Somewhere along the way I must have switched units." This statement leads Yahzee to tell Enders about the time he was punished for speaking Navajo in church—by being chained to a radiator in the church basement "for two days." The next thing we know, Enders is pleading, then yelling at his superiors. "Goddamn it! I can't do it! I can't perform my duty!" he yells, pushing his superior up against the wall. What I think he really means is: "I can't kill my Indian now that we've bonded." Is there supposed to be something here about shared oppression, like, ah, "we've both been betrayed by the Catholic Church, so . . . now I can't kill you if the enemy captures you?" Is it that easy to eliminate all those years of Catholicism, colonization, violence, betrayal, and allow the white man and the Indian to be brothers? Was a common enemy, in this case, God, all we ever needed to cross the great divide? I wish things were that easy in real life as in the movies. Oh, and just in case you forgot—some Catholic missions were indeed hell for Indians, but it was the boarding schools run by the U.S. government that rounded up children against their parents' will, sometimes even kidnapping them, taking them far away, and beating children for speaking their native languages. I guess Enders couldn't have bonded over that, though. He's a just-the-facts-ma'am kind of character.

In the case of John Nesbit's review of *Windtalkers*, it's the penis facts that do get noticed in "Woo Goes to War." He writes:

> One standard Navajo joke is translated loosely in a scene that doesn't play as funny in English, but it does indicate that one of the screenwriters was in contact with a Navajo. During the poker table scene, Injun-hating-Corporal Charles Rogers (Noah Emmerich) calls Yahzee "chief" and Yahzee humorously responds that he must have seen his "war bonnet" in the shower. It's much funnier in the original Navajo, which describes the tip of the penis as a "war hat" because Navajo soldiers saw similarities.

So . . . the film's makers can't be bothered with checking facts for military accuracy or Navajo religious ceremony and culture, but an authentic Navajo penis joke makes it?! What does this tell us about the film's priorities? It tells us that any expectations we had of *Windtalkers* telling a true story of Navajo Code Talkers are completely wrong. We can expect nothing like that from Hollywood. Hollywood is on a mission, all right, but its mission is to make money. John Woo threw in all the stock entertainment ingredients: revenge, plenty of violence, fight scenes, good over evil, underdog versus Nicholas Cage, but somehow the story just never came alive. *Windtalkers* is not a good war movie. It's not a good psychological thriller. It's not a good underdog-triumphs-over-prejudice movie (i.e., not inspirational). It's not even a good faux-Indian movie about the mystical and magical powers of being indigenous warriors. And it certainly is not a good movie about a small group of brave, dedicated, patriotic Navajo men who won the war in the Pacific for the United States.

That movie has yet to be made. This one rates four tomahawks down.

UGH!

— THE END —

What the Critics Said . . .

CHAPTER 1: THE SILENT RED MAN

The Vanishing American

"The Vanishing American," the photodrama presented last night in the Criterion Theatre before a brilliant gathering in which there were a host of celebrities, proved to be an inspiring production fashioned with infinite pains. The theme, of course, deals with the passing of the American Indian. . . . From a fleeting glimpse of the aborigines, glancing like dogs to right and left as they emerge from their recesses, one is taken to their skin-clad and paint-bedaubed successors, and then to the more interesting but slothful cliff-dwellers, who are pictured on ledges in the Grand Canyon, some dozing and others going about their toil listlessly. Energy then stalks along in the shape of the redskin, who mercilessly and easily defeats the inactive people . . ."

—"The Screen," by Mordaunt Hall. *New York Times*, October 16, 1925.

Redskin

"So beautiful are many of the natural color sequences in 'Redskin,' which was launched last Saturday at the Criterion Theatre, the spectators were impelled to applaud some of the lovely visions that greeted the eye. And, while this story is about as plausible as some of Douglas Fairbank's [*sic*] agile adventures, it is nevertheless most carefully cast and completely acted. The incidents, far-fetched though they may be, are usually more gratifying than annoying.

"Once again Richard Dix is to be seen as a man of copper hue. The last time he played an Indian was in 'The Vanishing American.' This time he appears as a Navajo, a fine athletic and agile person, who becomes smitten with the undeniable charms of a Pueblo maiden named Corn Blossom.

"Wing Foot (Mr. Dix) loves and is loved by Corn Blossom, but the Navajos and Pueblos can't see eye to eye. The Pueblo chieftains will that Corn Blossom shall marry a man from her own tribe, but help comes from the whites, and Wing Foot, who, during a chapter, goes to college, eventually escapes from the violent Pueblos, and so does his Pueblo girl.

"There seems to be an erroneous conception in the sequence where Wing Foot goes to college, for the students there are made to look down upon a redskin. This, in itself, is an incredulous notion and in a measure it is a pivotal point of the story. Certainly no white student would have been scornful of Wing Foot, who proved himself to be the fleetest of the fleet at the college . . ."

—"The Screen," by Mordaunt Hall. *New York Times*, January 28, 1929.

CHAPTER 2: JOHN FORD AND "THE DUKE" ON THE WARPATH

Drums along the Mohawk

"Walter D. Edmonds's exciting novel of the Mohawk Valley during the American Revolution has come to the Roxy's screen in a considerably elided, but still basically faithful, film edition bearing the trademark of Director John Ford, one of the best cinema story-tellers in the business. 'Drums Along the Mohawk' was tailored to Mr. Ford's measure. It is romantic enough for any adventure-story lover. It has its humor, its sentiment, its complement of blood and thunder. About the only Ford staple we miss is a fog scene. Rain, smoke, and stockade burnings have had to compensate. The fusion of them all has made a first-rate historical film, as rich atmospherically as it is in action. . . . Mr. Ford has been fortunate, too, in finding such externals to play his Mohawk people as those which go under the names of Henry Fonda, Claudette Colbert, Edna May Oliver, Eddie Collins, Arthur Shields, Ward Bond and Roger Imhof."

—"The Screen," by Frank S. Nugent. *New York Times*, November 4, 1939.

Fort Apache

"A rootin', tootin' Wild West show, full of Indians and United States cavalry, dust and desert scenery and a nice masculine trace of romance, has been honestly put together under the masterful direction of John Ford in Argosy's 'Fort Apache,' which came to the Capitol yesterday. Folks who are looking for action in the oldest tradition of the screen, observed through a genuine artist's camera, will find plenty of it here.

"But also apparent in this picture, for those who care to look, is a new and maturing viewpoint upon one aspect of the American Indian wars. For here it is not the "heavy" of the piece, but a hard-bitten Army colonel, blind through ignorance and a passion for revenge. And ranged alongside this willful white man is a venal government agent who exploits the innocence of the Indians while supposedly acting as their friend.

"Thus, for the standard white movie audience, 'Fort Apache' will chiefly provide a handsome and thrilling outdoor drama of 'war' on the American frontier—a salty and sizzling visualization of regimental life at a desert fort, of strong masculine personality and of racing battles beneath the withering sun. For, of course, Mr. Ford is a genius at directing this sort of thing and Frank S. Nugent has ably supplied him with a tangy and workable script."

—"The Screen," by Bosley Crowther. *New York Times*, June 25, 1948.

She Wore a Yellow Ribbon

"In this big Technicolored Western Mr. Ford has superbly achieved a vast and composite illustration of all the legends of the frontier cavalrymen. He has got the bold and dashing courage, the stout masculine sentiment, the grandeur of rear-guard heroism and the brash bravado of the bar-rack-room brawl. And, best of all, he has got the brilliant color and vivid detail of those legendary troops as they ranged through the silent 'Indian country' and across the magnificent Western plains.

"From the moment that Mr. Ford assembles the raw-boned troopers of Company C around the immortal guidon of the Seventh Cavalry at distant Fort Starke, thence to ride forth on perilous mission under Captain Nathan Brittles' firm command, the rifles are held at ready and the scouts are flanked wide on alert, for somewhere out there in the vast plains a Cheyenne dog-party is on the prowl. Custer is dead at the Little Big Horn, the buffalo herds are coming north and someone is making 'big medicine' among the strangely emboldened Indian tribes. And Mr. Ford being the admirer of the cavalry that he is, you may be sure that a plenty happens before the mission is brought to a close . . ."

"Bulwarked with gay and spirited music and keyed to the colors of the plains, 'She Wore a Yellow Ribbon' is a dilly of a cavalry picture. Yeehooooo!"

—"'She Wore a Yellow Ribbon,' at Capitol, Stars John Wayne as a Cavalry Captain," by Bosley Crowther. *New York Times*, November 18, 1949.

The Searchers

"'The Searchers,' for all the suspicions aroused by excessive language in its ads, is really a rip-snorting Western, as brashly entertaining as they come. It starts with the tardy homecoming of a lean Texan from the Civil War and leaps right into a massacre by Commanches [*sic*] and the abduction of two white girls. And then it proceeds for almost two hours to detail the five-year search for the girls that is relentlessly conducted by the Texan, with the ultimate help of just one lad.

"That is the story pattern on which Mr. [John] Ford and his gang have plastered a wealth of Western action that has the toughness of leather and the sting of a whip. It bristles and howls with Indian fighting, goes into tense, nerve-rasping brawls between the Texan and his hunting companion, explodes with fiery comedy and lays into some frontier heroics that make the welkin ring."

—"The Screen," by Bosley Crowther. *New York Times*, May 31, 1956.

CHAPTER 3: THE DISNEY VERSION

Peter Pan

"Such things as the innovation of a visit to the Indian Village by the Lost Boys (to the tune of a lively ditty, 'Tee Dum, Tee Dee') and a powwow there with the Indians to 'What Makes the Red Man Red' rollick with gleeful vitality . . ."

—"The Screen," by Bosley Crowther. *New York Times*, February 12, 1953.

Davy Crockett, King of the Wild Frontier

"[Mr. Disney's] legend of the Tennessee backwoodsman who fought Indians, outgrinned [*sic*] a b'ar, went to Congress to help Andy Jackson and died 'fer liberty' at the Alamo, is a straight juvenile entertainment with a story-line as simple as a T and enough poker-faced exaggeration to satisfy the most implausible fibber in school. The incidents are tall and transparent. No psychological subtleties to confuse. You know what's happening every single second. And all of it is okay."

—"The Screen," by Bosley Crowther. *New York Times*, May 26, 1955.

Pocahontas

"Fathers across American will soon be volunteering in record numbers to take children to the movies, and here's why: Pocahontas is a babe. She is the first Disney animated heroine since Tinker Bell with great legs—maybe *any* legs. She wears form-fitting, off- the-shoulder buckskin that would be as much at home in Beverly Hills as in 17th-century Jamestown. She's got sloe eyes, a rosebud mouth, billowing black hair and terrific muscle tone. And she is the centerpiece of a film that's as great-looking as its heroine.

"Blood will soon boil because of the Harlequin-style history dished out by this pretty romantic 'Pocahontas' which despite its origins is as much a fiction as any fairy tale. But for all the blatant liberties it takes with Pocahontas's story (and notwithstanding a slight taste for numbing pieties), it's still a success."

—"History as Buckskin-Clad Fairytale," by Janet Maslin. *New York Times*, June 11, 1995.

CHAPTER 4: MIXED-BLOODS IN DISTRESS

Duel in the Sun

"Reduced to its bare essentials and cleared of a clutter of clichés worn thin in a hundred previous Westerns, Mr. [David O.] Selznick's two-hour-and-a-quarter tale is that of a sun-blistered romance involving a half-breed Indian girl and two dagger-eyed Texas brothers, one of them good and the other very bad. That, as a plot, might be sufficient for a sort of O'Neillian frontier tragedy—and, indeed, once or twice it looks faintly as though this might turn it into a valid 'Desire under the Sun' . . ."

—"The Screen," by Bosley Crowther. *New York Times*, May 8, 1947.

The Unforgiven

"The gritty aspect of the ranching frontier, the tough, robust nature of its people, the touchiness of the mystery are all well and tensely brought together within Mr. Huston's crunching scenes. A wild lynching of the old hoodoo propels the stern drama to a height, and the challenge to settle the community's racial feelings toward the [Indian] girl is stark and clear.

"But at this point the screen play of Ben Maddow runs out of intellectual steam, and the idea that lies in the complex of human drama in a frontier settlement is lost. The writer and Mr. Huston take refuge in a Western cliché.

"It is a beaut of a raid. The ugly varmints come screaming out of the night, timed to Dimitri Tiomkin's booming and otherwise stirring musical score. The muskets crack. A grand piano, set out to trap the Indians, clangs. Fire burns the roof off the family fortress. It is an altogether hot half hour. But the only thing proved out of the complex that is carefully set up at the start is that blood is not so thick as being 'daughter.' Indian blood, anyhow. . . .

"Those who expect to see a settlement of the racial question will not be satisfied."

—"The Screen," by Bosley Crowther. *New York Times*, April 7, 1960.

The Last of the Mohicans

"'The Last of the Mohicans,' a rapturous revision of the schoolroom classic, follows the trail blazed by 'Dances With Wolves' and more recently 'Unforgiven.' A rousing frontier saga drawn from James Fenimore Cooper's 'The Leatherstocking Tales,' it looks back with longing on the savage Eden of 18th-century America, a lush old-growth wilderness from which mountains rise like sleeping giants wreathed in cloud. Painstakingly, breathtakingly re-created by director Michael Mann, this landscape makes room for heroes with principles greater than the circumference of their biceps—lean, smoldering, woodsy-smelling men.

"Set in the 1750s during the French and Indian War, 'The Last of the Mohicans' looks not only at the glorious possibilities of the New World, but at the violent collision of cultures that marked the beginning of European domination of the continent. The explosion brought about a sturdy hybrid represented by Hawkeye (Daniel Day-Lewis), the European-born adopted son of the patrician Mohican Chingachgook. That's not to say that Day-Lewis's portrait of Hawkeye isn't just a little bit Hollywood. A cross between Iron John and romance-novel cover boy Favio, the cerebral Brit promises to do for big hair what Don Johnson did for beard stubble in Mann's designer cop drama, TV's 'Miami Vice.'

"Part modern romance, part historical re-creation, the story no longer has much to do with Cooper's original, which Mann slammed as plodding, racist and shallow—especially when it came to its characterizations of Native Americans. Credited with the concept of the noble savage, Cooper would scarcely recognize Chingachgook, wonderfully played by American Indian Movement leader Russell Means. The story is based more on Randolph Scott's 1936 film of the same title, but Hawkeye has evolved from a celibate colonialist into a corset-popping proto-democrat."

—film review by Rita Kempley, staff writer. *Washington Post*, September 25, 1992. © The Washington Post

Hidalgo

"The much too long, primitively plotted family action adventure 'Hidalgo,' directed by Joe Johnston, has a handful of well-handled sequences but, given the young audience the film is intended for, the picture may be like having to finish an entire pot of broccoli to get a couple of jelly beans for dessert. 'Hidalgo' may yet be declared cruel and unusual punishment for kids of all ages. . . .

"The expansive and unbelievable movie follows Frank, who's persuaded to leave safety-defying re-creations of Native American battles at the late-19th-century Wild West show of Buffalo Bill (J. K. Simmons) to participate in the Ocean of Fire, a death-defying trans-Arabian race across 3,000 miles of desert. The prize is $100,000, and the competition is '100 of the finest horses,' probably bred to withstand the climate. . . .

"Eventually the journey of Frank and Hidalgo becomes a testament to Frank's need for validation, and it is so full of incident that the movie is finally about as colorful and convincing as one of those penny dreadfuls about Buffalo Bill's own life. There aren't many films that include the Wounded Knee massacre, a shot of the Statue of Liberty, a computer-generated sandstorm left over from 'The Scorpion King,' megasize locusts and a grand and incredibly staged rescue from a kidnapping, which logistically and storywise is the film's high point."

—"Film Review: Its Plot Written by a Mustang? It's Smart Enough Not to Say," by Elvis Mitchell. *New York Times*, March 5, 2004.

CHAPTER 5: YOU MEAN, I'M A WHITE GUY?

Broken Arrow

"In what appears to be an honorable endeavor to clear the public's mind of the traditional notion that the American Indian was an unprincipled and uncivilized brute, Twentieth-Century-Fox has manufactured a richly colorful romantic film, 'Broken Arrow,' in which the Indians come off better—much better—on the whole, than do the whites. As a matter of fact, one might wonder from this exhibit, now on the Roxy's screen, whether it isn't a white man, not the Indian, who should be regarded as 'good' only when he is dead.

"For here, in this high-minded story of a lanky veteran of the Civil War who tries to make peace between the white men and the Chiricahua Apache tribe of the great Southwest, it is the Indian chief, Cochise, who shows vision and noble character, and it is a group of snarling citizens of Tucson who show blind bigotry and ruthless hate. To be sure there are some good white men and some bad Indians—to wit, Geronimo, who refuses to bury the hatchet, to break the arrow—but, by and large, that's how it is."

—"The Screen," by Bosley Crowther. *New York Times*, July 21, 1950.

Little Big Man

"'Little Big Man,' the film adaptation of Thomas Berger's epic comic novel, is Arthur Penn's most extravagant and ambitious movie, an attempt to capture the essence of the American heritage in the funny, bitter, uproarious adventures of Jack Crabb, an irritable, 120-odd-year-old gentleman who may or may not have been the sole survivor of Custer's Last Stand.

"The film . . . tries to cover too much ground, even though Calder Willingham's script eliminates or telescopes events and characters from the Berger novel. Often it is not terribly funny, at just those moments when it tries the hardest, and it sometimes wears its social concerns so blatantly that they look like war paint. . . .

"'Little Big Man'—both in spite of and because of these failings—is an important movie . . ."

—film review by Vincent Canby. *New York Times*, December 15, 1970.

A Man Called Horse

"The film . . . places great stress on authenticity of ritual ('80 per cent of the dialogue,' say my production notes, 'is in Sioux, and in old Sioux at that!'), although a couple of odd faces turn up—quite at home—in the old Sioux camp.

"The ancient squaw, who looks like Mammy Yokum in a fright wig, is actually Dame Judith Anderson, whom publicists like to describe as one of the great actresses of the English-speaking theater. Here, however, she is restricted to speaking pure Lakotan, which sometimes sounds Yiddish. The Indian princess who wins Lord John's hand is played by Corina Tsopei, a Miss Greece who went on to oblivion as Miss Universe of 1964.

"In these details, 'A Man Called Horse' is conventionally absurd. However, [director Elliot] Silverstein has elected to tell the story of Lord John's survival largely in terms of Sioux rituals relating to such things as wars, weddings, deaths, and even spiritual deliverance. I must admit that I found all this interesting, although I'm the sort of Indian buff and tourist who gets a kick out of watching contemporary Navajos do their rain dances in tennis shoes.

"There are no tennis shoes in 'A Man Called Horse,' but there is a good deal of blood, as well as an emphasis on salvation through mutilation."

—"Richard Harris in 'Man Called Horse.'" *New York Times*, April 30, 1970.

Dances with Wolves

"'Dances With Wolves' has the makings of a great work, one that recalls a variety of antecedents, everything from 'Robinson Crusoe' and 'Walden' to 'Tarzan of the Apes.' Michael Blake's screenplay touches both on man alone in nature and on the 19th-century white man's assuming his burden among the less privileged.

"Its triumph is that it is never exactly boring, only dulled. It's a movie in acute need of sharpening."

—"A Soldier at One with the Sioux," by Vincent Canby. *New York Times*, November 9, 1990.

CHAPTER 6: INDIANS WITH FANGS

The Manitou

"That lump on Susan Strasberg's back 'The Manitou' isn't benign. It isn't malignant, either. Worse. It turns out to be the rapidly growing fetus of an Indian medicine man who lived 400 years ago. How come? Don't ask. . . .

"The conflict in 'The Manitou,' which opens today at Lowes State 2, the Orpheum and other theaters, isn't so much between good and evil spirits as it is between seasoned performers, among them Tony Curtis, Stella Stevens, Burgess Meredith, Michael Ansara and Miss Strasberg, and an absurd penny-dreadful script and a cheapjack production. It's another knockoff in the cycle of supernatural horror films that began with 'The Exorcist.'

"'The Manitou' is rated PG ('Parental Guidance Suggested'), probably because of its generally disagreeable subject matter."

—"Film: Return of the Native," by Tom Buckley. *New York Times*, April 28, 1978.

Wolfen

"'Wolfen' . . . is a sort of rich, thinking man's 'Alligator,' a supernatural monster movie of extraordinary stylishness in looks and sounds as well as performances. Its star is Albert Finney [who] plays a psychiatrically unreliable but brilliant Police Department detective who is called out of enforced retirement to help solve a series of mysterious murders that has stumped his colleagues. . . .

"The members of the supporting cast, most of whom are comparatively new to films, include . . . Edward James Olmos as a politically active American Indian, a highsteel worker who, after hours, likes to change himself into an animal or, sometimes, a bird. . . .

The strange 'wolfen' point-of-view sequences are the result of combining conventional photographic and unconventional electronic images, which are so good they demand better from the screenplay than the platitudinous mumbo jumbo we get about 'the balance of nature,' 'man's arrogance' and the all-too-easy put-down of today's wasteful, corrupt society."

—"'Wolfen' with Albert Finny," by Vincent Canby. *New York Times*, July 24, 1981.

CHAPTER 7: WALK A MILE IN MY MOCCASINS

Medicine River

"Filmed near Calgary, [Medicine River is] an engaging, funny romantic comedy about a man confronting childhood memories and a life he walked away from.

"A well-crafted screenplay by Thomas King and Ann MacNaughton gives the characters an edge, even in the funniest moments, and Graham Greene plays Will, a photojournalist based in Toronto.

"Unlike the Eddie Murphy character in the Beverly Hills movies, who gets all the best lines, Medicine River's Will (Graham Greene) is frequently left speechless by the collision of two cultures. Frozen like the proverbial deer in the headlights, nothing prepared him for his trip to Medicine River. He's an Indian, but he wears Bay Street suits, has a blonde girlfriend (Janet-Laine Green) in Toronto and spent most of his youth in Calgary. . . .

"It's a treat to see so many native actors in one production. And even though it's a story about a Blackfoot community, their individual performances suggest the TV industry might be moving closer to the day when Indian actors will be routinely hired just to play anybody, without a cultural peg. It's been taking too long."

—film review by Bob Blakey. *Calgary Herald*, October 17, 1993.

Smoke Signals

"Victor Joseph (Adam Beach) and Thomas Builds-the-Fire (Evan Adams) are Coeur d'Alene Indians living in Idaho, characters drawn by Sherman Alexie from his sharply etched, mordant book of stories, 'The Lone Ranger and Tonto Fistfight in Heaven.' Lighter and less bittersweet on screen (and adapted by Mr. Alexie into a splendid screenplay), three tales describe a contemporary American Indian culture coming to terms with its past in offbeat, unexpected ways. . . .

"Here is a first feature from Chris Eyre, a 28-year-old Cheyenne-Arapaho filmmaker, that has an American Indian cast and outlook. And it needs no dispensation for novelty: it stands beautifully on its own merits. Mr. Eyre presents an inviting, affectionate and witty look at contemporary Indian lives.

"Though this is very much a first feature, 'Smoke Signals' shows colorful style and a wisdom beyond precocity about its setting and its people."

—"Miles to Go, and Worlds Apart," by Janet Maslin. *New York Times*, March 27, 1998.

The Business of Fancydancing

"'The Business of Fancydancing,' the directorial debut of the novelist and screenwriter Sherman Alexie, is often affecting, low-budget melodrama that is occasionally sabotaged by its economy of means: the image quality is sometimes so poor that it's like watching the pixel breakup on digital cable. But although the film is initially clumsy and a little hard to follow, Mr. Alexie takes his time in setting his characters in play, and the visual clunkiness becomes secondary to the eloquent emotional desolation."

—"Film Review: A Poet Finds His Past Is Just Where He Left It," by Elvis Mitchell. *New York Times*, October 18, 2002.

CHAPTER 8: NDNS: THE YOUNG AND THE RESTLESS

The Indian in the Cupboard

"The best reason for children to see 'The Indian in the Cupboard' is illustrated by the film itself. It features a scene in which fighting breaks out between the title American Indian and his teeny cowboy counterpart after they happen to glimpse a violent western movie on television. We hardly needed further proof that viewers, especially young ones, are influenced by what they see. So here's a nice film that has nothing to do with greed, comic books or world domination. Children should be charmed by its fantasy world, and parents will be reasonably entertained."

—"Magic Furniture and a Tiny Friend," by Janet Maslin. *New York Times*, July 14, 1995.

The Education of Little Tree

"Can 'The Education of Little Tree' overcome its origins?

"The movie, adapted from a best-seller published in 1976 and republished in 1986, is a sensitive memoir about a Cherokee orphan's childhood in the backwoods of East Tennessee.... The author was Forrest Carter, who described himself in the years before he died in 1979 as a Cherokee cowboy, dishwasher and ranch hand and self-taught writer.

"But Mr. Carter's background was a hoax. Several accounts state that he was really Asa Carter, Ku Klux Klan member, violent white supremacist, anti-Semite and author of some of the most inflammatory speeches by former Gov. George C. Wallace of Alabama....

"What impact the author's segregationist past will have on the film's release remains unclear."

—"Movie With a Murky Background: The Man Who Wrote the Book," by Bernard Weinraub. *New York Times*, December 17, 1997.

The Doe Boy

"His name is Hunter. He is a young man of mixed-heritage, and the story of his complicated life unfolds in the heart of the Cherokee Nation in 'The Doe Boy.'"

—"Footlights," by Lawrence Van Gelder. *New York Times*, July 18, 2001.

Black Cloud

"To its credit, 'Black Cloud' manages to avoid much of the retrograde us-vs.-them stereotyping common to films about the Native American experience. Though the movie has its fair share of racial-epithet-spouting good-ole-boys and pious shamans, the protagonist's rash moral judgments are often proven wrong and a sheriff (Tim McGraw) who at first appears to be a proverbial white devil emerges as a more complex characterization. Yet such deviations from the expectation ultimately prove the exception in 'Black Cloud.'"

—film review by Scott Foundas. *Variety*, March 21–27, 2005, p. 24.

CHAPTER 9: DEATH WISH, INDIAN-STYLE

Navajo Joe

"'Navajo Joe' . . . is the latest of a succession of super-bloody 'Westerns' made by Italians and Spaniards in Spain with Italian, Spanish and American actors, this time led by Burt Reynolds, as the American titular superhero who dispatches troops of villains singlehanded."

"[The film was] shot in color but [is] decidedly colorless." —A. H. Weiler

—"The Screen," by Bosley Crowther. *New York Times*, December 7, 1967.

Tell Them Willie Boy Is Here

"Set in California near the beginning of the century, the story, based on fact, concerns a young Indian (Robert Blake) who after a long absence returns to his reservation and in self-defense kills the father of the girl (Katherine Ross) he loves. He flees with her into the mountains. . . .

"Most of the film is devoted to the chase. . . .

"'Tell Them Willie Boy Is Here' can be read on two levels, and has already been so read by critics who are delighted or displeased according to how they feel about that liberal genre, the message Western.

"[Director] Polonsky has his messages, tied to the white-Indian conflict, and they are delivered in a script that is not dialogue so much as a series of one-line monologues, to which characters may react but almost never effectively respond. With a moral victory or defeat registered every few minutes, the film is sometimes in danger of mistaking text for texture.

"The danger is generally avoided. 'Tell Them Willie Boy Is Here' lives most brilliantly on a third level, not unrelated to the action or the allegory, but deeper, more mysterious, more fully felt.

"Because it is a chase movie, concerned with clues and tracks, all signs must be read. And because the film is interested in questions of personal identity, all signs are doubly relevant. But the nature of the signs changes in the course of the movie, becoming always more intimate, elusive, meaningful, impenetrable."

—"Screen: 'Willie Boy Is Here' Opens," by Roger Greenspun. *New York Times*, December 19, 1969.

Billy Jack

"For a picture that preaches pacifism, 'Billy Jack' seems fascinated by violence, of which it is full. The title hero of this well-aimed but misguided drama is a muscular young Indian, an ex-Green Beret, who periodically appears to save a 'freedom school,' a group of idealistic young people from bald harassment by small-town bigots and worse.

"The violence commences to pile on predictably and endlessly, with an assortment of town bullies and psychopaths right out of Western stereotypes . . ."

—"A Misguided 'Billy Jack,'" by Howard Thompson. *New York Times*, July 29, 1971.

CHAPTER 10: LOVE, INDIGENOUS-STYLE

Waikiki Wedding

"Your enjoyment of it will depend largely upon your relish of Hawaii à la Hollywood. LeRoy Prinz, one of those sub-realistic dance directors, has his own ideas about the hula-hula and there are scores of young women willing to accept them. Mr. Prinz and his straw-skirted chorus are all over the place, caroling blithely along the beach, undulating around the tribal campfires, picking up some Robin-Rainger lyrics of 'Blue Hawaii,' 'In a Little Hula Heaven,' and 'Sweet Is the Word for You.' In no time at all, 'Aloha' will be just cold poi.

"But that's not really important though any of it is. What matters is that Mr. [Bing] Crosby, as the publicity man for Imperial Pineapple, has to convince the Pineapple Girl (a sort of Miss Birch Falls of 1937) that Hawaii really is a romantic place. Otherwise Shirley Ross would have written home some unpleasant things about the sunkis't tropic island. . . .

"It is, at least, a workable idea for a musical comedy . . ."

—"The Screen," by Frank S. Nugent. *New York Times*, March 25, 1937.

The Savage Innocents

"As presented yesterday in badly cut form as a neighborhood theatre second feature, this bitter drama of contemporary Eskimo life seems to offer little on the surface to capture the attention of a serious filmgoer. Neither the performance of Anthony Quinn and Yoko Tani as fur-clad primitives nor the stilted formality of the Eskimo dialogue would appear immediately promising.

"In addition, the story—the Eskimo inadvertently kills a missionary who disdains his hospitable offer of wife and igloo, then provokes a moral dilemma by saving the life of the trooper sent to bring him to Western justice—is, at first glance, conventional. Technically the Franco-British-Italian co-production released by Paramount is uneven, crudely matching studio sets with the sometimes splendid location color photography.

"Yet Mr. [Nicholas] Ray's highly individualistic preoccupation with moral tensions expresses itself in a series of unusually provocative scenes. Striking images of swimming sea lions turning a polar lake into a sea of blood, starved dogs lunging carnivorously at their masters, living worms writhing in a dish of edible meat, a water-drenched man visibly freezing before the camera eye, repeatedly emphasize the stark violence of the struggle for existence in the primeval wasteland. . . .

"The repressed brutality of Mr. Ray's screen play probes beyond the usual theme of natural instincts corrupted by civilization by suggesting that the primitive natural order is in itself so barbaric that our unnatural modern society, to still suffer by moral comparison, must have reached irrevocably abysmal depths."

—"'The Savage Innocents' Is Seen in Neighborhood Theatres," by Eugene Archer. *New York Times*, May 25, 1961.

Big Eden

"The gay romantic fantasy 'Big Eden' takes its title from the small Montana town where the principal character, the New York artist Henry Hart (Ayre Gross), was reared by his crusty but loving grandfather (George Coe). . . .

"[Director Thomas] Bezucha makes spectacular use of Big Eden's mountain scenery—the film was shot in Glacier National Park—but otherwise shows little interest in visual style. The movie is as flat and plain as a television program. . . .

"But there's no faulting Mr. Bezucha's benevolent vision of what it may someday be like to be different in America—which is to say, just as corny as everyone else."

—"Film Review: 'So Nice to Have You Back Where You Belong,'" by Dave Kehr. *New York Times*, July 13, 2001.

CHAPTER II: WORKIN' FOR THE GREAT WHITE FATHER

Distant Drums

"This outdoor adventure picture, which has Gary Cooper as its star all rigged out in a backwoodsman's outfit that looks great in Technicolor hues, has to do with a punitive expedition that goes into the Florida Everglades to knock off a gang of smugglers that sells guns to the local Seminoles. And what with the cries of swamp critters, the ululations of the braves and the frequent banging of gunfire, the din is terrific most of the time.

"So are the desperate adventures through which Mr. Cooper leads his band. It is just one tough spot after another, so far as these fellows are concerned. First it's a ticklish assault on the smuggler's fort in a midnight surprise and a fiery destruction of the arsenal, with Mr. Cooper the last man to leave. Then there's a long running battle with the Indians as the courageous band tries to work back to civilization through the unhealthy Everglades. And, finally, Mr. Cooper ends the struggle, single-handed, with the Indian chief in an underwater knife grapple—exotic but a little absurd. Needless to say, our people come out all right in the end, outside of those casualties chalked up to Indians, alligators and such."

—"The Screen," by Bosley Crowther. *New York Times*, December 26, 1951.

The Far Horizons

"The Lewis and Clark expedition to the Northwest never looked sillier."

—"The Screen," by Bosley Crowther. *New York Times*, June 5, 1955.

Thunderheart

"Though 'Thunderheart' is about a murder investigation and has the shape of a thriller, it also has a documentary's attentiveness to detail. . . .

"Filmed on the Pine Ridge Indian Reservation in South Dakota (which is called the Bear Creek Reservation in the movie), 'Thunderheart' is loosely based on violent events that took place there and elsewhere during the 1970's. The film employs many Indian actors, some of whose screen roles mirror their real lives. The fiery John Trudell, who plays an Indian activist suspected of murder in the movie, is in fact an Indian activist, as well as a poet and singer. Chief Ted Thin Elk, who plays an honored Lakota medicine man with a winning combination of courtliness and guile, is a Lakota elder himself.

"A film this intent on authenticity might easily grow dull, but this one doesn't; [Michael] Apted is a skillful storyteller. He gives 'Thunderheart' a brisk, fact-filled exposition and a dramatic structure that builds to a strong finale, one that effectively drives the film's message home. That message concerns corruption and reform battling for supremacy within the Indian community, widespread neglect on the part of the Federal Government and the urgent need for change."

—"Val Kilmer as an F.B.I. Agent among the Sioux," by Janet Maslin. *New York Times*, April 3, 1992.

Windtalkers

"'Windtalkers' has its own Navajo problem because it gives short shrift to the real dilemma: imagine becoming an elite marine during World War II only to be baby-sat. 'Windtalkers' invents an angle—kill the Navajos if necessary to prevent their capture, an act not known to have happened—and ignores the more compelling truth, that the Navajos are prevented from being front-line troops in the same war in which a Native American helped raise the flag at Okinawa. How do you prove you're a patriot if you're treated like a second-class citizen?

"Given the knee-jerk patriotism of recent war movies, it's discouraging to see 'Windtalkers' evade pertinent facts that could have recast the double-edged issues of racism and loyalty and made them relevant to contemporary lives."

—"Of Duty, Friendship and a Navajo Dilemma," by Elvis Mitchell. *New York Times*, July 14, 2002.

Ratings Sheet

Give the movie a rating using the following scale:

Don't bother with this one!

An element or two is working in this film, such as a somewhat comprehensible script, but most other elements are way off (e.g., bad acting, poor production values, offensive content, etc.).

This movie is not *so-o-o-o-o* bad. Several elements—its story, camera work, and/or its message—are working well together, but overall it's just not equal to the sum of its parts.

This is a pretty good film! A lot is working well (e.g., the acting is solid, there's a message in the film, production values are high), but perhaps not everything is lovable enough for me.

At last! What's not to like?

Now offer brief comments that support your rating:

❶ Provide a brief summary of the film. (Two or three sentences are fine; you don't need to include a lot of detail. For example, you might summarize the film *Jaws* by saying: In the heat of a late 1970s summer, a New England beachgoer is brutally attacked by a great white shark and havoc ensues.)

❷ State your opinion of the movie. What are its strengths and weaknesses? Provide specific examples (scenes, situations, shots, FX, etc.).

❸ What character(s) do you most identify with?

❹ In your opinion, what was the director's intention or message? (For example, you might argue that *Jaws* is more than just a summer blockbuster thriller: Of course the ocean bloodbath is disconcerting in itself. But when the beachgoer is brutally attacked by a great white shark after shark-infested Amity Beach is permitted to remain open, the movie forces one to recognize how the profit motive is typically perilous and rarely humane.)

❺ How does the film relate to American culture? Specifically, how does it relate to the era in which it was made?

❻ Final comments:

Post your comments and ratings on the Seeing Red—Hollywood's Pixeled Skins *website.*

Further Reading

Aleiss, Angela. *Making the White Man's Indian: Native Americans and Hollywood Movies.* Westport, CT: Praeger, 2008.

Bataille, Gretchen M., and Charles L. P. Silet. *Images of American Indians on Film.* New York: Garland Publishing, 1986.

———. *The Pretend Indians: Images of Native Americans in the Movies.* Ames: Iowa State University Press, 1980.

Berkhofer, Robert F., Jr. *The White Man's Indian: Images of the American Indian from Columbus to the Present.* New York: Vintage, 1979.

Bird, S. Elizabeth. *Dressing in Feathers: The Construction of the Indian in American Popular Culture.* Boulder, CO: Westview Press, 1996.

Buscombe, Edward. *'Injuns!': Native Americans in the Movies.* Chicago and London: Reaktion Books, 2006.

Churchill, Ward. *Fantasies of the Master Race: Literature, Cinema, and the Colonization of American Indians.* San Francisco: City Lights Publishers, 2001.

Csilla, Barkász. *Native Americans and Cinema: The Representation of Native Americans in Three Contemporary American Films.* Saarbrücken, Germany: VDM Verlag Dr. Müller, 2008.

Cummings, Denise K., ed. *Visualities: Perspectives on Contemporary Native American Film and Art.* East Lansing: Michigan State University Press, 2011.

Hearne, Joanna. *Smoke Signals: Native Cinema Rising.* Lincoln: University of Nebraska Press, 2012.

Herzberg, Bob. *Savages and Saints: The Changing Image of American Indians in Westerns.* Jefferson, NC: McFarland, 2008.

Hilger, Michael. *The American Indian in Film.* Metuchen, NJ: Scarecrow Press, 1986.

———. *From Savages to Noblemen: Images of Native Americans in Film.* Lanham, MD: Scarecrow Press, 1995.

Huhndorf, Shari M. *Going Native: Indians in the American Cultural Imagination.* Ithaca, NY: Cornell University Press, 2001.

Kilpatrick, Jacquelyn. *Celluloid Indians: Native Americans and Film.* Lincoln: University of Nebraska Press, 1999.

Knopf, Kerstin. *Decolonizing the Lens of Power: Indigenous Films in North America.* New York: Editions Rodopi B.V., 2009.

Marubbio, M. Elise. *Killing the Indian Maiden: Images of Native American Women in Film.* Lexington: University Press of Kentucky, 2009.

O'Connor, John E. *The Hollywood Indian: Stereotypes of Native Americans in Films.* Trenton: New Jersey State Museum, 1980.

Owens, Louis. *Mixedblood Messages: Literature, Film, Family, Place.* Tulsa: University of Oklahoma Press, 1998.

Prats, Armando José. *Invisible Natives: Myth and Identity in the American Western.* Ithaca, NY: Cornell University Press, 2002.

Rader, Dean. *Engaged Resistance: American Indian Art, Literature, and Film from Alcatraz to the NMAI.* Austin: University of Texas Press, 2011.

Raheja, Michelle H. *Reservation Reelism: Redfacing, Visual Sovereignty, and Representations of Native Americans in Film.* Lincoln: University of Nebraska Press, 2011.

Rollins, Peter C., and John E. O'Connor, eds. *Hollywood's Indian: The Portrayal of the Native American in Film.* Lexington: University Press of Kentucky, 2003.

Singer, Beverly R. *Wiping the War Paint off the Lens: Native American Film and Video.* Minneapolis: University of Minnesota Press, 2001.

Smith, Andrew Brodie. *Shooting Cowboys and Indians: Silent Western Films, American Culture, and the Birth of Hollywood.* Boulder, CO: University Press of Colorado, 2004.

Weatherford, Elizabeth, and Emelia Seubert. *Native Americans on Film and Video.* Vol. 2. Washington, DC: National Museum of the American Indian, 1988.

Contributors

Joseph Bauerkemper is Assistant Professor of American Indian Studies at the University of Minnesota–Duluth, where he teaches courses in politics, literature, and law. He has published in *Studies in American Indian Literatures*, *American Studies*, and the edited collection *Visualities: Perspectives on Contemporary American Indian Film and Art* (2011). After earning his PhD in American Studies from the University of Minnesota–Twin Cities, Joseph enjoyed one year at the University of Illinois as a Chancellor's Postdoctoral Fellow in American Indian Studies, followed by two years at UCLA as an Andrew W. Mellon Visiting Assistant Professor in the Department of English and in the program for the study of Cultures in Transnational Perspective.

Jeff Berglund is Professor of English at Northern Arizona University, where he frequently teaches indigenous-film courses. He is the author of articles on Blackfire, Sherman Alexie, Simon Ortiz, Esther Belin, and the pedagogy of American Indian literature. He is also the coeditor of *Sherman Alexie: A Collection of Critical Essays* (2010), as well as the author of *Cannibal Fictions: American Explorations of Colonialism, Race, Gender, and Sexuality* (2006).

Jodi A. Byrd (Chickasaw) is Associate Professor of American Indian Studies and English at the University of Illinois at Urbana–Champaign. Her articles have appeared in *Interventions*, *Cultural Studies Review*, and *American Indian Quarterly*, and her book, *The Transit of Empire: Indigenous Critiques of Colonialism*, was published in 2011.

Allison Adelle Hedge Coke's authored books include (American Book Award winner) *Dog Road Woman* (1997) and *Off-Season City Pipe* (2005), poetry; *Rock Ghost, Willow, Deer* (2004), a memoir; and *Blood Run* (2007), a verse-play. Hedge Coke has edited eight additional collections, including *Sing: Poetry of the Indigenous Americas* (2007), *Effigies* and *Effigies II*. Hedge Coke comes from Huron Metis, Cherokee, Creek, French Canadian, Portuguese, Irish, and Scots heritage. She came of age cropping tobacco and working fields and waters, and working in factories.

Denise K. Cummings is Associate Professor and Chair of Critical Media and Cultural Studies at Rollins College. Her teaching and research focus on film history, theory, and criticism; American and American Indian film and literature; and media and cultural studies. She is editor of *Visualities: Perspectives on Contemporary American Indian Film and Art* (2011), has curated numerous film programs, and serves on selection committees and juries for several film festivals, including the Florida Film Festival (Maitland).

Philip Deloria is Carroll Smith-Rosenberg Collegiate Professor of History and American Culture, and Associate Dean for Undergraduate Education at the University of Michigan. He is the author of *Playing Indian* (1998) and *Indians in Unexpected Places* (2004), and coeditor (with Neal Salisbury) of *The Blackwell Companion to American Indian History* (2002). Deloria is former president of the American Studies Association, a trustee of the National Museum of the American Indian, and the author of numerous essays, articles, and reviews.

Jill Doerfler (White Earth Anishinaabe) is Assistant Professor of American Indian Studies at the University of Minnesota–Duluth. She is interested in the diverse ways in which Anishinaabeg have resisted pseudoscientific measures of blood (race/blood quantum) as a means to define identity. She is the co-author of *The White Earth Nation: Ratification of a Native Democratic Constitution*, with Gerald Vizenor (2012), and coedited *Centering Anishinaabeg Studies: Understanding the World through Stories*, with Niigaanwewidam James Sinclair and Heidi Kiiwetinepinesiik Stark (2013).

Matthew Sakiestewa Gilbert is enrolled with the Hopi Tribe from the village of Upper Moencopi in northeastern Arizona. He is Assistant Professor of American Indian Studies & History at the University of Illinois at Urbana–Champaign. Centering his research and teaching on Native American history and the history of the American West, he examines the history of American Indian education, the Indian boarding school experience, and American Indians and sports. He is the author of *Education beyond the Mesas: Hopi Students at Sherman Institute, 1902–1929* (2010), and his articles have appeared in *Western Historical Quarterly*, *American Quarterly*, *Journal of American Indian Education*, and in edited volumes. Along with his scholarship on the history of American Indian education, he is writing a second monograph entitled *HOPI RUNNERS: Crossing the Terrain Between Indian and American, 1908–1932*. He received his PhD and MA in history from the University of California, Riverside, and holds an MA in theology from Talbot School of Theology/Biola University.

P. Jane Hafen (Taos Pueblo) is a Frances C. Allen Fellow, D'Arcy McNickle Center for the History of the American Indian, The Newberry Library. She is editor of *Dreams and Thunder: Stories, Poems and The Sun Dance Opera by Zitkala-Ša* (2005); coeditor, with Diane Quantic, of *A Great Plains Reader* (2003); and author of *Reading Louise Erdrich's Love Medicine* (2003). She is one of the Clan Mothers of the Native American Literature Symposium.

Gary Harrington is an enrolled member of the Comanche Nation, and a graduate of Cornell University (BA English 1983) and Harvard Law School (JD 1988). He has been practicing law in California since 1988, and started his own practice representing Native American clients in 1992. He began filmmaking in 2003. His films *Welcome* (2009) and *The Bouquet* (2007) have screened at film festivals. Gary has written, produced, and directed several other short films: *Kiddie Cam* (2004); *Killer Cat* (2005); *Chief Illiniwek Is Dead* (pre-production). In 2003, Gary wrote, produced, and directed *Driving 101* (2003), a 56-minute mockumentary about a

Chinese American teenage boy learning how to drive. Gary is currently completing a treatment for a feature-length movie, *Er Bai Wu*, in Mandarin; has begun work on another project in the Comanche language; and also is working on various other Native American–themed film projects.

LeAnne Howe (Citizen Choctaw Nation of Oklahoma) is the award-winning author of novels, poetry, screenplays, plays, and scholarship that deal with Native experiences. In 2006, she appeared as the on-camera narrator and screenwriter for the 90-minute PBS documentary "Indian Country Diaries: Spiral of Fire," which aired nationally. In 2007, she appeared on Jon Stewart's *The Daily Show*, in *Trail of Cheers* on Comedy Central, and fears this may be the pinnacle of her career. In 2010–2011, she received a Fulbright Scholarship to Amman, Jordan, to do research for a new novel. Currently a Professor in American Indian Studies, English, and Theatre at the University of Illinois, Urbana–Champaign, she makes her home in Oklahoma and Illinois.

Frederick Hoxie is Swanlund Professor of History, American Indian Studies and Law at the University of Illinois, Urbana–Champaign. He is the author or editor of more than a dozen books, including A *Final Promise: The Campaign to Assimilate the Indians* (1984, 2000), *The Encyclopedia of North American Indians* (1995), and *This Indian Country: American Indian Activists and the Place They Made* (2012).

Daniel Heath Justice (Cherokee Nation) is Associate Professor of First Nations Studies and English at the University of British Columbia. Along with essays on nationhood, sexuality, and decolonization in indigenous literary studies, he is the author of *Our Fire Survives the Storm: A Cherokee Literary History* (2006) and the indigenous epic fantasy *The Way of Thorn and Thunder: The Kynship Chronicles* (2011), as well as a forthcoming cultural history of badgers.

Rebecca Kugel (BA, University of Iowa; MA and PhD, UCLA) teaches Native American history at the University of California, Riverside. She is the author of *To Be the Main Leaders of Our People: A History of Minnesota Ojibwe Politics, 1825–1898* (1998), and coeditor, with Lucy Eldersveld Murphy, of *Native Women's History in Eastern North America before 1900: A Guide to Research and Writing* (2007). Her long-term research focuses on a number of aspects of Great Lakes Native history, including the operation of historic indigenous political systems in the eighteenth and nineteenth centuries, and the construction of political speech and its use of distinctive metaphors. She has additional research interests in the cultural constructions of race among Great Lakes Native peoples and in Native women's history.

Scott Richard Lyons (Leech Lake Ojibwe) is Associate Professor of English and American Culture at the University of Michigan, Ann Arbor, and the author of *X-Marks: Native Signatures of Assent* (2010).

Harvey Markowitz received a PhD in American church history from the Divinity School, the University of Chicago in 2002. He has held the positions of Associate and Acting Director of the D'Arcy McNickle Center for American Indian History, The Newberry Library. From 1999 to 2002 he served as Museum Specialist–Community Liaison/Fieldworker for the Smithsonian

Institution's National Museum of the American Indian, during which time he worked closely with the Florida Seminoles, Eastern Band of Cherokees, Kiowa Tribe of Oklahoma, the Blackfeet Indian Tribe, the Chiricahua Apaches, and the Tohono O'odham Nation. He lived for twelve years on the Rosebud Sioux Reservation in South Dakota. He is the author and editor of several articles and reference books, including *American Indians: Ready Reference* (1995), *American Indian Biographies* (coedited with Carol Barrett, 1999), and *American Indian Cultures* (coedited with Carol Barrett, 2004).

David Martínez (Gila River Pima) is Associate Professor of American Indian Studies at Arizona State University. He is the author of *Dakota Philosopher: Charles Eastman and American Indian Thought* (2009), and the editor of *The American Indian Intellectual Tradition: An Anthology of Readings from 1772 to 1972* (2011).

Carter Meland is a tall, left-handed man who teaches Native literature/film courses at the University of Minnesota. He writes fiction (which sometimes gets published) and an occasional journal article or two (which get . . . read? One hopes, but one does not lay any bets). Having read this far, you may be wondering why he has yet to list his various publications, but he figures with the way things are these days, it'd probably be quicker if you just Googled his name.

Deborah Miranda (Esselen/Chumash) is the author of *The Zen of La Llorona* (2005), *Indian Cartography* (1999), and *Bad Indians: A Tribal Memoir* (2013). Her poems and essays also appear in anthologies such as *In the Eye of the Deer* and *This Bridge We Call Home*. She teaches at Washington and Lee University. She is currently writing a collection of essays.

Dean Rader has published widely in the fields of visual culture, American Indian Studies, and poetry. His recent books include *Engaged Resistance: American Indian Art, Literature, and Film from Alcatraz to the NMAI* (2011); *Works & Days* (2010); *Speak to Me Words: Essays on Contemporary American Indian Poetry* (coedited with Janice Gould) (2004). He is the chair of the English Department at the University of San Francisco.

Jacki Rand (Citizen Choctaw Nation of Oklahoma) is Associate Professor of history at the University of Iowa. Her book *Kiowa Humanity and the Invasion of the State* (2008) places the Kiowa Indians at the intersections of federal Indian law and policy, material culture, and gendered work in the late-nineteenth and early-twentieth centuries. She is currently working on a book that examines tribal self-determination through the lens of violence, and Native women in the twentieth century.

James Riding In, a Pawnee and Associate Professor of American Indian Studies at Arizona State University, is the coeditor of *Native Historians Write Back* (2011), the author of numerous journal articles and book chapters, and the editor of *Wicazo Sa Review*. He is the chair of Pawnee Nation College's Board of Trustees, a former president of the American Indian Studies Association, and formerly a featured writer of the National Museum of the American Indian's writers series.

Paul M. Robertson is an anthropologist and currently president of Little Priest Tribal College in Winnebago, Nebraska. Before that, he lived and worked on the Pine Ridge Indian Reservation for thirty years, taught at Oglala Lakota College, and spent years as a community organizer working on a diverse range of issues ranging from family violence to land justice. He is skeptical about the notion of an apolitical intellectual and encourages students and teachers to engage with the pressing issues of the day.

Maureen Trudelle Schwarz is a cultural anthropologist whose scholarship focuses empirically on Native North Americans (especially Navajos) and theoretically on notions of personhood, issues of power, and representation. A professor of anthropology in the Maxwell School of Citizenship and Public Affairs at Syracuse University, she received her PhD in anthropology (1995) and MA in museum studies from the University of Washington. She has conducted ethnographic research on the Navajo Reservation since 1991, which has resulted in several articles as well as *Molded in the Image of Changing Woman* (1997), *Navajo Lifeways* (2001), *Blood and Voice* (2003), and *Choosing Life: Navajo Perspectives on Medical and Religious Pluralism* (2008). Her most recent research, focusing on how Native Americans use stereotypes of American Indians, is the subject of her book *Fighting Colonialism with Hegemonic Culture: Native American Appropriation of Indian Stereotypes* (2013).

Cristina Stanciu (PhD, University of Illinois at Urbana–Champaign, 2011) is Assistant Professor of English at Virginia Commonwealth University, where she teaches courses in U.S. ethnic literatures. Her work has appeared and is forthcoming in *American Indian Quarterly, Studies in American Indian Literatures, Wicazo Sa Review, Intertexts,* and *The Chronicle of Higher Education*. During 2008–2009, Cristina was a fellow in the American Indian Studies program at Michigan State University.

Susan Stebbins is of Mohawk and Metis descent. She received her Doctor of Arts degree from the University at Albany. She is professor of anthropology and Special Assistant to the President for Diversity at the State University of New York at Potsdam. She teaches Native American Studies classes, including Indian Images. Her research has focused both on Iroquoian ethnohistory and contemporary issues.

Pauline Turner Strong teaches anthropology and gender studies at the University of Texas at Austin, where she also directs the Humanities Institute. An award-winning teacher, she has published widely on representations of Native Americans in North American public culture. Her publications include *American Indians and the American Imaginary* (2012), *Captive Selves, Captivating Others: The Politics and Poetics of Colonial American Captivity Narratives* (1999), and a coedited volume, *New Perspectives on Native North America: Cultures, Histories, Representations* (2006).

Clifford E. Trafzer holds the Rupert Costo Chair in American Indian Affairs at the University of California, Riverside. He has published many books, including *Renegade Tribe: The Palouse Indians and the Invasion of the Inland Pacific Northwest* (1986), *Death Stalks the*

Yakama: Epidemiological Transitions and Mortality on the Yakama Indian Reservation (1997), and *Voices of the Dead* (1999). Since 1990, he has consulted with the Smithsonian's National Museum of the American Indian, and he has coedited two volumes with the museum, including *Native Universe: Voices of Indian America* (2004), and *American Indians/American Presidents* (2009). Currently he is researching a book on the medicine ways of Southern California Indians, and the intersection of Western and Native medicine in the region.

Theo. Van Alst is Assistant Dean of Yale College and Director of the Native American Cultural Center at Yale University. He is a former assistant professor and co-chair of Comparative Literary and Cultural Studies at the University of Connecticut. His most recent work, "Sherman Shoots Alexie," is currently available in *Visualities: Perspectives on Contemporary American Indian Film and Art*, ed. Denise K. Cummings (2011). His current book-length project is *Spaghetti and Sauerkraut with a Side of Frybread.*

Gwen N. Westerman comes from a long line of overactors. An enrolled member of the Sisseton-Wahpeton Dakota Oyate, she incorporates the languages and traditions of her family in her writing and art. Currently Professor in English and Director of the Humanities Program at Minnesota State University, Mankato, she is the author of *Follow the Blackbirds*, a poetry collection in Dakota and English, and coauthor of *Mni Sota Makoce: Land of the Dakota* (2012), a history of Dakota land tenure in Minnesota.

Jim Wilson is Assistant Professor in the Department of Language Arts at Seminole State College in Seminole, Oklahoma, and teaches creative writing in the Chickasaw Nation's Summer Arts Academy each July in Ada. He earned an MFA in creative writing from Spalding University, Louisville, Kentucky (2007), and an MA in archaeology (1987) from the American University of Beirut, Lebanon. He's at work on a memoir, *The Journeyman*, about love in the time of civil war in Lebanon.

Roll Credits

It would be a travesty for any book dedicated to movies to fail to credit all those who had a hand in its production. We therefore offer our thanks to the following individuals who made this book possible.

VISUALS: Elizabeth Teaff, Brandon Bucy
CONTINUITY: Gordon Henry
PRODUCERS: Gabriel Dotto, Julie Loehr
SCRIPT CONSULTANTS: Jon Eastwood, Craig Howe, Angel Lawson, Tom Litzenburg, O. Kendall White, Kristine Blakeslee, Annette Tanner, Rachel Schnepper, Elise Jajuga

No book of this kind would be complete without a special "shout out" to the actors in Hollywood films about Indians, here goes: Tonto and the Lone Ranger, his nephew's horse Victor, Cochise, Pocahontas, Henry Brandon who played "Scar" without a hint of irony in *The Searchers,* Debra Paget and Jimmy Stewart for their soulful performances in *Broken Arrow,* Kevin Costner as choreographer in *Dances with Wolves*, and Johnny Depp, for going where no other has gone before (being adopted into the Comanche Nation in 2012)—good luck, Dude.